INFLUENCING THE YOUTH CULTURE

INFLUENCING THE YOUTH CULTURE

A Study of Youth Organizations in Israel

JOSEPH W. EATON

In collaboration with MICHAEL CHEN

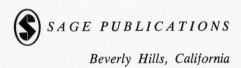

SAGE PUBLICATIONS

Beverly Hills, California

For information address:

SAGE PUBLICATIONS, INC.
275 South Beverly Drive
Beverly Hills, California   90212

Printed in the United States of America

Standard Book Number 8039–0052–X

Library of Congress Catalog Card No. 71–103015

First Printing

The research reported herein was performed pursuant to a contract (OE 4–10–010, Project No. 5–0375) with the Office of Education, U. S. Department of Health, Education and Welfare. Contractors undertaking such projects under Government sponsorship are encouraged to express freely their professional judgment in the conduct of the project. Points of view or opinions stated do not, therefore, necessarily represent official Office of Education position or policy.

ACKNOWLEDGMENTS

Behind every completed social research study are the enthusiasm and voluntary efforts of many persons. There were thousands who completed questionnaires, hundreds who responded to interviews and dozens who offered administrative and intellectual stimulation that enabled the research to proceed.

Data collection required cross-national collaboration of many persons. The United States Office of Education financed the study through a basic research contract. In a world in which government sponsorship often leads to close government surveillance, the United States government pattern for sponsoring basic research stands out as a model of free inquiry. It provides opportunities for research without prejudgment. Proposals are not accepted or rejected by some anonymous civil servant, however well intentioned. They are reviewed by a panel of citizens, many of them scholars in the field involved. In most cases, approval follows these expert recommendations. Persons outside the scientific community may be insufficiently aware of the freedom that investigators have in the conduct of research within this policy.

The Inter-University Research Program in Institution Building, with funds from the Ford Foundation, invited the study director to undertake a comparative survey of the planning process to institutionalize a youth corps in several countries where such programs have recently been organized. The Gadna Youth Corps of Israel offers a suitable laboratory for this purpose. Its staff and programs, with help from the Israeli International Cooperation Division, have been a model for adaptation in many countries of Africa, Asia, and South America. Most of the field work for this comparative survey remains to be done, but the association with fellow scholars of the Inter-University Research Program served to suggest a number of useful analytic guidelines, which are reported in Chapter 8, "Institution Building: The Gadna."

The Giora Josephthal Fund of Israel made a grant to the assistant director to examine the data collected in the city of Holon for its implication for Israeli youth program policy. A detailed analysis of certain educational concomitants of the data were made by Professor Michael Chen in partial fulfillment of the requirements for the degree of Doctor of Philosophy. Included was a factor analysis of most quantitative and dichotomous variables used in the area sample of the city of Holon, near Tel Aviv (see Chen, 1967: Appendix C, 160–184).

The Szold Institute of Behavioral Science in Jerusalem provided administrative services for the field work in Israel. Its two directors, Professor Moshe Smilanski and his successor, Dr. Chanan Rappaport, accorded to this study the same kind of concern as they would to projects directly sponsored by their own staff.

Joseph Meyouhas and Aryeh Kreisler of the Youth and Sports Department of the Ministry of Education and Culture in Israel helped to open many doors. They were always ready to share ideas and offer advice, administrative clearances, and other essential services. They read some chapters of the manuscript, particularly the one dealing with Beyond School programs, and made some important suggestions for its improvement. The Deputy Minister of Education, the Honorable Aharon Yadlin M. K., gave the study his encouragement. Mrs. Shoshanah Segal of the Holon Youth Department and the energetic mayor of that satellite city of Tel Aviv, the Honorable Pinhas Eylon, did much to facilitate our use of that area for making an intensive study of youth programs.

The investigators had equally satisfactory experiences with getting clearance from Israeli government sources for information that might be relevant. The consequence of the administrative relationship of the Gadna Youth Corps with the Israel Defense Forces (Zahal) was that some of the required data had to be obtained through official channels. When data were requested, they were usually furnished. And what was perhaps even more important, it was rare to find anyone who thought that his official role would make it necessary for him to defend the current policy. In matters related to youth work, Israeli officials within the Defense Forces or the Ministry of Education generally were quite free in discussing their own points of view.

Three former commanders of the Gadna Youth Corps, Colonel Akiba Azmon, Colonel Zvi Ben-Ari and his successor, Colonel Moshe Zohar, took a strong interest in the study. We were "adopted" by the Gadna without being asked to show filial obedience. The research staff was left free to seek relevant information from any available source.

Colonel Mordechai Bar-On, Chief Education Officer and the Liaison Department of the Ministry of Defense under the direction of Colonel Nachman Karni, with the support of Moshe Gilboa and Aaron Canaan, helped to resolve many issues. They were always available to discuss some of the theoretical, as well as analytical, problems that emerged during the data gathering process. Mr. Yehuda Kavish of the Jewish Agency Youth Department called our attention to a number of relevant activities of this body.

The collection and refinement of the raw data in the field would not have been possible without the dedicated efforts of Miss Dalith Ormian, Mrs. Hannah Weiner, and Mrs. Simcha Landau along with the late Mrs. Mellita Roth.

The writing of the report and the refinement of the statistical analysis was done largely at the University of Pittsburgh with the administrative support of Dean William H. McCullough of the Graduate School of Social Work and his Administrative Assistant, Mrs. Elizabeth Mazura. Mrs. Norma Feinberg served as Research Assistant. She was highly imaginative in working out technical details and did much to maintain the morale of the project staff. She did most of the data programming for computer analysis. Copyediting by Dr. Helen Jean Moore and Mrs. Wendy Almeleh helped to make the book more readable, just as Larry Thomas' index adds research convenience.

The writers owe an intellectual debt to those who critically reviewed a part, or all of the manuscript and who were always ready to discuss some of the fundamental questions involved in youth culture management. They were Menachem Horovitz and Gideon Levitas. Mrs. Katherine Falk was a most stimulating coworker, while making a thorough bibliographic survey. Professor Robert Mason of the School of Education at the University of Pittsburgh always found time to discuss with the junior author many of the questions of this study. Certain sociological issues were clarified in discussion with Professors Menachem Amir, Chaim Adler, Israel Katz and Moshe Lissak of the Hebrew University, Professor Alfred H. Katz, of the University of California at Los Angeles, Gavrush Nechushtan of Kibbutz Yezreel, and Martin Eaton of Kibbutz Yavne.

Parts of this book appeared in journal articles, titled "Education for Public Service" (*School and Society,* October 14, 1967: 358–360); "Reaching the Hard-to-Reach in Israel" (*Social Work* 15, No. 1, January 1970: 85–96); and "The Gadna Youth Corps" (*Middle East Journal* 23, No. 4: 471–483).

The most critical test of our findings came in conversation with young Americans and Israelis, who are concretely confronting a moral issue of great magnitude: national service, how and for what ends? Many ideas were suggested by and tested in interviews with adolescents who were considering the question: Shall I volunteer for public service? To them, this book is dedicated.

RESEARCH STAFF

Joseph W. Eaton, *Director*
Michael Chen, *Assistant Director*

ISRAEL FIELD STUDY STAFF

Hannah Wiener, *Administrative Secretary*
Dalith Ormian, *Research Associate*

UNIVERSITY OF PITTSBURGH DATA ANALYSIS STAFF

Mrs. Norma Feinberg, *Computer Program Specialist
and Administrative Secretary*
Mrs. Katherine Falk, *Bibliographic Survey*

ORGANIZATIONAL SPONSORSHIP

Graduate School of Social Work
University of Pittsburgh

and

Henrietta Szold Institute for
Research in the Behavioral Sciences,
Jerusalem, Israel

CONTENTS

TABLES

FIGURES

14

INTRODUCTION

Planned programs to influence the youth culture exist in all modern nations. This book is a case study of a comprehensive effort to get young people to identify with the core ideals of the parental generation through youth organizations. They supplement, through planned leisure-time pursuits, the socialization efforts of the schools and the family. The locale is Israel, where over ninety percent of the adolescents report an active involvement in one or more of three nationwide programs:

(1) Youth movements sponsored by political parties or by the Scouts.

(2) The Gadna Youth Corps, sponsored jointly by school authorities and the Ministry of Defense.

(3) Beyond School programs, providing group work, skill training education, and recreational services in community centers and in school buildings after school hours.

The continuity and survival of a social system depends on the capacities of each generation to meet challenges. Role training to assume these responsibilities is highly developed in the Israeli youth programs. They are coeducational, peer group oriented, with considerable emphasis on individual self-development and national service. The role uncertainty aspect of adolescence (derived from the Latin adolescere—to grow into maturity) is thereby reduced. Youth organizations provide a framework within which a large segment of the youth population is being motivated to spend part of its leisure time in task oriented groups. They combine fun-seeking, learning and comradeship with the acquisition of self-confidence, reinforced by the experience that their activities enjoy much social support.

The role of ideology as a national resource is discussed, as well as the achievement crisis that occurs whenever a revolutionary program for change succeeds, its leaders take power, and want to maintain the same innovative thrust in the oncoming generations.

No revolution is permanent. The Zionist ideology and action program for drastic change through "territorial therapy" of one generation of refugees cannot be transmitted to the refugees' native-born children once many

16

of the objectives of the parental social movement have been achieved. The youth programs, therefore, face the complex task of motivating young people to accept the status quo, while finding a new basis for public concern without which no planned social system can maintain a high level of morale and cohesion.

The youth organizations rely more on a strategy of co-operative control than on a directive strategy. There is much emphasis on voluntaristic participation, including the programs designed to prepare youngsters for both developmental and military forms of national service.

This study includes historical details, as well as an analysis of the planning process. Israel relies on planned control points rather than central comprehensive planning. There is no single source of power over the youth programs. Each political, religious, or politically disinterested adult-making agency is free to compete for the loyalty and concern of the next generation.

Recruitment, programming, and resignation of members as well as the role of peer group leaders and adults are analyzed. Special attention is devoted to efforts to reach the poor and new immigrants. The youth organizations try hard to interest children of population segments who have difficulty in meeting the requirements for achievement in a modernizing society. Class and ethnic group integration are problems that are consciously faced in Israel. This study examines the outcome of these efforts on the basis of extensive survey data of several large samples of the adolescent population and the leaders of the three major youth organizations.

The overwhelming mood of the youth of Israel is not alienation but identification with their country's past, its complex present and its uncertain future. There is criticism of the status quo, but it rarely takes the form of organized protest. Most young people seem to be co-opted by the existing adult-making agencies to work within the system. There is a minority of *idealists* who assign a high priority to national service, even at the price of inconvenience or neglect of more personal and family needs. They have an influence on the majority who are primarily occupied with meeting their self-centered requirements. These more *realistic* segments will support national service requirements on a routine basis during normal periods and with more enthusiasm during periods of emergency. The *detached* segments of the youth population, who are organizationally—and often ideologically —disinterested, also were studied in detail. Although lower-class youth are overrepresented in this group, the youth organizations reach out to them, integrate some and provide them with channels for upward mobility. In Part I, the general issues of youth culture planning are discussed and the role of youth organizations in the process of generational transition. The remainder of the book, Part II, presents the findings of an extensive field study of Israel's youth programs. The research procedures are summarized in Chapter Five. Readers less interested in the details of data collection and of analysis may wish to skip this chapter, though it does include a summary of the major sources of information.

In some respects, Israel's youth culture is unlike that of any other country. Israel is a garrison state, with a powerful army, controlled by a civilian and elected government. Its quasi-socialist economy has many capitalist features. Its origin is ancient, but its renaissance is very recent. Statehood began with a blueprint less than a century ago. Independence was achieved in spite of dedicated opposition from powerful competing Arab nationalist forces which claim the same territory as their patrimony. These and other facts limit, but do not preclude, the formulation of generalizations on the basis of Israel's experiences that may have cross-cultural applicability. No single illustration of how a social system works can prove a theory. Case studies can, however, suggest insights for the understanding of other complex societies, whose young people face similar social change realities. In all modern countries there are problems of generational transmission. An achievement crisis occurs whenever a social goal is realized. The book deals with such propositions and illustrates how the maintenance of a vital youth culture is facilitated by adult acceptance of the theory that the future is determined by the younger rather than their own generation. Organized co-optation of peer groups enables adult-making agencies to influence the youth culture with only occasional resistance to the generational transmission of esteemed social values. Ideological commitment is shown to be a powerful resource that can be harnessed for development as well as defense purposes.

More questions about youth cultures are raised than answered. Foremost among the latter is the challenge: Can social cohesion be maintained if and when peace comes and when material affluence replaces economic hardship? Or will adolescents in Israel begin to conform more and more to the criterion proposed by Sebald (1968: 502) for adolescents in the United States: "The prime condition for adolescence consists of *the discontinuity of socialization between the status of the child and the status of the adult*. This discontinuity stretches over a period of several years, a period of time that in fact is becoming progressively longer and that is beset with a corollary of status uncertainty and problems of identity." The youth culture of Israel conforms much more closely to the model implicit in the personal recollection of Cohen (1965: ix): "A few years ago it occurred to me that when I was a teenager, in the early depression days, there were no teenagers!"

A major issue posed by our findings is the question: Will there be a decline in public readiness to perform essential tasks that involve hardship, boredom and risk, if the common danger recedes? Or can societies, with a vital core-ideology, generate a *moral equivalent to war,* capable of inspiring the next generation with the cohesiveness necessary to sustain the public welfare?

Part One

YOUTH CULTURE AND

NATION BUILDING

Chapter 1

Education for Commitment

Co-optation

Countless generations of loving, untrained, and sometimes downright inadequate parents have kept the human race going. They have children and they influence them. This is never a haphazard process. Each family and local community follow cultural prescriptions to socialize the oncoming generation to become committed to ideals cherished by their elders. They introduce them to the facts as they see them and hope the young will respond in a conventionally approved way. In modern nations this challenge-response socialization process is planned. Adult-making institutions, such as the school and some form of national service, try to induce young people to internalize prevailing social norms.

This book discusses yet another organized socialization network: extracurricular, voluntary and peer group oriented youth programs. The power potential of youth groups explains the great temptations for adult-making institutions to influence young people. Much of the indoctrination is attempted through peer groups, where young people have a good deal of autonomy. Activities are often based on the fact that youths are biologically able to perform adult roles. And they want social acceptance of this fact. They can indulge in satisfying emotional and intellectual experiences with fewer restraints than adults, who are weighed down by family responsibility, who have a status to protect, and whose enthusiasm is often dampened by the caution that stems from experience.

In the United States, there are Scouts and the Four-H Clubs. The Soviet Union has its Komsomol, and Israel has its pioneer youth movements. These organizations, though they differ in many ways, have a common concern: they aim, in part, to challenge adolescents to give a high priority to the performance of public service roles. This includes the performance of acts of good citizenship, the discussion of social issues and consideration of the idea that, in an emergency, they should volunteer for difficult and dangerous assignments. They offer an organizational frame-work for young people to play approved adult-like roles, to acquire self-confidence, and to undergo a rite of passage into a more mature status. The program includes work and adventure, indoctrination and self-expression, study and instruction which the sponsoring adult-making agency views as relevant preparation for becoming a reliable person.

Youth organizations, much more than the schools, are willing to share power with the members or clients. This de-emphasis on adult coercion of young people fits the desire of most adolescents to establish their identity. Most youth programs attempt to satisfy this objective by co-optation—by delegating to participants a good deal of influence and power to make choices, provided they are ready to operate within general policies of the sponsoring agency.[1]

Modern societies, unlike their traditional antecedents, are self-consciously concerned with planning their future. They operate on the theory that the great society is not only built by great men. It relies greatly on an idealistic elite who can inspire support from less public service-oriented "realists." National development has never been just a matter of the availability of manpower and national resources. Development also depends on planned and carefully built social organizations. Some of the poorest countries, those in South America, for example, are rich in natural resources. Some of the least endowed areas of the world, like Switzerland, Israel, and Japan, have gone a long way to compensate for their lack of natural wealth by intensively developing their human resources.

The State of Israel, where a sense of social commitment is highly developed, will serve as a case study of youth organizations and their role in the youth culture. Young people cannot be treated as if they were mere targets for educational inputs of such skills as repairing a car or planting corn. As adults, their ideological orientation will be decisive for how the country will be governed in the future. Men are not machines who can be used by an impersonal state for very long without becoming inefficient. Each new generation must become committed anew to accept the responsibilities of public service.

There is no shortage of recipes of how this can best be accomplished. All social systems use a great deal of indoctrination and coercion, along with education. There is always some readiness to honor an adolescent moratorium on responsibility and to accept deviant behavior. Unusual dress, "sowing wild oats," and "dropping out" are regarded with indulgence, as long as such acts do not provide a fundamental threat to the established order.

This book will deal an added input to this network of social control: youth organizations with programs that accord social status to young people. The theory: Many young people will respond voluntarily to expectations that they assume limited responsibilities for the future of their society, long before they reach adulthood. Youth can be co-opted into socially and sometimes innovative activities as soon as the rapid pace of their biological maturation whets their appetite for parallel social acceptance of their capabilities.

Public service

Public service is a normative concept that defies operational definition. It implies social commitment and sacrifice. It can be defined as a *readiness to assign a high priority to the accomplishment of ideal-oriented objectives, even at the expense of competing personal convenience or preference.* Public service involves the acting out of good citizenship roles that make social norms operational. Nations and individuals vary in the degree to which public purposes are allowed to influence the determination of personal and family preferences.

The prevalence of honoring public priorities of a country, however defined, can balance discrepancies in population size, natural wealth and military hardware. It is measured less by what people say than by what they will do in circumstances when they can make a choice between actions that would be of private benefit and others which would serve public goals, to their personal detriment or inconvenience. The range is from relatively *detached* persons, who identify little, if at all, with public purposes to the *idealists* with the highest degree of commitment to assign priority to the accomplishment of social objectives. The rewards for what they do are internalized, often nonmaterial and spiritual. There is a high degree of voluntarism in their role. From this they may gain much public esteem, and at times they exercise power in the name of the cause which they serve.

The most dramatic instances of public service involve the risk of life for a cause. Lesser degrees of sacrifice involve the readiness to face imprisonment, forego a chance to hold a "safe" job, or engage in political activity for an unpopular cause, as John F. Kennedy (1964) documented well in *Profiles in Courage*. And there are "dollar-a-year" men, who give up remunerative and important positions to take complex government assignments. Other indices of public service orientation are charitable donations and working for the conservation of natural resources.

There was little reliance on public service incentives in the larger premodern states, with such notable exceptions as the Greek city states, the churches and other religious institutions. Governments did most of their business by relying on a system of material rewards and punishments. Princes depended heavily on the services of mercenaries or they resorted to coercion, serfdom and slavery to recruit the men needed to do their bidding. Modern states, especially democracies, rely to a greater extent on voluntary efforts to accomplish national objectives. They require the serv-

ices of public spirited minorities: people committed to give a high priority
to serving their community on the basis of self-motivation, far beyond any
material rewards that can be offered. Appeals for such commitments are
commonplace. Educational programs to nurture them require more planful
social action.

Dedication intensities

One of the objectives of youth culture management is to encourage
idealistic priorities on the part of the next generation and to discourage
detachment or cynic rejection. On the basis of their degree of readiness
to assign a high priority to public service needs, citizens can be divided
roughly into three dedication intensity categories—*idealists, realists* and the
detached.

Public spirited persons will disagree on many policies. But irrespective
of their political outlook, there is utility in differentiating between *idealists*
and *realists* on the basis of their relative concern for public rather than
private purposes.[2] There are those who will voluntarily vote for an increase of their own taxes to build better schools. Others will oppose such a
policy so that they can have more personal spending power. Public service
idealism is a major motivational ingredient among missionaries, persons
who join Catholic orders, Peace Corps volunteers and rebels of all types
(nationalists, conscientious objectors or journalists who refuse to disclose
their sources of information) who prefer jail to violating their principles.
But ideological commitment is always reinforced by other motives, even
when men risk their lives. For example in World War II, soldiers interviewed at the front for a study of combat motivation mentioned personal
values like "group solidarity," "ending the task" and "self-preservation"
more frequently than public service norms like "idealism," "duty" and
"self-respect" (Smith, 1949: 108). Public service attitudes can be expressed
in many social roles. In nursing, social work, teaching, civil service and
many other professions, personal preferences are expected to be subordi-
nated in favor of public priorities.

The importance of public service expectations increases during revolution, depression, or natural calamity; there are strong demands for higher
public priorities in the expenditures of resources, personal and social. It
might be noted here that the Chinese word for crisis is *Wei-Chi,* a philosophical combination of two characters, one meaning *danger,* the other
opportunity. This combination of alternatives is the essence of the crisis
situation. Some of the most dramatic crises are military. There are people
who will volunteer to defend their country; more will serve if drafted; and
there are some who will do all in their power to evade service.

At all times, the number of idealists is limited. They do not usually
control the political process. But social policies tend to be influenced by

them far beyond their numerical strength. Their potential for being influential is a function of their capacity to sustain a high level of civic enthusiasm during a state of crisis, while keeping resources needed for personal needs at a minimum.

The idealistic elite has to rely for support on the much larger (and therefore politically important) *realistic* segment of the community. Particularly during sustained crisis, idealists are not sufficient to meet manpower requirements. Realists balance public needs with a strong emphasis on their personal needs.

Publicity of the Peace Corps, for instance, takes a realistic approach. In recruiting personnel, it emphasizes what the Peace Corps can do for its volunteer as much as what the volunteer will be required to do in his job. The following (Shuldiner, 1965: 73–75) are examples of both types of emphasis:

Idealism	*Realism*
There is nothing that the developing countries need so much as people with trained hands who can pass along their skill to others.	The Peace Corps is the working man's Rhodes Scholarship,—it gives a person an opportunity to live and work in culture different from any he has known.
After a cyclone, Roger Hard, a bricklayer in Pakistan along with seven Pakistani volunteers rebuilt 171 homes and two schools. What's more: his planning and instruction of Pakistani in bricklaying (when it was again possible to get bricks) led to the rebuilding of Kumire into the model community it is today.	Hard left Pakistan soon thereafter . . . this work had also given him administrative experience he expects to use in a new career. Today he is studying labor relations at Portland (Oregon) State College.
	The Peace Corps does not guarantee any improvement in future earning power, but service does open new opportunties. Many colleges award academic credit for Peace Corps experience and more than 1,000 scholarships are available to former volunteers.
	Private industry is also becoming increasingly interested in former Corpsmen. I.B.M. President Thomas J. Watson says that volunteers who complete their service are particularly employable. They have demonstrated the ability to do tough jobs under difficult circumstances, and there are never enough people of this kind available.

Realists conform to Almond's (1950: 53–60) generalization about Americans: "They prefer to combine idealistic explanations with pragmatic justification. It must be good for an abstract selfless cause but also be 'good business' . . . Americans would appear to be happiest when they can cloak action motivated by self-interest with an aura of New Testament unselfishness . . ." In the words of the ancient Hebrew proverb, which is also the text of an Israeli popular song (Babylonian Talmud, 1935: 8):

> If I am not myself, who will I be?
> If I am only for myself, what am I?
> And if not now—when?

Realists and idealists differ from the more detached segments of the population who are not interested in public priorities. In many of the newly emerging countries the detached represent a majority of the citizenship. Identification with national objectives is weak. The energy of most people is concentrated on personal, family, local and tribal needs. During a crisis, this condition changes only slightly. The detached feel they have little reason for identification with the larger social order. Many of them are poor, culturally disadvantaged, emotionally ill or feel discriminated against. Emergency measures like rationing or licensing will be viewed as antithetical to their needs.

Even in the world's richest country, a Presidential Commission (The President's Task Force on Manpower Conservation) in 1964 reported that many young people have good reasons for not identifying with the interests of national security. In the United States one-third of all young men in the nation turning 18 would be found unqualified if they were to be examined for induction into the armed forces. Of them, about one-half would be rejected for medical reasons. The remainder would fail through inability to qualify on academic achievement and mental tests.

Usually there is a tendency to keep this disaffected or detached segment to a minimum. Those in power or the opposition wishing to replace them exhort young people to be idealistic. And if not idealistic, they expect young people to show realism in balancing social and personal needs.

Voluntarism

A key element in public service is voluntarism. It can be defined as the degree to which a task is performed in response to normative or idealistic power, rather than remunerative or coercive power (Etzioni, 1961: 4–6). Volunteers often achieve an elite status by virtue of their readiness to sacrifice for public purposes. This differentiates them from more established elites, whose power is derived from wealth, the accident of birth into a prestigious family or control over military resources. Idealistic elites represent an important avenue for social mobility. Even young people can gain considerable influence by virtue of their identification with an idealistic cause that enjoys public esteem and by their willingness to sacrifice for the actualization of these ideals. Removal of mines from a battlefield is forced labor if enemy civilians are required to do it. It is idealism of the highest order when soldiers volunteer to do it as a public service. Voluntarism can give social prestige to otherwise menial, difficult or dangerous jobs (Eaton, 1968: 129–134 and 1967: 358–360).

The actual tasks performed by volunteers are often the same as those performed by some non-voluntaristic employees. What differs is the social meaning attached to what is done. When a job is regarded as a public service, those who perform it can more easily demand and receive social support to insure their success. This access to social support is the reason why so much youth work is organized on a non-profit basis. Their voluntaristic aspect endows the programs with symbolic meaning for the survival of cherished social values.

Young people are primarily *consumers* of other people's attention in their home and school. They can be *producers* of attention for other people when they serve as volunteers. In this role they are often allowed to perform services the adult society values, but would not pay for. Volunteering opens up new opportunity structures that enable youths to practice adult roles and begin to be recognized for them. It is hard to criticize, discipline or fire a volunteer. As a result, the frequently competitive rules under which men work are modified. A volunteer youth leader who conducts a swimming class will get help from other citizens who think that his job is also theirs. Since he asks little for himself, he can demand that others help out with donated labor, rent-free quarters or whatever else is needed. The commercial swimming school cannot count on such support. Its owner will have to be licensed and pay taxes.

Planning

National development requires planning, *the determination and enforcement of public priorities*. Detailed planning is usually done only for selected *control points* of the social system, as in the allocation of budgets or rationing. Many plans are implemented voluntarily. Under emergency conditions, planning will become more comprehensive. In war, it becomes nearly total. In peace time, for instance, manpower needs tend to be planned only on the basis of making broad determinations of how much labor should be allocated to one or another segment of the economy. In war, many citizens will work on jobs that are assigned by the government. They are drafted to serve in the army or to perform specific civilian tasks.

Our generation has witnessed the attainment of independence by nearly all countries of the world. Some of them, formerly ruled by colonial powers, had barely emerged from the iron age. They expected to become transformed quickly into twentieth century nations once their flag was raised at the United Nations. Unfortunately, they lacked the manpower to work planfully for national development. The component tribes, races and religious groups had been unified on a purely negative basis—hatred of the former rulers. Once this unifying scapegoat disappeared there was no new idea to replace it. In the pursuit of tribal interests, or to support the dreams of empire of their dictators, millions have been killed in civil wars. Others were forced to become refugees. Many of these new nations have experienced a drop in their standard of living.

This type of *achievement crisis* was particularly pronounced in Indonesia, Egypt, the Congo and in Nigeria. In repeated revolutions, some of the most idealistic and well educated persons were forced into inconsequential posts, had to flee or were murdered. The nations concerned are now having difficulty in motivating young people in sufficient number to work hard for positive developmental objectives.

In Israel, whose youth organizations are the subject of this book, the achievement crisis has been of more modest dimension. Conflicting interest groups have learned to coexist. Unity is not only encouraged by the existence of military threat from the outside; it is nurtured by the existence of a Zionist ideology that is widely shared by the Jewish population. It provides a normative basis for positive planning. Major policy issues are being debated openly. Decisions, once made, can be implemented by technicians, who can appeal for support in the name of public service values, that enjoy widespread sanction.

Competing priorities

The core values that support planning for socioeconomic development are never perfectly integrated. There are always multiple criteria, public and private, by which the desirability of an action can be judged. This fact gives rise to an often unmentioned variable of the planning process: its competing priorities. There are always values opposed to those on which a plan is predicated. They introduce an inefficiency factor, that must be taken into account, unless those responsible for a plan have the will and capacity to ignore all competing cultural values and to silence those who support them. For instance, the objective of educating young people has to be dealt with in terms of traditional families who have a prevailing belief that girls, the future mothers of the society, will be corrupted if exposed to too much education. Sometimes this means that girls are kept out of school altogether. Other parents at the least will impose restriction on their children's participation in peer group programs.

A high rate of development can occur even with a sizable inefficiency factor. The planning process in a democracy can never be fully unidimensional so that all alternate cultural deterrents will be ignored. Planning involves more than the determination and public enforcement of technically relevant priorities. Allowance must be made for the fact that there are traditions—many of them widely cherished—even though they require actions which are technically irrelevant or contrary to a plan and its implementation.

Military versus developmental priorities

The issue of competing priorities is highlighted in the confrontation of military and developmental priorities in the national planning process. All nations maintain military establishments for reasons of prestige, as well as security, internal or external. In some, the priority assigned to the purchase of complex military hardware and the training of necessary experts is so high, that major developmental projects are shelved. Children die of minor infections for the lack of penicillin pills, costing pennies, while their governments maintain million-dollar fleets of supersonic planes, flown by pilots who could have become physicians.

No implication is intended that all military expenditures can be dispensed with. Some countries might not survive without military deterrent forces against internal or external enemies. But if a high rate of socio-economic development is the goal of a national plan, military priorities represent an inefficiency factor. And if the only formal demand for public service to young people is to engage in compulsory military training, a potential resource of great magnitude is lost to the cause of development.

True, when young people are drafted for military service, this does not entirely exclude their utilization in developmental tasks. All modern armies are contributing incidentally to nation-building objectives by offering supplementary and technical education, by building roads and through emergency aid to civilians. They can stimulate much general economic activity in all sectors of the economy. But the essence of most military service programs is negative—the prevention of conquest by an enemy or the enhancement of internal security. Military activities receive greater publicity than the achievement of a high yield by farmers. Few countries have as yet learned to have an independence parade honoring those who create products of farms and factories that will give substance to their new sovereignty. Only military men are rewarded medals, though their work can affect a nation's development capability only indirectly.

Public service can be rendered through both military channels and developmental programs. Under a military system, planning priorities are set and enforced by command from above. Developmental programs generally allow for more citizen participation in the process of determining priorities. Another fundamental distinction is that planning for nonmilitary development tends to be less comprehensive. It is often restricted to control points through an allocation budgeting or a licensing system. The distinction between the two types is highlighted by the following conceptual model:

Conceptual Model of Public Service

Functional variable	Military	Developmental
Goals	Destructive or the prevention of destruction	Creative—addition to existing resources
Risks	Life, limb, health and property	Comfort, convenience and limitation on self-centered pursuits
Time	Limited to period of a military service	Less limited—can require lifetime dedication
Skills	Military emphasis with only incidental carry-over to civilian life	Production oriented, with carry-over to military capability
Planning	Priorities determined publicly and affecting all aspects of living	Public determination of priority usually limited to control points of the system
Decision-making	By command; very limited public participation	Considerable public participation

In Israel, where a high proportion of the national income is devoted to defense, there also is a strong emphasis on economic development. Technical planning requirements are often modified by competing cultural priorities. The coexistence of these functions in the youth culture will be examined in detail.

Search for a moral equivalent to war

Readiness to give public service seems to be related to the degree of crisis in a society. When the frontiers are developmental, idealists and realists are not easily distinguishable. When there is enough income to pay them, both pay their taxes. Both work to meet self-needs, while doing something to fulfill public requirements. The distinction between idealists and realists becomes most evident during an emergency, especially a war, when individuals must make fateful choices between what they can expect from the nation and what they must be prepared to give to it.

In the hope of counteracting the reduction of public service readiness during peace, *a moral equivalent to war* strategy was first advocated by Professor William James (1940: 193–194).[3] Before World War I, he urged in a now classic essay that youth be conscripted for peaceful, rather than military, purposes. They would be assigned to

> hardship tasks of social significance in a war against poverty and a natural calamity to get the childishness knocked out of them and to come back to society with healthier sympathies and more sober ideas.

They would have paid their blood tax, done their own part in the immemorial human warfare against nature, they would tread the earth more proudly, the women would value them more highly, they would be better fathers and teachers of the following generation.

There are those who would dismiss James' proposal as utopian. In all countries, national service has been and continues to be largely related to warfare. Real or imagined threats of war are being utilized by those in power to maintain sizable military establishments and to call upon young people to serve in them (Levin, 1967). Little of their youthful capabilities are directed towards peaceful and developmental objectives. But there are some exceptions. A part of the military manpower and equipment are siphoned off for peaceful purposes (Glick, 1967). Among Israelis, as Hanning (1967: 119) reports, there is much interest in harnessing the military national service machinery to the achievement of developmental objectives because "the need for military readiness is matched by a comparable need to mobilize the nation against a harsh and unrewarding physical environment. To this need they have responded by building on tradition and modernizing the concept of the soldier-farmer."

The existence of real or imagined military threat in so much of the world has constrained the few voices who would shift at least some of the priorities in national service towards peaceful objectives. The idea of non-military public service through building a recreation area in a national park or by teaching in an urban slum has less drama than guarding the sky against a possible attack from hostile airplanes. But minorities among young people in many parts of the world are expressing an interest in relating to public service challenges in which the goals are developmental rather than military. They are willing to serve the cause of peace.

Commitment education

Young people everywhere must learn to see their world in five dimensions: Length, width, height, time and *purpose*. The first four dimensions are well defined. Not so the fifth dimension: the purposes for which men strive and for which objects are used. An adolescent can use a stopwatch to time himself to the length of a hundreth of a second in the hundred-meter dash. But there is no single standard for deciding why he should run so fast. To keep physically fit? To win glory for his team? To gain personal fame? Would he be better off if he were to use his time studying accounting and competing in the job market?

What for is a question that applies to every activity of individuals and societies. Answers are never simple. But they are essential for personal and social stability. Existence without personal goals is demoralizing, even pathological. Social life without fundamental consensus yields anarchy and anomie. Agreement on basic values is particularly difficult to arrive at in a modern society, in which there is a rapid rate of change. New ideas compete with traditional values. Confusion about the purposive dimension of living is common.

One of the characteristics of traditional societies is that parents feel secure in their beliefs. There is little ambivalence in indoctrinating their offspring. Modern parents are generally less sure of themselves. They have problems in transmitting a well-defined philosophy of life to their children because they have experienced our modern era as Churchill (1930: 74–75) described it in his biography:

> I wonder often whether any other generation has seen such outstanding revolutions of data and values as those through which we have lived. Scarcely anything material or established which I was brought up to believe was permanent and vital, has lasted. Everything I was sure or taught to be sure was impossible, has happened.

Education not only involves knowledge and skills, it includes indoctrination of young people to embrace the nation building beliefs, hopes and values that sustain the planning process. Commitment education answers the question: "What for?" It occurs not only in schools, but in churches and synagogues. It can never be divorced too much from the real world. Doctrinaire pressure to serve unrealistic causes may be applied to young people by well entrenched power figures; however, in time, senility and death will force them to yield to succession by the youth whom they once controlled. Stalin, for instance, like other megalomaniacs before him chose priorities that were symptoms of a paranoid personality and often defeated national planning objectives. His successors redefined him from being a national savior to a criminal psychopath.

The inevitability of generational succession is an ever-present social reality, no matter what power of persuasion, control or terror is employed to retard its impact on social change. Stalin's own daughter (Alliluyeva, 1969) left Russia to campaign for civil liberty at home. And still younger Soviet citizens have sought martyrdom by publishing what they believed but knew to be officially frowned on. In commenting on the current evidence of rebelliousness of Soviet youths, Edward Crankshaw (1968: 9), a British Kremlinologist, notes:

> For decades anyone who dared speak up in the Soviet Union, even privately among friends, would find himself taken away in the middle of the night, imprisoned, interrogated, sent to forced labor, if not shot. Why, then, has the sequestration of a few young writers so profoundly shocked a society for so long accustomed to terror? The answer is that the young genuinely believed that the spirit of the highest authority had changed, and that all that was necessary to make the Soviet Union a fit place for honest men and women was a show of the boldness and determination they found lacking in their elders.

Ideology as a national resource

Idealism makes men willing to plant trees that will benefit only the next generation. It will support a heavy program of saving and taxation to raise capital for development. It will induce a significant minority to sacrifice for commonly shared values in more substantial ways, economic as well as personal. *Ideas Are Weapons,* is what Lerner (1940) proposes in a seminal book which examines the impact on ideologies that become internalized by people.

There is a tendency to exaggerate the significance of material possessions for social change and national development. This bias has been reinforced by the valid observations that the actions of men are influenced by economic considerations. How men are related to the means of production no doubt affects their lives, but this Marxian theory must not blind anyone to the fact that individuals and groups also act with economic irrationality. Without commitment education, even generous economic incentives may be insufficient for rapid nation-building. Remunerative incentives provide a very limited basis for development, as has been indicated in Libya, Iraq and Ghana. While these countries are relatively rich in natural resources, their population includes as yet few who are also highly responsive to strong idealism for nation-building. In contrast, Israel and Japan, while poor in natural wealth, have populations that include strong minorities of idealists who give high priority to public needs, even at the cost of some personal inconvenience and loss (McDiarmid, 1966: 136–143). Their challenge by adversity after World War II was great; but so was the response of their nation-building elites. These countries lead the world in a rapid rate of development.[4] Many other variables, like investment and technical aid, affect development. But commitment also is a concrete socioeconomic resource.

The basis for normative or patriotic consensus is eroding in many countries which are experiencing rapid social change. Migrants or their parents moved from a farm to a village; from village to a city. Or they have emigrated to a new country. They question the "old" ways without having alternate standards to replace them. Young people grow up without being able to accept the traditional values held by their grandparents, values about which many of their parents already had doubts. For instance, honesty is seen as a "good policy," but men who get ahead without honesty can become leaders of the community. Patriotism may be extolled verbally, but only a minority of parents want *their* children to enter national service. In each country there are many men uncertain if there is any public issue for which it is worth sacrificing for. They are primarily addressing themselves to family, neighborhood, and tribal concerns.

The requirement of missionary service of Mormon Youths, Quaker work camps, Russia's Komsomol, Ethiopia's University Service, Germany's "Wiedergutmachung" (Reconstruction) Labor Projects and Israel's Gadna Youth Corps are all applications of the theory that public service is good both for society and for the person. Comprehensive commitment is expected of members in these *elite* youth organizations. They aim at more than member self development. They have as their objective the moral revitalization of and/or political influence on the larger society.[5] Premature resignation is not merely a matter of canceling a membership. It involves a loss of status, even to the extent of being viewed a "deserter" of common ideals. Members are expected to identify largely or totally with the movement, at the expense of other peer group loyalties. As a Director of Training of the Peace Corps (Kauffman, 1963: 155) points out, "Public service is different from the pattern of careerism, that begins in early high school for many U. S. youths. They learn to plan every move of work, study or pleasure, within the context of building a 'record,' curricular and extra-curricular."

Conclusion

The relative success of a plan for nation-building is not only a function of its technical perfection but is also dependent on its inefficiency factor. No planned social change can ignore the existence of competing priorities. Culture is not rational. Every plan has to take account of alternate interests and deterrent social forces. Their containment to a realistic minimum is the challenge that differentiates nations that do well from those which do poorly in planning and implementing an actual program.

This generation is witnessing the emergence of new nations at an unprecedented rate. Local populations have attained sovereignty in most areas of the world. But after their flag is raised and the new national anthem has stirred the citizenry, they wake up the next morning to face the challenge: Nationhood for what?

In India, the Congo, Nigeria and Indonesia independence was followed by sectional and tribal struggles. In Egypt and Ghana, the end of colonial rule led to efforts to restore ancient empires. Many resources were allocated to meet competing military priorities. Others were destroyed in civil riots between competing power cliques. Military and prestige expenditures compete with developmental investments in the national budgets of all new nations.

This book will proceed from an assumption that the pace of planned nation-building or of development is never simply a function of natural resources. Their scarcity can be more than compensated for by planning with a low inefficiency factor. This is possible because competing priorities are kept down to a reasonable degree by an elite with a strong public service commitment, an active minority who are ready to give high priority to the satisfaction of agreed upon public needs even at the inconvenience of alternate and more person-oriented priorities.

Such an elite is neither hereditary nor a function of privilege. It is self-selected and voluntaristic. It is unlikely to emerge without deliberately planned programs, like youth organizations, for the utilization of national service volunteers. Volunteers must be trusted with responsibility and held to standards of performance. Their impact on the country is a function of the intensity of their commitment, their number and the balance between what allocations are made by these elite to military and developmental needs. These two utilities are not mutually exclusive. But when high value is placed on military gains, many of the society's resources and its most gifted and dedicated officials are less available for the implementation of developmental requirements (Brenan, 1968).

In a modern society, the recruitment of idealistic elite is not left to chance. It is facilitated by adult-making institutions, which include commitment education among their functions. These adult-making institutions include the school, the army and the youth organization. The latter, unlike the school or the army, relies largely on voluntaristic recruitment. Its programs are directed by adults, but day-to-day operations are also influenced much by its youthful leaders and members.

The theory that a dedicated minority of idealists can help inspire other more realistic segments of the population to work together to achieve public purposes is a specific instance of a more general sociological proposition: what social groups want to have happen, can happen, if their desire is accompanied by a plan to bring about the change. This theory has also been described as the self-fulfillment theory (Merton, 1964: 421–436).

This book will deal with informal educational programs designed to challenge a proportion of the country's youth to volunteer for public service and to motivate much of the remainder to contribute to public purposes within the limits of their more personal and family requirements. It will also deal with what is being done organizationally to reduce to a minimum the proportion of detached youths who feel no identification with these nation-building priorities. It will examine the balance between military and developmental objectives in the commitment education program of Israel, a country with a serious and chronic security problem, as well as a core ideology that places much value on social-economic development.

Chapter 2

Youth Organizations

Adult making and the youth culture

Education for public service is part of the function of an interrelated network of social institutions. They include the family, school, religious groups, and in many lands, a national service. They have the purpose of *adult making,* of socializing the young. Each of these institutions is adult directed, with a plan to influence the youth culture.

Youth culture is the web of normative directives in a society that are enforced among the young—their rules, customs, fashions and fads. These norms often differ somewhat for the young than their parents, particularly in rapidly changing societies. Modern adolescents who can take a tranquilizer before an examination or a "pill" before a date, or who will hear their President psychoanalyzed by a television commentator face life problems with which their parents had no experience. Innovation has always been the privilege of youth as well as its destiny. Even in less rapidly changing cultures, young people must learn to take adult roles under circumstances that are different from those their parents experienced. They must separate psychologically and residentially to form their own families of procreation. They must enter the world of work, learn to make decisions and take risks. This process of generational transition is universal, but it has taken on added significance in modern times. Its young people grow up in a world where the adults fail to take account of the rapid pace of social change.

Commitment education for conformity to adult expectations begins in the family, as does every aspect of social identity. This is where the young begin to learn answers to the questions "who am I, what am I and what purpose do I serve?" The national language is acquired and emotional links are developed with a historic sense of community. Attitudes of readiness for patriotic and communal service are most likely to flourish

36

if supported by the family. But the means for their expression require a larger social framework than the kinship group.

Commitment education is continued and reinforced in the public school. But such indoctrination is not the school's primary function. Its curriculum tends to be focused on pragmatic subjects, learning skills and acquiring of knowledge. Much of the time is devoted to "how to do it" courses. Less time is given to history and civics, which if properly taught, acquaint students with nation-building issues that confront the body politic.

The school rarely has a partisan ideological impact, especially in democratic states, where different political parties compete for power. In such countries, controversial political and moral issues that young people must confront are often deliberately avoided in the curriculum. Such omissions also occur in totalitarian states where teachers fear to discuss them openly. Schools and universities more often become the seedbeds of change because students become involved in clandestine study and discussion *outside* the official curriculum.

Voluntary youth organizations are under no such constraints for neutrality. They can be and often are frankly partisan. They do not try to appeal to everybody. Some espouse a specific political or economic philosophy, such as "free enterprise," socialism, anarchism or some form of nationalist revival.

School and youth organizations

The first step taken in modern societies to contain the youth culture was universal compulsory education. In recent decades, young people are also offered more informal programs like the Scouts, group work programs, extracurricular activities and recreation services. They generally stress neutral civic virtues. They avoid major public controversies, very much as the public schools do. This similarity may help to explain why they are sometimes closely related administratively to the schools.

There are few activities of such youth programs which could not also be sponsored by a school. Both can conduct sports activities, discussions and hikes. They can sponsor clubs, help develop leadership and organize the idealistic elite for public service programs. When two institutions coexist, the question naturally arises: "Why are there several organizational alternatives for accomplishing the same objective?"

The answer may be related to the different prerequisites for participation in each of these institutions. Schools cannot go far in co-opting peer groups. They cannot yield much power to the students. Their primary task is technical, the counteraction of illiteracy and ignorance. Teachers and principals, being in full charge, organize what they regard as optimum conditions for the acquisition of skills. Students are evaluated by how much they know. Fierce competition is generally encouraged.

In contrast, peer groups follow a set of different rules. Courtship, intramural sports, debating, the enjoyment of music or other "fun" activities are priority goals. Participation is not conditional on comprehensive examinations or grades. In few groups, high value is placed on emotionally laden experiences like comradeship, participation and loyalty to shared ideals. Schools are therefore often supplemented planfully by a separate informal education network. The latter does not have the built-in limitations of schools for counteracting peer group influences.

This is why two frameworks, the school and the youth organizations, can and do coexist. They serve different functions. Youth leaders, unlike teachers, do not have to demonstrate their skill on the basis of competitive accomplishments of their charges. Success involves such variables as who participated, the frequency of participation and whether the involvement helped in the formation of the adolescents' social identity.

Of the two institutions, the school is the more firmly rooted in most parts of the world. There is where the young study skills and "safe" ideas. In totalitarian and even in many democratic countries, there are nationally planned educational systems. But youth-serving institutions speak less often with a single voice. Certainly, in multiparty states with democratic governments, there is no central source of power, even when government and semipublic bodies support many of the youth programs. In school systems, uniformity is often imposed by such devices as nationwide textbooks accompanied by teachers' manuals and workbooks, performance testing and final examinations. Young people cannot resign from school without considerable opposition from adults. They can leave a youth organization with much less and sometimes no loss on status. Such organizational flexibility facilitates the involvement of young people. To be a pupil in good standing, a student is evaluated by adults on the basis of how well he acquires specific occupational skills, technical knowledge and formal study. In youth organizations the "curriculum" is much less formal. Young people can take part in programming and policy making. In a woodworking class in a vocational high school, the teacher prescribes what is being done; in a woodworking group in a youth center, the activity is defined as a hobby. Training in personal hygiene occurs in both schools and youth movements, as do discussions of recent history, ethics and philosophy. But in voluntary youth organizations, unconventional ideas, such as the use of LSD, sexual freedom or political change can be discussed without Ministry of Education-level clearance. New youth culture patterns can be developed and tested. Fashions, fads and protests can and are tolerated.

In youth organizations, there is also less competitiveness than in schools. Voluntary youth programs can appeal to youngsters who get poor grades in school. Leadership, a sense of humor, athletic skills and sex appeal can give such youths peer group status they cannot get in school if their knowledge or skills are marginal. In youth organizations, performance will be rated by a different set of criteria. There is an expectation that youths are important and that most of them will succeed. In school, only a minority are expected to do well.[6]

Formal youth organizations were rare in ancient or medieval times. Nor do they exist in contemporary traditional or, what Eisenstadt (1956) calls, "nonkinship or universalistic" societies. In these predevelopment cultures, adolescence is a brief interlude between childhood and adulthood. There is not too much role uncertainty, although romantic observers have been apt to exaggerate the bucolic simplicity of these so-called "simple" societies. However, identity is taught early and unequivocally. Adult responsibilities are to be assumed early, especially in the area of work. Marriage can take place right after puberty and full employment often begins before it. Levels of aspiration of young people are realistic, not far removed from what could be achieved with moderate effort. Each person is born with an established status. Semi-slavery, indentured service and corporal punishment—even abuse have at times been quite acceptable as means of controlling the next generation (Aries, 1962).

In the more modern social systems, there are an increasing number of organizational mechanisms to postpone adult status. Youths are sent to college, in part to "find themselves," not just to train for specific adult roles. The status transition from childhood to adulthood is slow, resulting in many role uncertainties. Adolescents are expected to postpone marriage for several years after puberty. The state grants voting status years after young people think they are qualified for it. Except in times of dire emergency, such as war, youths are not made to think they have a real part to play in the ongoing social system. Quite often schools serve as institutions for the prolongation of "nobodyness." Controversial questions have to be handled gingerly. Many modern adults are ill-at-ease about or totally opposed to the public discussion of moral, sexual, religious and political controversies. In some circles, such questions are barely thought to be appropriate for adult consideration. The public school tends to reflect this lack of normative consensus.

In the 1950s, 90 youth organizations were reported [7] in France, 141 in the Netherlands and 115 in the German Federal Republic (*European Seminar on New Methods of Working with Youth Groups,* 1955: 15–20, 1956: 15). Hundreds of youth-serving agencies exist in the United States at national, state and local levels, under both governmental and voluntary sponsorship.[8]

The diversity of organized youth groups in the multiparty states stands in contrast to what exists in highly controlled societies. In newly emerging nations, the expansion of both schools and youth organizations are among the many signs of modernization, but most of the youth organizations are sponsored by the same government that also runs the schools. This is true of the Ghana Workers Brigade or the National Volunteer Service programs in Kenya, Ethiopia, the Ivory Coast, Jamaica, the Philippines and Thailand (International Peace Corps Secretariat, 1964: 1; Hailie Selassie I University, 1966; *Commandant Levy Aperçu Sur Les Activités Du Service,* 1967; Lawrence, 1962). In the more authoritarian lands, there is not only a single organizational framework, but young people are bluntly discouraged from becoming interested in political action generated by peer groups. Spontaneous youth leadership is suppressed. To give an extreme case, when Hitler assumed power in Germany, all the country's youth organizations were either dissolved or *gleichgeschaltet* (integrated). In single-party countries, like Poland and the U.S.S.R., only one major youth organization is allowed, but there are many less formal "circles," especially in the universities. Participation in the state-sponsored youth organization is a virtual must for youths planning a career in politics, education, or public service. It smooths the path to upward social mobility, to higher education, and to other career advantages. There are always exceptions to this controlling tendency, but, at least in theory, youth organizations in single-party countries are seen as instruments to be controlled by the central government. These organizations do not stress what youth organizations can do for young people; they ask what young people do for the party. In the name of "national interest," young people are expected to work under adult direction to support the political and/or religious principles of those in charge of the government (Fainsod, 1951: 18–40).

Peer groups—informal and temporary—differ from all these adult-making institutions because much of the initiative and power is in the hands of youths. Young members can compete with the better entrenched adult authority figures, such as parents, school and government officials. Friendship groups, cliques and gangs which stress sociability but have no clearly defined programs, provide youth-controlled environments for learning new social roles. Youth culture innovations emerge in such settings and are expressed in a variety of group activities, including sports, dancing, dating, music, hiking, adventure, "hanging out," crime or political protest. There is little long-range planning and no hierarchy of formal leaders. At times, peer groups adopt an action program such as a hike, a dance, a delinquent rumble, a sit-down strike against racial discrimination, or other pressing problems. But they rarely develop a stable organizational structure.

The spontaneity and voluntarism of peer group associations give them a basis for having great influence on the youth culture and on individual youngsters. Old patterns are tested; new ways of dealing with life problems are likely to emerge. Adult-making institutions are, therefore, tempted to sponsor youth groups. Many parents, favoring such indirectly controlled programs, will encourage their children to join them.

Unlike the schools, youth organizations are elective. This is their most distinctive feature. They are age- and sometimes sex-limited. Children can choose to belong or resign, be active or nominal in their participation. Some have ideological selection criteria. Others are more activity centered or stress the learning of skills and hobbies. Overall policies, even when determined by adults, reflect more youth power than in other social role-training programs. Training for approved adult role behavior is an incidental rather than an explicit objective. Youth leaders without professional qualifications can serve as volunteers. Unlike teachers, social workers and army officers, they need not be adults. Their actions are less often predicated on the expectation of making this work their career.

The schools are too formal to be informal as well. But youth work, both inside and outside school auspices, is also becoming professionalized. In the United States few ministers run church clubs. The job is turned over to educational directors. Group work and recreation leadership are subjects of graduate level training programs. The importance of amateur citizens in the youth services is declining.

An expansion of youth programs, personnel, buildings and equipment can be expected, regardless of the organizational development that will be used. The management of the youth culture is a "growth industry." This can be observed universally, in the more developed as well as the less developed countries, where leisure is thought of not only as a luxury but also as a "problem."

There has been little systematic study of this organizational network to influence the youth culture. This book aims to identify some of the issues and provide data to facilitate their examination.

Control strategies

Patterned relationships between young people and the adult-making agencies vary considerably. Traditional parents tend to object to the symbols of the emerging youth culture, which conflict with their way of life. Somewhat more permissive traditionalists will consider each youth culture innovation on its merits. Parents decide unilaterally which fads they will tolerate or disapprove. In more modern families, a feedback process exists between parents and their children. Although the parents retain veto power, they will allow their children to engage in innovative fads as long as they do so within limits set by the parents. When the parents lose control over their children, a revolutionary family situation is created.

Similar variations in patterned behavior can be observed at the organizational level. Those responsible for youth culture management operate on the basis of a variety of strategic models.

(1) Lowest on the scale of peer group power is a *negative* strategy.

It views most separatist youth culture manifestations as dangerous, if not antisocial. Youth culture patterns are downgraded or opposed.

(2) Next on the scale is the *directive* strategy. It accepts the development of a youth culture as inevitable. But it relies on close adult supervision of peer-group activities to encourage socially acceptable behavior and to compartmentalize or anesthetize dissident practices. Direction is made tempting by the fact that all youth organizations are *temporary social systems* (Miles, 1964: 437–490). Members change frequently as one cohort gets older and a younger one takes its place. Only the adult leaders and organizers remain active for a long period and thus provide organizational continuity. In any temporary social system, those who are organizing it can easily control potentially competitive peer groups. Unless they encourage it, little or no feedback from the young people needs to be tolerated.

(3) A more positive acceptance of an autonomous youth culture is implied when a *co-optation* strategy is used. Peer groups are incorporated by an established adult power elite into an organizational framework that the adults have established. The incorporated youths surrender their autonomy in return for delegated posts of secondary leadership and the right to participate in policy formation within a general framework acceptable to the adult power group. Youth culture innovations are rarely rejected unilaterally without prior consultation with the young people. Co-optation differs from cooperation, in which a coalition of equally powerful groups work together to accomplish a common objective. Neither group surrenders its autonomy.

(4) Finally there is the *revolutionary* strategy. The youth culture tries to displace the existing establishment. Revolutionary youth groups aim to wrest power from the adult-making agencies. This can be done in a variety of ways, such as overthrowing the government or abandoning parental ways in favor of new institutions that coexist with those they intend to replace. The latter path was chosen by the contemporary Zionist kibbutz movements and the utopian communal societies in the United States during the nineteenth century. Theirs was not a revolution by violence, but a setting up of alternate social systems, which was accomplished by hard work (Eaton and Katz, 1942).

The differences among the four strategies are crudely symbolized by different expressions used in English to characterize adolescents.

Adult strategy for youth culture management	Terminology to characterize adolescents
Negative	Being "a nothing"
Directive	Teen-ager
Co-optative	Young Adult ⎫ Being "a somebody"
Revolutionary	Pioneer ⎭

The negative approach

Power- or tradition-oriented adult-making agencies tend to give a high priority to objectives of preventing alienation, deviancy, and delinquency. This is the principal concern for relating to the emerging youth culture of their society. The popular press will often applaud a "firm" local ordinance that attempts to discourage disapproved youth culture manifestations. They may forbid beards, short skirts, smoking, or beer drinking in school, not to mention drug taking and sexual acting out. Negativistic youth culture control agents may become obsessed with even minor fads and other innocuous youth culture innovations. Some school principals devote their talents to administrative measures to outlaw such symptoms of deviancy as sneakers for boys or slacks for girls. Negativism toward youth culture fads is prevalent among a not uncommon species of high school principal, who enforces his rules with a vigilance not used when the issues are educational.

The negative strategy toward youth culture innovations is complicated by its inconsistency. Outside school, sneakers and slacks *are* acceptable forms of clothing. When young people are warned against indulgences— smoking, drinking, alcohol and premarital sex—they are being asked to forgo experiences that are meaningful, if not highly valued, by some of their parents. In institutions in which the negative strategy is pushed strongly, for example, some orphanages, reformatories, and residential schools, the outward acceptance by adolescents of what adults demand of them is accompanied by a secret and very deviant youth culture.

The negativistic approach to the youth culture becomes particularly contradictory in change-oriented societies. How can one expect young people to develop initiative while withholding from them the ability to make choices, which is associated with the possession of adult, physical, intellectual, and emotional capacities? Young people cannot be expected to participate in school student governments with enthusiasm if they are only "play" governments with no decision-making power. One cannot root out smoking when parents consume several packs. Nor is this particular problem made easier by the fact that the cigarette industry spends billions of dollars in the mass media to counteract medical evidence about the dangers of cancer with advertisements that seduce one into "letting go."

No generation can conform entirely. Few parents will exercise as much control as is theoretically possible on their children. Many accept an adolescent moratorium on deviancy. The Hutterites, for instance, postpone baptism until after adolescence to give young people a chance to try out forbidden experiences without the serious indictment of mortal sin (Eaton, 1952: 331–340).

Conservatives everywhere tend to idealize the compliant youth culture.

But their objective is unrealistic in any rapidly changing society. Everywhere today young people must face a world their parents barely understand. Adult-makers are unsuccessful even in highly controlled one-party states in nurturing a passive youth culture. In spite of their well-oiled social control apparatus, they have not succeeded in imposing a truly negativistic approach to youth culture innovations. Young people, including the children of Russian leaders, are attracted by such "deviant" goals as American jazz. A significant minority imbibe alcohol irrespective of adult disapproval. Many prefer materialistic rewards to Komsomol esteem. And those with intellectual and idealistic aspirations are fascinated by many of the ideas their government views as subversive.

The directive approach

Few American adult-making agencies espouse a purely negativistic strategy toward youth culture management. For example, church groups will sponsor a dance and schools will hold a debate on drug use. The progressive high school principal or church youth leader will avoid moralizing with young people about their dress and manners. In all modern societies, adult-making institutions are under pressure to encourage young people to think about change. Many a high school has a youth council that adopts a code of behavior which will then be enforced administratively. But the organization protects itself by investing the principal with the power of veto over youth council decisions.

The directive approach requires that adults take note of youth culture innovations and accept some of them, such as a new dance or fashion of dress, which they regard as innocuous or socially acceptable. But directively oriented youth leaders will strongly oppose those changes that they think "go too far" such as the dance that is too wild or the abolition of rules on boy-girl meetings without adult chaperons.

The brakes on youth power are generally strong when there is a directive strategy. The feedback system has a one way bias. Innovative ideas from young people quickly run into a wall of preestablished expectations. For instance, the school has a formal curriculum. How far can students be allowed to modify it? The church has sacred ideals, preordained by charismatic men in the distant past. Such ideals are not subject to change, except through very gradual generational reinterpretation. The school or church can sponsor a "way out" dance, but attire will have to be much more modest than if the dance were held without official sponsorship. There, a higher degree of youthful initiative is usually tolerated. A controversial subject will be discussed more cautiously in a public school than in a political forum.

The co-optative approach

Co-optation involves the incorporation of an already existing institution for the attainment of new functions. In co-optation there is more of a two-way feedback process. In return for accommodation to the goals of the controlling institution, the co-opted program is given a chance to influence what occurs. The process is well illustrated by the educational system of the kibbutzim, communal villages where "peers exercise informal, semi-formal and formal control" (Spiro, 1965: 308). Teachers and youth workers use a variety of devices to influence adolescents, including appeal to reason, threats of deprivation, shame and orders. But most of the techniques used by these youth workers do not include the exercise of formal authority. Instead, they manipulate "the situation so that the responsibility for insuring conformity devolves on the group or the individual" (Spiro, 1965: 308). If, for example, a difficulty or a problem arises and the teacher feels it ought to be met, he calls a meeting of the class, poses the problem, and asks them to suggest a solution. Hence, although it is the teacher who usually initiates the process, it is the group that imposes the sanction so that instead of exercising authority himself, he delegates it to the group (Spiro, 1965: 312–313).

This co-optative arrangement is often used in modern societies when an adult group wishes to challenge young people to carry out highly approved objectives so that they can develop a sense of self-confidence and commitment. This is true in every club, sports group and other extra-curricular activity organizations, where the goal is to nurture spontaneity and leadership. There must be a readiness to accord young people a fair amount of status and influence. Young people often select their own leaders, help determine programs and negotiate with adults. Through co-optation, the youth culture can sanction the trying out of many a fad and fashion. Young people are being challenged to perform established as well as innovative adult-like roles. But room is left for adults to exercise influence on them to prevent a generational gap that is regarded as "excessive."

The revolutionary approach

Peer groups generally sanction conformist as well as some deviant behavior. Much of the deviance is transitory, such as the violation of school rules, sex before marriage and the withholding of information from adults about events in which young people are involved. Innovations may be designated as revolutionary if they involve major change of social as well as personal significance. Revolutionary ideas are justified by an ideology devoted to changing the social system. Their expression can be, but need not necessarily be, violent. Nor is all violent change revolutionary.

The Zionist pioneer youth groups of Europe, which will be discussed later, began as nonviolent but revolutionary youth movements. The kibbutz settlements which they established were revolutionary in their challenge to the established order. But unlike the protesting college youths of our era, they had an action program to live a different, and what they regard a better life of communal labor. Their influence was based and still rests on primarily their spiritual appeal to utopian socialist values within a framework of national renaissance. By labor, not coercion, they sought and achieved a major break between the social order in which they had grown up and the new Jewish state they were determined to build.

Rioting young crowds are common, but actively revolutionary youth programs are rare. They tend to have a short existence (Kohn, 1934: 516–521). For example, the *Wandervögel* of Germany were swallowed up by World War I when their ideals for a purer and less bourgeois fatherland gave way to unqualified acceptance of their country's demand for military service in defense of their Kaiser. Youth movements also will suffer if their programs succeed. Their leaders then are tempted to perpetuate themselves in office. Young leaders must grow older. As they mature, marry and have to think of making a secure living, they can continue to remain active only by turning their youthful agitation into a career. Like labor leaders and leaders of other social movements who are oriented to "revolutionary change," they assume more and more control in order to stay in power over what had been a spontaneous and revolutionary social movement. The revolution becomes "stalinized"—that is, professionalized.

Transitory youth movements emerge periodically which frighten the adult-making agencies because they advocate radical change. In the United States there are youth groups who take a firm line on civil rights, advocate the use of LSD, or espouse active opposition to the Vietnam war. In underdeveloped countries like Indonesia, such groups burn the embassy of an unfriendly country or organize a demonstration against the government. This power-potential reinforces the efforts of some governments to sponsor youth groups responsive to a more co-optative or directive strategy. This is seen as an "antidote" to the revolutionary potential inherent in more autonomous peer groups who want to replace the old order or wish to try a disapproved experience.

Youth culture management

The negative, directive, co-optative and revolutionary models are logical abstractions. They are analytic concepts that facilitate the comparison of different universal organizational arrangements. Youth culture management rarely relies exclusively on a single control strategy. In the United States, a few policy makers advocate a negativistic strategy, which would be in opposition to youth groups and restore the predominance of school authorities and of the family over the emerging youth culture. Many more favor a directive approach. It is a strategy of official encouragement that young people play a role, provided it is closely monitored by "responsible" adults. In contrasting these institutional alternatives, Coleman (1961: 312) describes the first one as highly impractical:

> One strategy . . . is to bring the adolescents back into the home; to reduce the pervasiveness of the adolescents' society and to return to a state in which each boy and girl responds principally to parents' demands.

Coleman expresses more support for the directive approach:

> The other possible strategy is just the reverse of this: to take adolescent society as given, and then use it to further the ends of adolescent education. Rather than bringing the father back to play with his son, this strategy would recognize that society has changed, and attempt to improve those institutions designed to educate the adolescent toward adulthood.

Israel, as will be shown, relies heavily on a third pattern, the strategy of peer group co-optation. There is a two-way feedback system between the adult-making institutions and the youth groups. In return for power to determine major policies, public institutions provide financial support, pay youth leaders and sponsor informal educational programs. But in day-to-day programming they rely heavily on initiative and leadership of peer group leaders. Even when adult authorities exercise more direct influence, as is the case in the Gadna Youth Corps, it is often exercised with sufficient passivity to leave young people some degree of freedom to innovate peer group patterns. Antiadult and antischool attitudes are treated with considerable tolerance, as long as they do not become an imminent danger to the established order. Should this occur, the police are called in. Such "innovations" would be defined as delinquent and suppressed as they are elsewhere.

We encountered few professionally oriented youth workers who would settle for a largely negativistic or directive policy for the control of youths.[9] Few viewed their jobs as being primarily concerned with the prevention of deviance or the teaching of a well defined code of behavior sanctioned by their church, the Scouts or a technical club. This "no trouble" outlook fails to take note of the fact that modern countries are dependent for their future on a minority of innovative activists—people ready to try out new adaptations in the light of major social changes. There is a need for altruistic persons who are willing to take risks. They must be ready to give a relatively high priority as public officials or as volunteers to the achievement of public purposes, even at the inconvenience—if not detriment—of competing personal and family preferences. Without such altruists no democratic nation can implement plans for change. In times of crisis or war, the readiness of citizens to show such a public-service orientation through military service will be a variable crucial in determining survival.

Conclusion

The world of the young includes a highly diversified range of associations, which are less formal than the school and which help in socializing young people into adults. Youth organizations coexist with friendship cliques, local gangs and the many ties of affection, or distrust between the generations.

Youth organizations supplement other adult-making institutions in their effort to influence the oncoming generation. They are part of, but not equivalent to the youth culture. They are linked to other social institutions. Adults can try to influence them by a variety of strategies, such as negativism, directiveness, co-optation and revolution.

In singling out youth organizations for special study, one must keep in view their special functions. They are only one of several adult-making agencies which aim to influence the future citizens and leaders of the social system, but they are the most elective and voluntaristic. These qualities enable them to be more selective and exclusive than the school, the army or the family. Youth organizations can cater to special groups and interests. They can become concerned with controversial issues. They are open to youngsters who do poorly in school. Unlike the army, the school and the family, in which young people are automatically relegated to low status by reason of their immaturity and dependency, adolescents have preferred status in youth organizations. In fact, only they have full status. There is much scope for the development of leadership talents, the testing of innovations and the development of new social roles.

Coleman (1961: 328) expresses the view that few American youths get enough experience either in daily life or in school with the impersonal world of large institutions. He thinks that "a boy or girl growing up never has a chance to practice" with many of the difficult problems which will face him as an adult, because they are not interpersonal problems. He proposes computer games to be used in schools, as they have already been used in management training, to condition him to the world he will face. The Israeli youth organizations often use something other than games. They use real life situations.

In a planned society, youth organizations are being given much attention. In the emerging countries of Africa and Asia, they sometimes are monitored by a high-level civil service official or a cabinet minister. In one-party states, the official organizations try to maintain a monopoly. In multiparty states, youth organizations can be sponsored by many different adult pressure groups. This is true of Israel where youth organizations are quite diversified. The sponsoring adult-making agencies, the leadership and the membership have been studied to identity some of the variables that affect man's capacity for youth culture management.

Chapter 3

Co-optative Planning

A natural laboratory

Complex social events are often analyzed in terms of the leading dramatic personalities who participated in them. When this is done, the fact is easily overlooked that there is more to the Vietnam war than the views of the late Ho Chi Minh and former President Johnson. Nor can events in the Middle East be properly understood by focusing on what Abdel Nasser, Moshe Dayan, and Prime Minister Wilson are willing to say for publication. Without wishing to suggest or imply that personality variables are irrelevant to social change, this case study is based on the theory that complex social change can be planned organizationally over a long period of time by selective attention to limited institutional variables, "control points," without considering other features of the social system in the planning process.

The Zionist idea is as old as the Psalms. It was first conceived in antiquity by men who had to leave their homeland and yearned to return there. It did not survive because of the impact of any one individual, but became an inherent part of the Jewish religion and culture. Yearning was turned into reality when men organized to implement the idea. Israel as a state, represents an unusual case of successful social planning, much of it voluntary, within a network of competing ideological and political forces. However, the planning process always was limited by developments outside the control of Zionist institutions. Therefore, Israel also illustrates the probably inherent limits of the planning process—the effort to use past and present events to influence the future for the purpose of achieving a concretely formulated objective.

No plan is self-enforcing. It has to be implemented, often in competition with alternate models. This process can be studied in depth by focusing on a limited institutional sector. This study is focused on youth culture management through organizations, each with a program for influencing the process of generational transition. In choosing organizational variables for special analysis, no implication is intended that they are necessarily the most important or even the most effective means by which one generation can influence another. The family and the public school probably has a much more direct impact on the future of a social system. But youth organizations provide a planful way by which a government or political parties can try to influence large segments of a population.

In Israel, there are three major adult-directed youth programs aimed at influencing adolescents: youth movements, the Gadna Youth Corps and Beyond School activities. Youth movements preceded statehood and did much to help it come into being. Gadna and Beyond School activities also serve socialization functions. Sports clubs, social clubs, and the national service further contribute to the goal of planful youth culture guidance by perpetuating society's core ideology and public service objectives.

Israel is a self-contained society, small enough to permit intensive observations of the way social planning is related to implementation. Planning alternatives are often discussed openly in the press and in the parliament before they are resolved. Public priorities for nation building are balanced with openly acknowledged vested partisan interests.

Citizens of many new countries are impatient about reaching a modern level of living. Their leaders aim to shortcut the slow evolutionary process of the more developed lands. They think in terms of a series of five- and six-year plans to leap into the twentieth century. Israel stands out among the new nations because it has come close to achieving some of its planned-for cultural, spiritual and material goals.

It is also an unusually troubled land. Military priorities compete severely with socioeconomic development objectives. Alone among the members of the United Nations, Israel's very right to exist is openly challenged by Arab states. Young Israelis have never known peace, as was also the case with many of their parents. The possibility of physical extermination is not an abstract concept, but a concrete fact of daily life. Early in life, youngsters learn to be silent during hourly news broadcasts which might spell out damage, injury or death of someone they know. They are experiencing in immediate ways an implication of modern life: the technology that brought man to the moon and help to build a material utopia can also be employed to plan for the total destruction of a society. Radiation pollution, atomic holocaust, overpopulation and the other real dangers to human survival are generally understood by few. In times to come, they may become clear and present dangers.

The challenge of evolving a normal social life, geared to such pursuits as work and fun, to dating and mating and to the pursuit of spiritual experiences is generally being met. Indeed, the danger to Israel's existence may be helping to unify its divergent ethnic elements in ways that may help to explain the curious paradox that, as an emerging nation, Israel has moved rapidly, in spite of a depreciated legacy. Palestine, the "promised land" of the Bible, has few natural resources. Its soil was seriously neglected during hundreds of years of Turkish rule. For many generations, the population had to subsist in the abject poverty that still characterized so many of the neighboring areas of the Middle East.

What the country lacks in natural resources has, in part, been compensated for by a high rate of investment of human talent. Included in this "input" is a sizable cadre of idealists who are ready to give a high priority to public requirements, even at the price of neglect of many personal and family requirements. Youths and youth organizations play a major social role in nurturing these nation-building values.

The utility of analyzing Israel's experience with co-opting youth power for nation building is heightened by the fact that this is one of the major components of the country's foreign aid program. African and Asian leaders often were invited to Israel even before their land achieved independence. Many left, impressed by the programs for educating adolescents, to espouse public service values and requested help in evolving similar programs. Since 1959, more than 800 Israeli youth advisors have served in twenty-five countries. Over 300 educators came for brief study tours and fact-finding visits to study Israeli youth organizations and national service programs. More than 950 trainees graduated from three-month courses in Israel organized to meet the special requirements of young leaders in Africa, Asia, Latin America and three Middle East countries, Iran, Cyprus and Malta. Additional thousands of youth leaders were trained in their own countries in courses conducted by Israeli instructors, in English, French, Spanish and Persian. The curriculum stressed group leadership, scouting, discussion group techniques and methods of organizing work camps.[10]

These mutual aid programs deal with such questions as the following: How can new countries train an idealistic elite who will give high priority to public priorities? Can women as well as men take part in public service programs? Can there be governmental financing of youth organizations without imposing an unacceptable degree of central control? More generally, can the co-optative practices of Israel be adapted to the needs of tradition-oriented countries where most people are illiterate, with little experience in self-government and only an incipient tradition to serve as a common bond for voluntary public services? Can public support for national service be maintained when no military threat exists and when the only enemy is man's capacity to plan effectively for matching his aspirations to his capabilities?

At the beginning there was planning

No one had to build France, Albania or Ghana. They have always been, although they achieved their present national status by differently tortuous routes. Only Israel, in contrast, began as a mere idea. Its impact is summed up in Theodor Herzl's (1960: dedication page) law of social change:

If you will it, it is no fairy tale.

In sociological terms this is known as the self-fulfillment theorem (Merton, 1964: 521–536): When men regard something as possible, their belief generates social action designed to realize their social objectives. Nationhood was attained in Israel by a social movement called Zionism, which was able to mobilize manpower and economic resources to solve a worldwide problem—the pariah status of Jews in many lands and their frequent persecution.

Planning for the return of Jews to Israel can be said to have begun in the year 70 A.D., when the Romans destroyed Jerusalem and put an end to Jewish sovereignty. The chief control point of the planning process was the Jewish religion. One of the Jewish religious leaders, Jochanan Ben Zaccai, was able to obtain Roman assent to assemble surviving scholars at the village of Yavne. It was there that the Jewish holy scriptures were finally codified. A daily routine of prayers was prescribed. "Return to Zion" became one of the recurrent themes of their content. At least six times a day, morning, afternoon, and evening, and after every meal orthodox Jews include a plea to God that Jerusalem be rebuilt and the Jews be returned to their ancient patrimony.

The vitality of this religious reinforcement of Zionism was not dimmed by the passing of many centuries and the settlement of Jews all over the world. In each country, synagogues were built facing in the direction of Jerusalem. In death, many Jews are buried with a small sack of soil from the Holy Land. There was a never-ending migration of small numbers of Jews to Palestine.

Political support for the idea that a Jewish state be reestablished in Palestine began to appear early in the 19th century. There were Christian statesmen like Napoleon and Jean Henri Dunant (founder of the Red Cross), Sir Laurance Olipant, Colonel Henry Churchill, and Anthony Ashley Cooper. As outsiders they could not stir the Jewish masses, as did the call for a return to Zion by such Jewish leaders as Leon Pinsker, Moses Hess and Rabbi Zvi Hirsch Kalischer (Learsi, 1951: 21, 50). They advocated Zionism for many different reasons, including religion, socialism and the urgency of finding a territorial solution for the homelessness of the Jews.

Beginning with Napoleon's rule in France, many anti-Jewish laws in Western Europe were formally repealed. Jews streamed out of the ghettos to greet the dawn of a new era of enlightenment. Acculturation and assimilation proceeded at a fast pace. But anti-Semitism did not disappear.

Violent persecutions persisted, especially in Eastern Europe. Even in France, the slogan "Death to the Jews" became respectable a century after Napoleon had emancipated them. Millions of European Jews reacted by giving up hope of ever becoming full-fledged citizens of the lands of their birth. The majority migrated to America, Australia and other overseas settlement areas. Only a trickle of thousands went to their ancestral home in Palestine.

It was in reaction to the disillusionment with universalism that Theodor Herzl, a young Viennese newspaper correspondent and play-wright wrote a book entitled *Der Judenstaat* (*The Jewish State*). In 1897, eighteen months after it appeared the first World Zionist Congress con-vened in Basel, Switzerland. The Congress adopted a plan for a Jewish home in Palestine that was to be more than refuge. It was to be a better world, where social justice would replace man's exploitation of men. Not only Jews, but the resident Arab population were to benefit and live to-gether in peace. Fifty years later the United Nations voted, by a large majority, to partition Palestine into an Arab and a Jewish state. The few thousand Jews in 1897 had grown by 1947 to a population of 650,000. It was not large, but it was big enough to set up a viable government and to defend its territory.

This transition from blueprint to fulfillment was facilitated by a good deal of closely coordinated technical planning. For instance, the Jewish National Fund was set up in 1901 to purchase land, reclaim swamps, and plant forests. The Palestine Office of the Jewish Agency, a socioeconomic planning agency, was organized in 1908, but it never had a monopoly over development.[11] Many specified projects were organized autonomously, in industrial development, the building of new communities and the en-couragement of immigration. The Hebrew language was adopted as the medium of communication to replace the many languages that the immi-grants brought with them.

The idea that planning cannot be total or highly centralized was accepted widely. Different political and religious groups as far apart as Marxist utopians and religious fanatics maintained their independent ini-tiatives. They could work together cooperatively on such common control points as land purchase, economic development and defense.

They did not attempt to impose uniform land use patterns, labor standards or ways of recruiting volunteers needed to guard their villages. Coordinated planning was also made easier because of external opposition from powerful nationalist stirrings among the Arab people of the area. Israel and most Arab states achieved sovereignty at about the same time. While the Zionists were always ready to negotiate—and for years were ready to accept a binational state in Palestine, there was no recognized leader among the many Arab factions who could or would negotiate an

TABLE 1

Paradigm of Israel's Core Ideology

Public Service Objective	Areas of Agreement	Areas of Major Controversy
Jewish Renaissance An unbroken cultural chain links modern Jewry throughout the world with the ancient Hebrews and the land of Israel.	The Bible is Israel's common heritage; its language is once more the common means of discourse. Festivals and memorials are national holidays. Israel should be a spiritual center for Jews everywhere.	Many differences exist about the meaning of the Bible. Religious groups want a theocratic state. This is opposed by the country's more secular majority, who vary in their outlook on traditions.
Ingathering of Exiles Unrestricted immigration brings Jews from everywhere in the world irrespective of their capacity to support themselves.	It is proper that about two-thirds of the heavy absorption cost must be paid out of Israel's national income. The remainder comes from overseas contributions.	There is disagreement on the extent of incentives and social welfare services and opposition to giving newcomers more generous help to find housing and schooling than is given to old settlers.
National Defense All citizens, male and female, young and old, must be prepared to fight for their country.	In the event of an attack, Israel would have to do battle in the territory of its hostile neighbors. The country is too small for a more defensive strategy.	There are many proposed strategies on how much occupied territory should be kept. There is opposition to military exemptions of some women and rabbinical students from orthodox families.
National Resources Development Israel is poor in natural resources. It cannot support its population on a modern standard of living, absorb immigrants, and maintain an expensive army without optimum exploitation of its resources.	No man should think only of making a living for personal enjoyment. The government has the right to enforce a general development plan. Economic activity should be related to the national needs.	There is little agreement on the best means of socio-economic planning. Socialism has many adherents, but even among them there is much diversity about the role of private and cooperative enterprise.
Individualism There is to be opportunity for self-fulfillment and maximum freedom of choice for every person within limits set by the needs of others.	Agreement exists on a very abstract level that each man must be free to pursue his and his family's happiness.	There are questions on the limits of individualism. Each of Israel's cultural and ethnic groups has some different prescription for the "good life."

accommodation between the two national movements, each with persuasive claims to the same area.

The role of ideology

Volunteering for public service seems to be a function of the acceptance of a core ideology, the common beliefs shared by diverse segments of the population. Israel is a unified, yet divided, country. Communists and nationalists, orthodox Jews and Atheists have fought side by side during each of Israel's three wars since 1948. Groups associated with all these parties lease land from the Jewish National Fund and help absorb immigrants from abroad. But in most public matters, alternate policies are advocated by these groups that reflect fundamental ideological differences (Eisenstadt, 1967) so that more than a dozen major parties and factions within parties exist.[12] Many sponsor their own youth movements, competing with others for the mind and soul of the oncoming generation. Loyalty to the state does not require loyalty to the government in power.

If the Israel experience with national planning has any general significance, it lies in the fact that its noteworthy results are being obtained in spite of considerable partisan divergence in goals and priorities. A high rate of development occurred without resort to totalitarian control, which characterizes so many underdeveloped nations, and some more-developed ones. As Professor Gross (1966: vii) points out,

> Israel has been a dramatic exception. In 1948, it was a poverty-ridden land of sand and rock, swamped by enormous immigration and threatened with imminent destruction. Since then, while remaining in the "powder keg" of the Middle East, it has been transformed into an industrial, technology-oriented society. Living standards have reached Western European levels.

Planning is sustained by a core of widely shared social goals which are regarded as being above politics. There might never have been a State of Israel had the situation been otherwise (see Table 1).

Planning has its limitations and many of them are highly visible in Israel. There often is insufficient information to anticipate future contingencies. For instance, many Zionists in Europe and Russia, who had been thinking of leaving for Palestine, postponed their departure beyond the time when their government was allowed to leave. Israelis still accept Ottoman land laws. Workers sometimes strike against labor saving devices that will cut costs of products needed for export, as Akzin and Dror (1966: 19) observe:

> One of the surprising paradoxes in Israel—shared to some degree with other new developing states—is the contrast between the rapidity of organized social change and the conservative tendency to protect the internal characteristics of administrative institutions.

Pioneer manpower

The chief instruments of Israel's planned renaissance were the so-called *Halutzim*—settlers oriented to public service. Over 100,000 came from Eastern Europe, especially from Poland as young volunteers from countries where Jews were second-class citizens.[13] From among tens of thousands of Jews who experienced such insecurity, the Halutzim were a self-selected elite dedicated to a mission rather than to make a mere living. A much smaller number of Halutzim came from western countries, where the integration of Jews in general public life was more advanced. Between 1931 and 1952, just over 3,000 immigrated from the United States, Canada, England, South Africa, Australia and New Zealand, establishing twenty-five collective villages (Morris, 1953).[14]

The majority came to build a socialist society. But there was no single acceptable model. There is much genuine experimentation with alternate ways to apply socialist principles to the real world. Among these Halutz volunteers were some who had tried to take part in the reform movements of their native lands. A few had even attained positions of influence. But many of the European socialists were also responsive to the nationalist and religious prejudices. They defined Jews as outsiders. Many of the idealistic Jewish socialists migrated to Israel to build a utopian working class society of their own near the river Jordan rather than settle for being second-class participants in the socialist endeavors of the lands of their birth.

For religious socialists, there was an added sacred inspiration. Re-establishment of a Jewish national home in Palestine would be the fulfillment of the prophetic visions in the Old Testament. For a hundred generations, Jews included in their daily prayers the vow: "If I forget thee Jerusalem, may my right hand wither" (Psalm 137).

For all Halutzim, irrespective of their political philosophies, the old homeland was to be more than a refuge for Jews. It was to become a more perfect society. There would be no capitalist exploitation. Men would live from the fruits of their own labor, particularly labor of the soil.[15] Jews with diverse religious orientations and ethnic backgrounds were to live together in peace, in harmony with the resident non-Jewish, mostly Arab population. Being a Halutz was like joining the Peace Corps for life, but without guaranteed minimum pay.

The Halutzim planfully set about to create Israel's basic institutions. For many years there was no harbor in Palestine where seagoing ships could tie to a dock. Immigrants had to be transferred offshore to small boats or be carried to shore on the backs of Arab stevedores. They were coming to a land of historic ruins, swamps and deserts. Before World War II, Zionist literature dealt almost exclusively with these developmental challenges. Mutual aid, scientific agriculture, democracy and social justice were key values. Through cooperatives, the children of capitalist merchants set up modern consumer services, transportation, and banking institutions. Under the guidance of experts in development, the Halutzim laid out hundreds of new settlements. Walter Clay Lowdermilk (1944), a chief of the U. S. Soil Conservation Service, who devoted some of his retirement years to providing consultative services in Palestine described their developmental doctrine as follows:

> Thou shalt inherit the holy earth as a faithful steward, conserving its resources and productivity from generation to generation. Thou shalt safeguard thy fields from soil erosion, thy living waters from drying up, thy forests from desolation, and protect thy hills from over grazing by herds, that thy descendants may have abundance forever. If any fail in this stewardship of the land, their fruitful fields shall become sterile, stony ground or wasting gullies, and thy descendants shall decrease and live in poverty or perish from the face of the earth.

The Halutzim did not build the state by themselves. They always were a numerically small elite who helped to sustain a larger social system that was able to absorb larger numbers of ordinary refugees, who could not live safely in the lands of their birth. Halutzim provided an uncommon type of manpower: Highly idealistic and generally well educated persons who were willing to engage in "blue collar" labor and viewed it as having as much dignity and status as "white collar" work.

They were organized in small groups, often from the same part of Europe. There were no officers or generals, only members. Within each group decisions were by majority vote. They worked while others just talked and hoped. They represented a major capital and developmental asset, not to mention their spiritual influence. They were bound by no contract. Each year there would be dropouts, who felt that they had sacrificed enough, whose health was impaired, or who found themselves in disagreement with members of their group. The number who remained Halutzim for life was only a fraction of those who originally volunteered to join this unique development corps. But their impact on the country was far out of proportion to their number.

Adversity as an incentive

As suggested previously a crisis can be defined as a social situation in which danger coexists with opportunity. In the last three decades the Zionist settlers were confronted with a series of polarized alternatives: to perish or fight. No compromise that would have permitted the Jewish community to survive could be negotiated. As George Simmel (1955), Lewis Coser (1956: 104) and many others have pointed out: "outside conflict increases internal group cohesion."

These harsh realities occurred in Palestine after World War II, under the shock of awareness that the world had stood by with no more than token objection to the highly organized Nazi campaign to exterminate all persons of Jewish ancestry. The pitiful half-living remnants, discovered in Dachau and Auschwitz, highlighted the enormity of the catastrophe that had befallen the Jewish people. Most Israelis of European origin had lost almost all their relatives. Thousands of Jewish communities in Europe were wiped out. The centers of recruitment of pioneers by Zionist youth movements no longer existed.

Only in places where the Germans failed to achieve total control, as in the Soviet Union, did Jews survive in large numbers. Half a million Jews fought in the Soviet armed forces. A high proportion of these were officers, including fifty generals, and hundreds of colonels. One hundred twenty-one Jews received the coveted Soviet decoration called "Hero of the Soviet Union." But when the war ended, Zionism remained illegal there as it had been before World War II (Elkins, 1968: 15). Jews were not allowed to migrate to Palestine. Many prominent Jewish leaders were arrested: some were executed in a new wave of Stalinist anti-Semitism.

In England, the British Labour party, when out of power, had been pro-Zionist. But after winning the election in 1945, its leaders decided to enforce a prior government policy of 1939 that halted nearly all Jewish immigration and land purchases. Arab nationalism had gained much self-confidence and power during World War II. The Arabs regarded the Jews as alien intruders, without rights to statehood. Sentimentalism regarding the tragedy of the Jews seemed hardly a sufficient reason to antagonize so powerful a geopolitical force.

Peace in Europe permitted the stationing of over 100,000 British troops in Palestine. Their purpose was once and for all to convince the Jewish population that there would be no alternative to acceptance of Britain's decision to freeze the status of the Jewish national home. The full powers of the British army and navy were mobilized to halt the un-authorized immigration of Jews who were being smuggled in superannuated boats and across land borders by volunteers of several countries. This policy was enforced ruthlessly even against the survivors of German death camps, who some of these same British soldiers had helped to liberate in Europe. The ship *Exodus*, for instance, was intercepted by the British navy and forced to return to Germany, its decks packed with refugees.

The British policy lacked nothing in resoluteness. Nor was it un-reasonable in terms of the way British officials defined their long range strategic interests in the Middle East. But it left the Jewish community without a reasonable prospect for growth and development. Its very exist-ence seemed in danger. Units of the Trans-Jordan Arab Legion, officered and equipped by the British, were stationed *inside* Palestine, while Jewish self-defense units were disarmed. The alliance of Arab nationalism and British power left no alternate policy except surrender and the ultimate evacuation of Jews from Palestine. The surviving relatives of those who had perished in Europe were driven to desperation. They decided to rebel. Unlike their dead relatives in Europe, in Palestine the Jews had a territorial base. Most of the young people were experienced in self-defense; tens of thousands had fought with the British against Germany, others had been trained clandestinely.

Halutzim who had come to Palestine to build, planned secretly to fight. New farm settlements doubling as military strongpoints were set up overnight in forbidden zones. Ships filled with refugees sailed the Mediterranean Sea, forcing the British navy to attempt their interception. Bridges were blown up to delay British troops rushing to intercept those who reached the beaches. Military force was employed in carefully selected guerilla actions.

Israelis did not struggle alone. Help came from some dissident British officials. Thousands of Jews from all over the world came as reinforcements and there was active support among many non-Jews everywhere. Much of this response reflected sympathy for the universalistic ideals of the Zionist movement, its concern with the rehabilitation of refugees, the rebirth of an old-new country and the Halutz ideology that men can build a better world if they are willing to do it for themselves.

By 1947, the British government decided to give up its Mandate over Palestine rather than continue the expensive and unpopular war against the Jews. And in 1949 when the Israel flag was hoisted at the United Nations, admission was supported by a most unlikely political coalition led by the United States and the Soviet Union, where Zionism continued to be outlawed. The Vatican was unsympathetic; yet most Catholic nations voted for Israel.

United Nations membership did not end the threat to Israel's physical survival. The Arab states continue to refuse to recognize her right to exist. Over two decades of guerilla warfare have passed, interspersed with major military confrontations in 1956 and 1967. Each could have resulted in the destruction of the State and most of its citizens. The Jewish community, however, was able to mobilize enough force to prevent this. The end of this fifty-year-war is not yet in sight. In the past each major battle left the Jewish state in a better strategic position. While the future has uncertainties, most Israelis are sustained by confidence that even before peace comes, development of their country can proceed rapidly.

Today almost every Israeli family is involved and has personal recollections about their involvement in these events. Only a minority came as volunteers. Many were refugees who could not continue to live in dignity or safety where they had been residing. Even after their arrival they had to live under hardship conditions. Most of them had to learn new occupations, form new social relationships and experience the transition from immigrant to citizen.

"Israel has proven itself the most successful intruded state of modern times," commented Sulzberger (1968) in a news dispatch about the country's twentieth anniversary as a sovereign state: "None had such a flamboyant inception."

Arab nationalists respond to this reality with denial quite different from what has helped to solve sensitive territorial disputes, of which there are quite a few in the Middle East, not to mention the rest of the world. The policy as enunciated most recently in the Khartoum Conference in 1967 requires that there be "no recognition (of Israel), no negotiation and no peace." Voices of moderation or of compromise, when they are heard, are generally opposed vehemently by Palestinian irridentists. Extremists among them will use every means at their disposal, including assassination, to frustrate even exploratory discussion of a political settlement (Hudson, 1969).

Israeli leaders would like peace. They want to shift their planning priorities from war to development, but not at the price of giving up their country and of undoing what to many represents a fulfillment of biblical prophecy:

> Fear not, for I am with thee; I will bring thy seed from the East and gather thee from the West. I will say to the North, give up; and to the South, keep not back. Bring my sons, from far, and my daughters from the ends of the Earth. (Isaiah 43: 5–6)

Secular Jews view their achievements more as the sound application of social planning principles. The fate of Jews vindicates the Zionist theory of how to solve the problem of Jewish homelessness. Many see themselves as having had historic foresight. In Palestine a fraction of about 10 percent of the more than six million men, women and babies, who in Europe died helplessly, stood their ground to create a territorial entity, where Jewish children can grow up to acquire self-respect. There is pride in the country's cultural and social welfare achievements.

The mood is much more sober with respect to its military successes. Even the Six Day War in 1967, which freed the population from a grave military threat, is widely viewed in the perspective of its human cost, 830 dead and 3,000 wounded. To the outsider this will appear to be a small price to pay for survival. But these casualties are "higher than the proportionate total of United States casualties in the Korean and Vietnam wars put together. And this was all in six days, not fifteen years" (Rabin, 1968).

Conclusion

Israel is a garrison democracy[16] in which young immigrants have played key roles in transforming idealistic blueprints into a much more complex but real present. National planning is characteristic of all modern countries. In Israel it preceded statehood. Without sovereignty, there could be no governmental coercion. Co-optation of diverse interest groups was the predominant pattern. Much of the planning involved voluntary co-operation among an idealistic elite of Halutzim who, by virtue of their willingness to work hard and in a disciplined way, were able to dominate the emerging social system. Key elements in the implementation process were young people, members of youth movments, most of whom were recruited in Europe. They emigrated to Palestine as volunteers, who were part of a Halutz peace corps, which expects lifetime service rather than a short-term commitment. They embraced many different utopian and socialist ideas. Often they clashed with those of others who were equally dedicated. But there was enough of a core ideology around which a sense of national purpose could develop. Unity was also reinforced by outside opposition to Zionism by Arab and British forces. Military priorities often overshadowed the nation-building objectives of the Zionist movement, but few Israelis hate their enemies. National unity depends far more on common developmental objectives. Utopian ideals retain much of their appeal although they are viewed with a realism that comes from daily practical confrontation.

Zionism succeeded on the basis of a voluntaristic control point planning process that included a high inefficiency component owing to competing priorities. It would appear that successful implementation is not dependent on total coordination. Men cannot predict the future well enough, nor assess all relevant details, to anticipate complex social events with the precision of an architect at his drawing board. The Israeli experience suggests that planned national development can occur in spite of the existence of many competing priorities in the planning process.

The young people of Israel are continuing to show much readiness to assume responsible roles for the realization of the parental core values of planful nation building. There is agreement that Israel's primary mission continues to be the nurturance of a promised land where men can live a decent life, within a framework of Jewish traditions, universalistic ethical values and with a modern standard of living. The threat to physical extinction that faces all young people in Israel, who mature into adulthood in the "no-peace, no-negotiation-and-no-recognition" atmosphere of the Middle East has not yet turned the country into a modern-day Sparta, where military feats are honored beyond all others. The development pioneer—the Halutz has retained some of its halo, though this model has lost its prior monopoly in the youth culture. In the words of a non-Jewish British scholar (Sykes, 1965), reviewing the confrontation of political forces in the Middle East: "Zionism was from the beginning a movement of Jewish self-criticism. The salt is still there and the consequence is no diminution of self-criticism, especially among the younger generation."

Every nation would like to arouse such concern for public service and for nation-building among its youths. The relative success of the Israeli society in achieving this objective makes it all the more instructive to study some of the organizational arrangements within which this phenomenon occurs.

Chapter 4

Generational Transmission

Territorial therapy

When the twentieth century began, two Jews, who were to leave their footprints in world history, labored side by side in Vienna, Theodor Herzl and Sigmund Freud. Both founded worldwide social movements. Each, in his own way, wanted to bring about a better world. Freud explored, among other things, the psychodynamics of hatred, while Herzl addressed himself to its politics. Their theories, while not mutually exclusive, called for radically different methods to reduce the incidence of human hatred.

Freud showed that individuals who wanted help in overcoming pathological emotions could be helped by individual therapy, a permissive relationship between a gifted human healer and the sufferers of fear and anger. But the Nazis who destroyed Freud's world and many of his relatives, wanted no help. Psychotherapy could not cure German and Austrian anti-Semites of their corrosive hatred. At the age of 82, Freud had to resort to Herzl's territorial solution. He had to change his environment. A serious problem (pariah status) was solved by territorial change. Some of the attributes that made Freud a deviant in Austria, without the right to live, were the basis of defining him as a welcome resident in England (Jones, 1963: 500–506).

Freud's fate gives irrefutable testimony to the limits of his own theory in solving intergroup problems. By taking refuge, he resorted to a form of milieu therapy: stress reduction by a change from a political jurisdiction where a group problem appears to be insoluble to a new and more supportive environment where the problem can disappear.

Intergroup relations specialists have sometimes been over-impressed by the potentialities of psychological approaches to the management of group conflict. Without much supportive evidence, they cherish the hope that racial or ethnic hatred are subject to resolution through more personal contact and by means of appeals to "brotherhood." This theory tends to short-change the power variable. Ethnic minority groups who lack a territorial base are often exploited by the majority. This is a social fact applicable to many groups. It can be changed if the social system is modified through political power that can be generated most strongly in an area under the political control of the disadvantaged ethnic group.

Contemporary Black Power advocates use the same theoretical approach in staking their claim to America. The urban slum is their territorial base. Within it they can organize a more general strategy to right the wrongs of many generations. Through the ballot and their numerical weight, black ghetto inhabitants can demand, rather than request, justice. As it has done for other American ethnic groups, neighborhood power has achieved gains for blacks that are more concrete than those previously negotiated by "intergroup" techniques and goodwill gestures.[17]

Territorial therapy has its limitations. The dramatic substitution of first-class citizenship for being powerless and outcast, is no small achievement. But improvements in legal status will not, at once, wipe out the personal consequences of being brought up in a disadvantaged family. Conditions reflecting the accumulated impact of centuries of low caste existence cannot be reversed at once by the mere act of migration and the acquisition of political power. This becomes all the more apparent once the original political objective is achieved. New goals are then needed to answer the question: Power for what ends?

The achievement crisis

As was just mentioned, the limits of political solutions become particularly apparent after a social movement has been successful. Success clears the deck for concern about problems that may have always existed but were given a low priority when there was an intense struggle to achieve a unified purpose. The fervor of such a movement, be it for freedom or to remove discriminatory laws, cannot remain unchanged after the objective is attained. Liberated people often turn against each other in a fierce struggle for ascendancy. The change in outlook may not always take such an extreme form as in the shift from radicalism to the status-quo preference of the leaders of Russia under Stalin. But any revolutionary change has to be followed by a change in focus.

Achievement of a hard-to-reach goal is the occasion for great celebration. But when the festivities are over, problems previously played down take on a higher priority. Native-born Israelis, who now defend their country's borders, were never in need of territorial therapy. They cannot feel the awe of their parents and grandparents who were reared in a European ghetto tradition and who suffered the consequences of organized anti-Semitism.

The present generation has different priorities. They are concerned with what kind of state is desirable. They want to change some of the institutions their elders created. This outlook is directly traceable to the success of the previous generation in meeting so many of its objectives. While struggling for statehood, this political objective was invested with an idealistic halo that involved the deliberate exclusion of certain realities, such as the fact that statehood alone will not bring about peace or prosperity. Halutzim, feeling the breath of history on their brows, often denied themselves goals of a more personal nature. They accepted long separations from their families. Few could think of starting a savings account to take care of their old age. Many gave up opportunities for professional education.

But when victory was won, they could begin to think of themselves and their families. Kibbutz wives, who felt too constrained by group demands, now felt free to press their husbands to move to a city in order to set up their own households. Departure could no longer be interpreted as running away from common dangers. Workers could strike more freely and place fringe benefits above competing demands for efficiency at lower cost. Tax rates are high and progressive, but managers could devote some of their talents to the elaboration of fringe benefits, as shown in the following excerpts from the Israeli State Controller's report (*Jerusalem Post,* 1969: 7):

> In Israel there are 14,757 company managers, generally receiving both a salary and income from shares. An examination of the four biggest tax districts revealed that 672 were classified—contrary instructions—as wage earners, so were liable in some cases to be taxed only on their salaries and not on other emoluments.
>
> In many cases company managers receive benefits to cover expenses, mainly for local travel, for running a car, for trips abroad (with members of the family), for life insurance, for entertainment or for the rent of an apartment. Some of these outlays are private expenses and not company expenses, and should be denied tax exemption.

Political opponents, who had collaborated to face a common danger felt freer to oppose each other openly.

These self-advancement activities had never been entirely absent. But after the attainment of independence, they rose in the priority scales of many people. The resulting achievement crisis condition reflected the fact that during the long period of emergency, the ideological common ground which had united a whole generation was eroded by a new balance of national and personal priorities. Utopian hopes about the glories of the new freedom can be more easily entertained as long as achievement was not in sight. After independence some of the immigrants whom Jews had struggled hard to bring into the country were found to share no concern with Zionist ideals. Crime rates rose, requiring an expansion of the prison system (Eaton, 1962).

Thousands of volunteer soldiers who had rushed to Israel from America, Europe and South Africa returned home. They could not adjust to the complexities of making a life in Israel. Competition for jobs was keen, at times even underhanded. White lies—and some outright falsehoods—were broadcast to assure a job for friend and deny it to someone better qualified. Charismatic qualities ascribed to leaders became tarnished, when the leaders shifted roles. Instead of being heroes in opposition to British rulers, they had to assume governmental responsibilities in which they had to say "no" to demands, some of which were being made in the name of partisan rather than public interests.

Young Israelis are growing up to view Israel without embellishment. They talk less about Halutz pioneering and more about red tape in the bureaucracy of the Labor Federation. Revered national leaders of the independence are described as "old men," who should have retired long ago to make room for new blood. Bus cooperatives are seen as a monopoly, more concerned with profits for their members than service to the public. Indeed the uninformed reader of the Israeli press might easily be misled by the large volume of published complaints and vigorous controversies to conclude that the country is in grave danger. There are many serious problems, indicating that the achievement of one generation cannot yield a utopia. However, past achievement allows the next generation to concentrate its attention on new issues.

The nonrecognition of Israeli sovereignty by neighboring Arab states perpetuates some sense of crisis. There is a high probability that the country's Left-to-Right coalition government would break up, if the Arab states were to agree to permanent peace. Peace would make it unnecessary for Israel to live in a perpetual state of military readiness for war. But Israelis now feel secure enough to sustain many major controversies even on matters that once were regarded as almost "sacred." The Zionist movement is being attacked as outdated, both organizationally and ideologically. There is much dissatisfaction with the present political parties, the lack of efficiency of many bureaucracies and the country's sparse economic resources.

No generation which achieved one epic objective can expect to transmit its own emotions and fervor to its children. Many people find it easy to make public service oriented choices in an emergency situation. If personal and national priorities conflict, they choose the latter. But after the emergency has passed, their priorities begin to shift. Herein lies a dilemma for recently emerged countries. Nation building does not end with independence. This memorable event only allows the nation to begin. The enthusiasm that can unify a people when combating an outside enemy is not automatically transmitted to the developmental challenges which face the postindependence generation who must deal with less dramatic challenges of working forty-four hours a week every week of the year for wages that are always lower than desired.

From idealism to realism

In the United States it has become quite respectable for a public servant to announce his resignation in order to return to private business so that he can recoup his personal financial stability. Public service is highly regarded, but it is accepted as limited in duration. The principle of rotation is incorporated in most posts that call for voluntary sacrifice and national service.

This was less true in the Zionist movement. Before Israel achieved sovereignty, all important settlement, military, and civic functions were performed by volunteers. There was a chronic shortage of pioneering personnel. People for whom pay and organizational status were secondary considerations were hard to replace.

After independence, Israel became a land of great opportunity for upward mobility. The Jewish population expanded fourfold during the two decades between 1948 and 1968. The number of children aged 10 to 17 who are eligible for schools or youth programs increased about sevenfold. The supply of Halutzim and other idealism-oriented public servants was not equal to this great demand for leadership talent.

The heavy logistic demand for public servants occurred on top of a serious loss in qualified manpower. Somewhat over four thousand soldiers and two thousand civilians were killed in the War of Independence (Lorch, 1961: 450). Nearly 2 percent of the Jewish population over 15 years old was lost. Many of them died when they volunteered for dangerous assignments. Halutzim who had made their reputations planting new varieties of fruit trees and spraying them against disease were called on to become diplomats. Social workers became mayors of new towns built to accomodate immigrants and underground military leaders became managers of new industries. Few of the present heads of the vast industrial and commercial enterprises of the Israel Labor Federation had any formal education in the fields of their specialty.

The growing size and complexity of the country has shifted priorities from ideological to technical prerequisites. The recognition of this shift has led to suggestions that future managers be better trained (Shapiro, 1968: 5). In the government this policy is being applied more and more widely. Even political appointees are often sent to school to gain technical competency. As professional competency is emphasized, ideological and party affiliations are given less weight.

Israel, like all nations after the attainment of independence, experienced a letdown in civic morale. In 1966, a year before the Six Day War, the country experienced a severe recession. Unemployment reached a high level. Israelis were confronting the questions: What will be the public service equation of the next generation? Will there be a balance between the generation's concern for the community's welfare (especially for tasks that are arduous and carry special risks) and their desire to advance themselves and their immediate families? How can public enthusiasm be maintained when the balance of national priorities is shifting from the primitive issue of "Survival or Extinction" to the less dramatic setting of guaranteed and secure borders and the attainment of development goals?

Sacrifices are still demanded, but more on an allocated basis. Youths can work out a realistic balance between their personal needs and those of national service. Emergencies are planned for. Service in the active army and the civilian reserve is no longer voluntary; it is required by law. Voluntarism is still utilized, but only for the staffing of some of the hardship and glamour posts. Volunteers have to meet appropriate qualifications that have been determined by a comprehensive testing procedure. This routinization has divested public service of much of the emotional intensity that characterized it before Israel became a state.

Only a dozen of the hundreds of new towns and villages established since 1948 were settled by pioneers who volunteered for this task. Most new settlements are inhabited by immigrants who are assigned to go there by the Jewish Agency, which financed their journey (See, for instance, Weingrod, 1966). They were induced to accept a pioneering assignment in return for free living accommodations and a chance to become economically independent. Problems that exist are thought to be solvable without a radical reorganization of the status quo. No new symphony, but only variations on a theme already composed, seems to be required.

The Halutz idealist is thinning out in the Settlement Department of the Jewish Agency. Quite a few have aged into career officials with a bureaucratic orientation to their jobs. There is a shortage of personnel who are willing to make their career in the merchant marine. The Histradruth Central Federation of Labor has become a cumbersome political machine, with entrenched functionaries who are showing some of the universal attributes of the "organization man." In the public school system, teachers with formal qualifications will generally advance even without charismatic qualities. What Max Weber has called the "bureaucratization of charisma" is increasingly in evidence.

Crucial pioneer tasks are still filled quite often by volunteers, but the desire to serve is not always a sufficient basis for ensuring proper performance. Not all Nahal pioneer members are volunteers. Only a minority have the intent to settle in a kibbutz. More and more, youth leaders have to be hired for pay. Hardship posts in development towns often remain unfilled for long periods. The hospital in Beersheba cannot maintain all its departments for lack of properly qualified physicians. Israeli policy makers, still much under the influence of their pioneer tradition, are ambivalent

PIONEERING NOW REQUIRES REALISTIC INCENTIVES.
(Israeli Government advertisement in the *Jerusalem Post*, February 22, 1968: 3)

about supplementing idealistic incentives with realistic material benefits. But more merit-oriented organizations like the army and the Ministry of Labor have learned to do this. Their career personnel get fringe benefits in the form of low-cost housing, tax reductions and civilian education to keep them in the service.

It has been traditional among Jews to resolve the conflicting views of ancient rabbis with the Talmudic concept of *Teikuh,* which means "the Messiah will answer all such questions." But this theological resolution will not satisfy modern-day Israelis who openly air many dissatisfactions.

Some react to the discrepancies between their aspirations and their achievement in terms of an ad hominem explanation, typified by a story that made its rounds during the term of office of the late Prime Minister Eshkol.

> The Prime Minister, Minister of Finance, and Minister of Social Welfare were flying to a conference in Europe when their plane fell into the ocean. "Who was saved?"
> —"The State of Israel!"

When viewed in a larger context, Israel's sobering mood has something in common with similar sociological trends in the United States, the Soviet Union and other modern nations. In spite of the high degree of accomplishment of the parental generation, young people everywhere are turning away from ideology and slogans. Even in the United States, which has reached a level of prosperity unknown in human history, many young people are dissatisfied and some are alienated. They see the problems many of their parents chose to ignore.

All these trends support the theory that the achievements of one generation cannot provide satisfactions to another. Different circumstances prevail in large part because of what the parental generation accomplished. Every successful social revolution or major planned change has to confront the issue. Will their children's fervor diminish? In the words of one American Halutz (Isaacs, 1967: 84):

> Me, I can say I participated in creating the Jewish state, a homeland for the Jews. That's what we did, I mean those who came to fight or to take part in the Kibbutz movement before the war. The guy who came after all of that can't say as much. I'll also say that my kids won't get out of this what I've gotten out of it.

But for the continued opposition of Arab states to peace, the achievement crisis of Israel would probably be more intense than it was once described by Foreign Minister Abba Eban (Jewish Agency, Youth Aliyah Department, 1964: 23):

> Pursuit is movement, pursuit is dynamism. Attainment on the other hand is conservative and static. Many Israelis and many Jews looking back

to the heroic struggle of the past three decades, now ask themselves the burning question: What happened to our dream? It abandoned us. And in the vacuum now there sound no strong voices speaking in mutual unification of one hope and will.

He went on to indicate that his country must somehow recapture its "morning feeling." Among the tasks still to be faced are the following:

(1) How can economic freedom be achieved with economic justice?
(2) How can tradition be revered within the exercise of free intellect and free conscience?
(3) How can the youth of Israel and of the Jewish dispersion be drawn together?
(4) How, within an organized and increasingly industrialized society, can the special serenities and solid virtues of rural and agricultural life be preserved?
(5) How can a society be built which, while fostering its own heritage, will in some modest measure be a portent for all mankind?

Neo-Zionism

Contemporary Israeli adolescents still have reasons to feel important. They saved their country in the Six Day War of June, 1967, while many of their elders listened to the battle news in safe shelters. The struggle for secure and recognized borders has displaced territorial therapy as one of the core ideology elements around which national unity can be sought. Socialism continues to be a vital force in the country. But the problem of modifying socialist theories on the basis of practical experience needs attention. The General Labor Federation is in need of revitalization.

There are also many opportunities for innovation. In Israel new institutions can still be built without being limited by too many traditional practices. "Experimentation" remains as a highly valued quality, be it in the army, education, social welfare, water supply control or the administration of customs duties.

Israel has not lost the functions of territorial solution and of social rehabilitation. More than twenty years after Hitler committed suicide with Eva Braun, Jews are still persecuted in several countries. Nazi-type cartoons have appeared in Russia. Jews are the only national minority prevented from maintaining their own cultural institutions. The few remaining Jews in Arab lands are harassed. Many feel out of place in South Africa, with its apartheid policy.

Unfinished business is big business in Israel. When immigrants arrive, they need housing, vocational training, health care and education. Some of them need help in making the transition from a primitive way of life into the twentieth century with its contradictory values. Thousands of teachers, social workers, doctors, employers, foremen and youth leaders participate in the task of social welfare rehabilitation. And their number is insufficient to meet existing needs. Young people are, therefore, not without opportunities for creativity.

Idealism as an export

The idea that people need to identify with development oriented public services has universalist implications. Every year thousands of young men and women come to Israel to do volunteer work, mostly in communal farms (kibbutzim). The Government, the labor movement and the kibbutzim are subsidizing this program of *Sheruth Le'umi*—the Hebrew term for public service. Israel has become a Mecca of people trying to find themselves.

The supply of volunteers sometimes exceeds the country's organizational capability to make full use of them. Not all are pioneer material. Some are young adults who enjoy bohemian living, will shirk work and who are lost souls in need of help rather than being capable of giving much of it. But many more volunteers make a pilgrimage in search of self-fulfillment. Approximately 1,200 of the many thousands who hurried to Israel when its existence was threatened during the summer of 1967 have made arrangements to stay permanently. They helped gather the harvest, recover military equipment from the desert or repair damaged settlements. A Jewish Agency report (*Jerusalem Post,* January 9, 1968: 1) indicates that about one-half of them were members of a Zionist youth movement in their countries of origin and they declared that they would have come to Israel in any case, and only came earlier because of the war. But others have more universalist ideals.

These neo-Zionists "dislike, even resent" being told they must come to Israel because the future of the Jews elsewhere is uncertain. They want to show independence and are impatient with the country's complex bureaucracy. Few of them seem to have any interest in existing political parties.

Why do they come? One clue comes from a report of the Masada excavation. Masada is where Jews had made their last stand before the Romans ended their national sovereignty in the year 73 A.D. Volunteers came from twenty-eight countries when Yigal Yadin was ready to wrest the secrets of Herod's desert fortress through archaeological study.

Most of the volunteers in Masada had to perform the tedious manual labor of excavating by hand and with small tools. They had to pay their own fares to and from Israel and were required to stay for at least two weeks. They were told in advance that living would be rough—in tents, each with ten beds. This was no soft vacation junket. But there were more than enough applicants from all over the world to run twenty-three two-week shifts during two winter sessions, with an average three hundred participants, ranging from priests to vagabonds, professors to butlers.

One official from London was allowed to come with his 16-year-old son, although the boy was too young to be accepted. The father explained (Yadin, 1966: 262): "My object in bringing (him) is partly education, but mainly that he may be shown by example to give of his time and labor without financial regard, for the joy of a worthwhile venture alongside young people from other nations."

There is some doubt that unskilled work done by volunteers is less expensive than the hiring of paid local labor. But the process of volunteering does act as a self-selection mechanism to recruit the kind of young men and women whom Israel hopes to attract as permanent settlers. By reserving certain tasks with inherently idealistic meanings for volunteers, officials create opportunities for local or foreign personnel to feel part of the historic enterprise of nation-building. Some will remain; others will go home but will return later.

The organization of work camps, volunteers and youth services also has become one of Israel's principal foreign aid programs to the emerging countries of Africa, Asia and South America. The pioneering accomplishments of Israel are inspiring leaders of these nations with the hope of replication. Did not Palestine become transformed from a destitute wasteland to one of the world's most progressive countries, and was this progress not achieved within a period of decades, rather than centuries?

Here and there Israeli mutual aid provides military training, but the major part of such aid is devoted to developmental rather than military objectives. Laufer (1967: 213–214), who studied Israel's mutual aid programs, found that this new nation symbolizes to many the attainability of the cherished hope for rapid development.

> Israel's cooperation program is not without its flaws, failures and continuing problems. In many important respects the problems are similar to those that other donor countries face. Yet by virtue of its almost charismatic appeal, Israel, the symbol, has largely remained untouched by these difficulties. The traveller in Africa or Latin America is repeatedly struck by contrasting reactions on the part of his hosts: mention the United States and it brings to the fore uneasiness, suspicion, a plea for more capital, a question about U.S. intervention in the Dominican Republic or the war in Vietnam: mention Israel and it evokes a cordial smile, questions about the Kibbutz, Israel's accomplishments in a specific sphere or declarations of how much better things would be if only the Israeli spirit were present.

The foreign aid program also serves to reinforce the prestige of pioneering inside Israel, at a time when it is losing some of its charisma. It embodies the powerful spiritual message that what is being accomplished need not be viewed as a unique case of nationalistic rebirth. Herzl (1960: 129–130) envisioned such a universalization long before Israel became a state.

In 1902, in his novel describing the Zionist movement as a universalist utopian effort, the hero exclaims:

> Now that I have seen the restoration of the Jews, I should like to pave the way for the restoration of the Negroes—that is why I am working to open up Africa.

The Israeli foreign aid effort, of which the development of youth programs is a major part, adds a strain to Israel's large foreign exchange deficit. Only by postponing some urgent domestic measures can the needed dollars and skilled manpower be allocated. The governor of the Bank of Israel reported in 1965 that there were two thousand students from under-developed countries who were in Israel for training. The number of Israeli experts abroad is at a rate of more than twice that of those from the much more developed European Community states (Horowitz, 1965: 10).

The decision to concentrate heavily on foreign aid involves a variety of factors. Certainly, Israel's foreign aid program has helped to break down the wall of diplomatic isolation from newly emerging countries which Arab states tried to erect. Foreign aid jobs have enabled many Israelis to see the world beyond their confining borders. Many of these foreign aid experts return home with renewed enthusiasm to their youth work. The recipient countries often pay a large part of the cost of the aid. One of the distinctive attributes of Israel's foreign aid program is the emphasis on pioneering attitudes in the selection of personnel, the majority of whom are young. As Laufer (1967: 56–57) reports: they have earned an image at home and abroad for speed, pragmatic improvisation and social idealism. They identify with their host country as if it were their own. In the words of one of them:

> We worked with the local people and wore the same work clothes they did. We treated them as we treat our workers in Israel. We let them come into our hut, which no Englishman would do . . . work schedules aren't a holy matter. If necessary, one works at night. . . .

Cross national comparison: utility and limits

In a world where so many countries devote a disturbingly high proportion of their national incomes to support a military establishment, Israel's experience with co-optatively planned change stands out because a high rate of development has been achieved in spite of the necessity to maintain a large army. Can there be generational transmission of the enthusiasm, fervor and voluntarism which inspired the parental generation who succeeded in bringing about a major change? Can national morale be maintained when the military emergency begins to lessen or disappear? These are universal problems of long-range national planning.

TABLE 2

Schematic Comparisons of Selected Institutional
Variables in Israel and the United States
Relevant to the Question:
Shall There Be a National Service?

Noncomparable planning variable	United States	Israel
Size of program	Large population over 200 millions	Small population of about 2.5 million
Political support for comprehensive national service	Opposition to be expected	Strong support. National service is not a controversial political issue
Supportive economic resources	Very large per capita gross National Product	Much more limited per capita gross National Product
Defense necessity	Borders are not fortified. There are no hostile neighbors next door. The defense of the United States has been maintained by other means than comprehensive national service	Surrounded by hostile neighbors Israel relies primarily on comprehensive national service for its defense
Eligibility	All citizens, irrespective of race or creed who favor a strong country	Only Jewish and Druze Arab citizens. Other Arabs are exempt to spare them potential battle with Arabs across the border
Opportunity structure for young people	Large and diversified	Small and more limited mobility

Something can be learned about these questions from a cross national comparison, although no two historic circumstances are ever identical. In the United States, as in Israel, the idea of a universal military service to recruit a civilian militia in time of war has become traditional. But American programs to recruit young people for developmental tasks, the Peace Corps and Vista domestic service are of recent origin. Their expansion into a universal national service to employ the approximately three million eight hundred thousand youths who come of age each year would be a mammoth undertaking (see, for example, Eberly, 1966; Tax, 1967). In urging some degree of expansion to cover more of the youth population, former Labor Secretary Willard Wirtz told the National Advisory Commission on Selective Service (1967: 62–63): "I think that life will have more point to it if every boy and girl has in his or her life a chance to spend two years doing something for some reason other than what is called 'breadwinning'—that is, for some reason better than money and on a pure service basis."

This is indeed what Israel expects from all its young citizens. There is a universal national service. It has many consequences for the total social system, but they are not necessarily the same as those which would emerge if the same idea were to be implemented in the United States.

There is much variance between the United States of America which spans a whole continent and postage stamp size Israel. For instance, compulsory education in Israel ends with the eighth grade. The government is committed to extend the period two more years, but has been unable to finance the implementation of the plan. In 1969, there were still 21,000 teenagers without any formal schooling between the ages of 14 and 18, somewhat less than one in seven. Many postelementary school training programs, academic as well as vocational, require tuition payments from all but the poor and youngsters living in frontier and development areas.

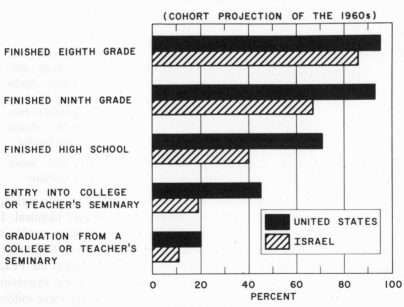

FIGURE 1.

Israel has a long road ahead to equal the educational attainments of the United States at the high school and university levels (Braham, 1966) (see Figure 1).

In spite of major differences (other than those mentioned) between conditions in Israel and in the United States, there are in both countries common administrative considerations in planning for a comprehensive national service, such as the following:

(1) The need to challenge the on-coming generation and to develop an affinity for public service. A high ideological value is placed on voluntarism but only a minority of the population will actually respond to a call for a purely voluntary national service.

(2) The need for opportunities for young people to discover themselves, their capacities and skills. Many of them feel they are growing up under achievement crisis conditions. The parental generation attained a high degree of success in some areas of life; their children must identify new challenges to give meaning to their lives.

(3) The presence of a sizable segment of the population who grow up in poverty. This includes many insufficiently educated youths especially from culturally deprived ethnic groups. Under ordinary circumstances, they enter adult life without meaningful experience in the performance of social roles that have status in the youth culture or in the adult society.

(4) The need to integrate the deprived and to motivate some of them to take part in public service programs.

Conclusion

The mission of creating a cohesive citizenry out of Israel's polyglot population is facilitated by a network of public service, welfare and educational programs. Prominent among them, as will be shown, are youth organizations. They serve many functions, such as creative use of leisure time, utilization of skills and leadership training, along with the nurturance of nation-building enthusiasm. Sponsorship is by a variety of agencies including political parties, schools, the army and some private groups. But there is no central control. The possibilities and limitations of nationwide planning for youth services can, therefore, be studied easily in such a diversified laboratory.

When Israel became a sovereign nation, there was an achievement crisis. It involved a shift from idealism to realism, a change in priorities among many of the country's pioneer elite. Halutzim left collective settlement to pursue more individually and family centered careers. When there were conflicts between personal and public priorities, the former often were in ascendancy. Crucial posts were filled on the basis of personal and party loyalties, sometimes with little regard for technical merit. Many vital developmental programs, such as the new harbor at Asdod, were delayed by jurisdictional conflict and strikes aimed at imposing featherbedding practices.

The severity of the achievement crisis was mitigated by the continuation of external conflict. The Arab neighbors of Israel view its destruction as a necessity. Relationships are based only on a cease-fire agreement. It is often broken, as such "no peace, but no war" arrangements are always likely to be.

There has, however, been a dramatic change in the nature of the country's mood. The revolutionary fervor of their parents cannot be felt by the younger generation in the same way. Young people born in Israel do not experience anti-Semitism. They do not have to make the transition from being a refugee to being a citizen of a new land, learn a new language and work in a new occupation. The emerging youth culture cannot remain what it was before independence.

Like children everywhere, Israeli children are concerned with their personal development and with having fun. Daily conversations are filled with excitement about the next soccer game or who is courting whom. And they get angry at bus schedules and are frustrated by school assignments. They want many things somebody thinks they should not have. As in all developing countries, aspirations for personal achievement are high, but there is little room at the top. Opportunities for higher education for important jobs and for comfortable jobs are very limited. Young people must work many years to finance their own apartment. Many have more than one job. One paycheck is usually too little to be the basis for supporting a family at a middle class standard of living.

In one sense, this is what the parents struggled to give their children, a chance to grow up normally. But the country's political leaders and educators are also concerned with perpetuating the ideals which brought them from all parts of the world. There is much unfinished business in Israel to transform the country's promises into a more stable state of fulfillment. The remainder of this book will deal with the organizational arrangements that have emerged to influence the country's youth culture through peer group programs guided by adults. As will be shown in subsequent chapters, they retain much of the organizational structure of the pre-independence struggle. But the day-to-day programs reflect, in part, the fact that Israel is no longer a vision but an accomplished fact. The present generation, much like young people in other rapidly changing countries, are growing up in a system run by well-established adult-making agencies. Their ideology and structure were fashioned before they were born, to meet requirements of an era quite unlike the conditions that pertain now.

In such a setting, it is possible to investigate a general problem of institution building: How can innovative thrust be maintained when, in order to survive and to protect its interests, an organization must maintain stabilizing alliances with other segments of the social system? How can the officials in an open, democratically governed country, who are in control, maintain their influence, while allowing a sufficient exercise of power to each cohort of young people to make their program relevant to them.

Even in traditional or in dictatorial societies, generational transmission has always been an occasion for change. In the hydrogen age, in which the computer, the tranquilizer and the birth control pill have become commonplace, generational transmission is even more complex, all the more, for a successful parental generation, who implemented much of what they set out to achieve. Their children face some very different problems, even if others remain the same, such as the question of sheer survival. The Israeli youth organizations that are rooted in the pre-independence period provide a useful natural laboratory within which these issues of societal change can be examined.

Part Two

THE ISRAELI
PROGRAMS

Chapter 5

The Research Setting

Organizational mapping

The principles of planned youth culture management were analyzed by relating three elements:

(1) Major youth organizations in Israel;
(2) Leaders who staff their programs;
(3) Members who participate in them.

Selected variables were chosen for more intensive study. In social system research, as in planning, it is a good strategy to survey the total network of related institutions but to concentrate detailed attention on key variables or control points of the larger system. Computers can handle intricate multivariate analysis of quantified data. But the statistical output must also be related qualitatively to the total complex of cultural, socioeconomic, political and psychological factors.

The research began with a survey of nationwide organizations and government ministries concerned with youth problems. Descriptive reports, census data and available research studies were reviewed. Key policy makers were interviewed by the American study director or by his Israeli collaborator. Interviews with these informants helped to formulate questions which were pretested before being included in one of our several schedules. Large-scale data collection and analysis were focused on three national youth programs; the youth movements, the Gadna Youth Corps and the Beyond School programs. There was also a considerable amount of participant observation. The research staff was invited to visit many organizations, sometimes to give lectures or to be available for consultation. These requests provided access to important sources of data.

Two different methods of sampling were necessary. Leaders and policy makers were selected from lists of leaders furnished by each organization on the basis of their accessibility and their readiness to be inter-

TABLE 3

Schematic Outline of Activities of Israeli Youth Programs

Activity	Youth movements	Gadna Youth Corps	Beyond School programs	Sports clubs	Street worker programs	Zahal national service
Hiking and touring	Often	Often	Occasional	Rare	Occasional	Often
Sports and games	Noncompetitive	Noncompetitive	Noncompetitive	Competitive	Noncompetitive	Noncompetitive
Discussions	Often	Occasional	Often	Rare	Often	Often
Arts and Crafts	Rare	Occasional	Often	—	—	—
Group Singing	Often	Often	Occasional	—	Rare	Often
Teaching of vocational skills	Rare	Rare	Often	—	Rare	Often
Premilitary conditioning	Incidental	Major goal	Incidental	Incidental	—	Major goal
Coeducational groups	Yes	Yes	Yes	No	No	Yes
Leadership	Professional or nonprofessional	Professional or Nonprofessional	Often professional	Non-Professional	Mostly professional	Highly selected and trained
Social Work with problem youngsters	Occasional	Rare	Occasional	Almost none	Often	Occasional
National Service	High priority	High priority	Minor emphasis	—	—	High priority

viewed. Information from adolescents was obtained on an area sampling basis. The area chosen was Holon, a metropolitan suburb of Tel Aviv. Efforts were made to reach all youths in the sample, including those not active in any youth program.

Every modern society tries to influence the next generation through organizations. Youth program participation in Israel is almost as common as school attendance but much less regular. Over 90 percent of all Israeli youngsters reported themselves as having participated—for a shorter or longer time—in one or several of the three major youth organizations selected for study. The proportion was 95 percent among the adolescent tenth grade cohort in Holon, which has an above-average participation rate.

All of the collected data were related to the presence or absence of reported membership. This is a crude index at best, since it fails to measure the meaning of participation for each respondent. Some become deeply involved in a youth program while for other members, participation is nominal. Youngsters experience the membership personally rather than organizationally. For many, it is more than a matter of going on hikes or engaging in sports and in discussions. In contrast, many of the adult policy makers and leaders think of their work in more jurisdictional terms. They discuss them administratively as youth movements, the Gadna Youth Corps, the Beyond School programs, sports clubs, street clubs or the national service of the Israel Defense Force. Each plans specific activities in terms of the ideological and administrative expectations of the sponsoring adult-making agency. Many of these programs, as shown in Table 3, sponsor the same activity. There is some overlap also in their organizational objectives. But there is no single administrative unit which could aspire to exercise overall control of the youth culture or furnish the data needed for this study.

All these programs offer leadership roles to young persons, but there is variation in how much initiative can be exercised by them. There is directiveness in all programs, but the element of co-optation—the incorporation of competing and conflicting youthful elements in leadership and policy formation—is more varied.

Youth movements

Several of the youth movements will soon celebrate their fiftieth anniversary. That is a long time for peer group and age-limited organizations, which must recruit from a new group of eligible persons each year. As will be shown in Chapters 6 and 7, they are losing some of their predominance in the youth culture, but they retain much public esteem. They now reach about three-quarters of the adolescents at some time of their lives. But only a dedicated minority will still be associated with them when they reach adulthood. Structurally the youth movements have changed little, nor have their official ideologies changed much in spite of major changes in circumstances of their operation. Youth movements remain in the forefront as organizations recruiting for public service, especially in kibbutzim, but there is also much talk about their being outdated.

The youth movements, in contrast to the other youth organizations that will be discussed in Chapters 8, 9, and 10, had their origins in Europe, where program leaders recruited Halutzim and facilitated their emigration to Palestine. They still have some overseas branches, but they now rely on nurturance from Israel to flourish. All of the ten movements, with the exception of the Scouts (*Zophim*), are sponsored by political parties. But they are quite similar structurally. Each is composed of small dens (groups) of age mates, federated regionally and nationally.

Each youth movement began with a "radical" program to build a new social order. With the success of Zionism, they have now become "establishment" oriented, with the exception of a handful of members of a Communist youth group who failed to take part in our survey. Ex-members of the other youth movements are prominent in the government. Overall policy on "principles" is formulated by adults, who prefer to exercise their influence indirectly. Youth initiative in day-to-day operations remains relatively high. There is a good deal of reliance on voluntary and amateur leadership. Paid coordinators are employed increasingly for central posts that cannot be manned by volunteers.

At one time the youth movements had a near monopoly over organized peer groups. They still reach more members than any other youth organization but participation is short lived for all but an idealist elite. Early adolescence is an age when many satisfactions are derived from group activities. But they tend to decline generally during the later years of puberty when there is an increasing tendency for boy-girl pairing and the desire for courtship-oriented activities competes increasingly with programs for a larger group. Even among long-term members, a decline of ideological impact is reported by many of the leaders who were interviewed.

The Gadna Youth Corps

Gadna had originated as a para-military volunteer corps prior to the country's struggle for independence, as a cooperative program of the high schools and the then underground Haganah army. As will be shown in more detail in Chapters 8 and 9, Gadna's bi-organizational structure has been retained. Minimal participation is now compulsory in most post-primary schools, including weekly or monthly drills, hikes and endurance training. There also are voluntary out-of-school Gadna clubs devoted to sharpshooting, airplane model building, first aid, marine scouting and/or an orchestra. About 60 percent of youths between 14 and 17 years of age are now enrolled.

There is very limited youth culture initiative in Gadna. The top level organizers are army career officers or Ministry or Education officials. They supervise a well-organized curriculum taught by full time youth leaders. Eighty-two percent were former youth movement leaders. A large minority are women. Students are taught to accept discipline, but are expected to exercise a good deal of peer group control in place of externally enforced commands. A selected elite is invited to enroll in vacation courses on leadership. Like its sponsoring agencies, the Army and the school, Gadna is nonpolitical.

The Beyond School programs

There are many local cultural enrichment and recreational programs subsidized and/or coordinated by the Ministry of Education. They include a range of amateur sports, dancing, supervised recreation, hiking, hobby and art classes, films and other informal educational offerings. There are also extended day school programs and after-school clubs in school buildings. As discussed in detail in Chapter 10, they reach in excess of half the adolescent population. Known by many administrative labels, they will be designated in this book as Beyond School programs. They have to be taken into account in any assessment of organizational efforts to influence the youth culture.

There is no central control although different bureaus of the Ministry of Education and Culture along with local youth departments are planning and financing them. Those located in elementary schools are officially designated as *Supplementary Education programs* (*Hinuh Mashlim*). In high schools the *Social Education* (*Hinuh Havrati*) Department of the Ministry of Education is responsible for encouraging their expansion through a subsidy program. In separate buildings one will find *Neighborhood Centers* (*Moadonim*) programs, *Technical Clubs* and community-wide *Youth Centers* (*Batei Noar*). There are also detached youth work programs. Municipalities furnish leaders to guide self-generated social clubs and induce them to locate in one of the youth centers. Leaders are more often career officials than in any of the other organizations. About two-thirds are male. Few are under 20. The program is more professionalized than the Gadna or the youth movements.

For several decades now, the adult-making institutions in Israel have sponsored three nationwide youth programs, each designed to supplement the efforts of the family and school system in specializing on adolescents. As will be documented in more detail later, none of them use a negative

strategy. They do not openly oppose youth culture manifestations as dangerous or antisocial. Nor are any of the contemporary programs revolutionary
in their objective.

TABLE 4

Schematic Outline of Adult Control of
Adolescent Youth Programs in Israel

Program	Adult-making institution attempting to exercise control	Control strategy	Degree of initiative by youths
Cliques or gangs[a]	Parents; also social workers and probation officers if clique or gang is engaged in antisocial activities	None or co-optatively influenced	High
Youth movements	Political parties; the Youth Department of the Ministry of Education and the Youth Department of the Jewish Agency provide some subsidies	Co-optative	Moderate
Beyond School programs, municipal and rural youth centers	Local schools, local departments of recreation and political parties. Some centers are also sponsored by voluntary organizations and youth movements	Co-optative	Moderate
Sports clubs[a]	Political parties, municipalities, plus earnings from national lottery and sale of tickets to spectators	Directive but voluntary	Low
Gadna Youth Corps	Gadna Departments of the Ministry of Education and the Ministry of Defense	Directive and Co-optative	Low
National service[a]	Ministry of Defense	Largely directive; co-optatively controlled Nahal units	Low

a. Not included in our field survey.

The Gadna Youth Corps and the national service are inherently directive in their outlook. Their military structure gives the leaders a great
deal of formal control in deciding organizational objectives. But within

this control structure, young people are given many opportunities to volunteer and to serve on a co-optative rather than on a command basis.

Those working with youth movements and the Beyond School programs rely in part on co-optation, since young people are recruited for key leadership and policy-making posts. There is a positive acceptance of some youth culture innovations. There is a regard for the need for autonomy on the part of young people in deciding on the use of their leisure time.

Additional youth activities are provided by sports clubs and local social clubs. The national service of the Israel Defense Forces also provides an organized framework for adolescents. These programs were studied, but not included in our analysis. Sports clubs have a specific athletic mission. They are not aiming to exercise a general youth culture influence. Local social clubs are not sponsored by an adult-making agency. They form spontaneously by youths in neighborhoods and are largely devoted to companionship and social dancing. The Army's national service makes a determined effort to have an impact on the youth culture. But it drafts youths at 18, beyond the age range of the population samples available for our study.

Our research attention was restricted to the three nationwide youth programs which have a well formulated strategy for influencing the pre-army age-group youths. They have a strategy for recruitment and training of leaders to educate and to indoctrinate them. But to get a more complete picture of the total network of leisure time services, it will be useful to outline the youth programs that were excluded from our analysis (see Table 4, p. 86).

Sports clubs

Soccer is the king of organized sports in Israel. It is likely to be played whenever boys can be gathered together in a neighborhood lot. Most localities have a local team. They play to crowds of spectators and engage in regional, as well as national tournaments. Two hours of physical training instruction a week are required in most schools above the third grade, including gymnastics, soccer, other sports and walking trips. Swimming lessons in school are compulsory in the sixth grade. Hikes, noncompetitive basketball, swimming, track and field sports are also part of the program of youth organizations and the Gadna Youth Corps.

Sports are activities in which adolescents generally outshine everybody else. They are viewed as fun more than an object for single-minded devotion. The stress in Israel is less on training a few outstanding athletes than on widespread participation. In the 1968 Olympics in Mexico, as well as the 1964 Olympics in Tokyo, not a single Israeli athlete won a medal. "None showed that vitally important 'push,' that supreme Olympic effort.

that breeds best 'performers' and brings about the upsets" (Raphael, 1964: 3).

Most sports clubs are sponsored by a political party. Each party contributes funds and provides adult sponsorship but it is rare for political criteria to be used in the selection of players although the party gains prestige from its club. Many localities make contributions from tax revenues.[18] Members also pay small fees. The Ministry of Education contributes to the improvement of facilities. Funds are also raised through a national lottery.

Physical education teachers as well as amateur sports leaders are trained at a specialized school, the Orde Wingate Center. It has excellent facilities, located on the seashore between Tel Aviv and Natanya. The center conducts a two-year teacher training program in sports for elementary and high schools. There are also brief courses on specific sports for leaders of amateur clubs.

Sports clubs are less coeducational than the other youth programs. The sex ratio of our sample of tenth-grade-level youths in Holon was four males for every female.[19] Sports seemed to attract ex-youth movement members much more than those who were still activists in youth movements in the tenth grade. Since many of the games take place on Saturdays, sports clubs compete for time with youth movements, which also use that day for many of their programs. Nevertheless 35 percent of the active members in the Left Socialist Hashomer Hatzair youth movements in Holon also reported being members of a sports club.

About one in ten adolescents in our Holon area sample is a sports enthusiast. While 17 percent said they belonged to a sports club, only two out of five (7 percent of the total group) rated sports as their "most preferred leisure activity." On this basis they were designated as sports *enthusiasts*. In addition, there were 3 percent who were unaffiliated sports enthusiasts. These youths also designated sports as their favorite type of recreation, but did not report themselves as belonging to a club.

In sports clubs, as in all autonomous peer group programs, good students from European families predominate. About one-half of the sports club members were enrolled in an academic high school; nearly two-thirds had fathers born in Europe. But achievement in sports is not dependent on intellectual capability. Sports clubs did reach youths who fail to do well in school. Nineteen percent of those who received failure scores in the eighth grade screening examination reported being a sports club member. Of the youth movement members who were *not* in a sports club, about 60 percent were good students, in contrast to only 45 percent of the youth movement members who were also active in a sports club.

Sports clubs have a high attraction for those who think of themselves as physically fit. Only 3 percent of the sports enthusiasts (those who were sports club members and who rated this activity first among leisure-time activities) thought they would be deferred from the army for health reasons. Expectation of deferment was mentioned by 13 percent of those who were youth movement activists but not sports club members. Of those who belonged to no organized youth program, 49 percent thought they would be deferred from the army for health reasons.

Sports clubs are activity centered. They do not advocate pioneering-type tasks. Sports enthusiasts, those who rate sports above all other recreational programs, reflect this fact. Less than 3 percent thought they would join a kibbutz, as against 14 percent of the mildly interested sports club members, whose first preferences for recreation was an activity other than sports.

Local social clubs

All young people belong to informal cliques. Membership tends to be spontaneous and local, reflecting friendship patterns among age mates in a school or neighborhood. Most youngsters belong to one or more of these groupings. Some acquire enough identity to adopt a name and to sponsor scheduled programs, especially dances or excursions. Others retain more fluidity. While these cliques are an important part of any youth culture, they were outside the range of our field study, which dealt with programs to intervene *organizationally* in guiding adolescent leisure time activities.

Many a school class, especially in middle class neighborhoods, will begin to be divided socially as they near the end of grammar school into two major strata: youth movement members and social club (Havuroth Noar) participants. The latter place a higher priority on clothes, keeping up with movie stars and other popular culture activities. They are exclusive for youths in a specific area or school. Their members rarely pay dues; they just belong. Use of lipstick among girls, smoking by young students and social dancing are acceptable. They meet in each other's homes, on the beach, the street or in neighborhood cafes, especially on Friday and Saturday night.

In later adolescence, local social groups gain more adherents than the youth movements. They explore the world that unfolds to their curious minds in all its facets, including jazz and classical music, literature and pornographic magazines. The cliques will also do some "things" their elders would disapprove. Their programs are fun, social and courtship oriented. Much of the time members just sit and gossip. They may serve additional functions such as helping to bring food to lonely aged persons or the pursuit of delinquent activities. The difference between the local clubs and youth movement activists is not absolute. It is a matter of degree. Peres (1967: 62) found that two thirds of the youngsters oriented towards the popular culture thought "elegant dress helps in making a good impression," an attitude shared by only 44 percent of the youth movement members.

Cliques are highly resistant to adult control or co-optation. A street club program began to take shape to reach deviant cliques while our survey was in process. Social workers were employed in the Tel Aviv area to seek out and befriend individuals and groups among the under-privileged, who often engage in disapproved, if not illegal, activities. The street worker's main objective is to co-opt these potentially dangerous cliques so as to control their violations of socially acceptable values. The street club worker does not wait for an invitation. He seeks out a group which he thinks is in need of socialization. He befriends them, often by first "hanging around" in slum cafes where shadowy figures meet to gossip, do business or plan antisocial acts. Few of the lower-class social club members are enrolled in any adult-controlled youth program. They are primarily *detached* from the social system and its reward structure.

Over the months, the good street worker becomes accepted as a valued outsider. He will give advice, intervene in family problems, assist in obtaining employment, help in court cases, and apply his know-how about military service problems (Leissner, 1967). He has many opportunities to be present in situations which could easily deteriorate into a major fight or a criminal act. He knows when a car is stolen or with whom a local girl is sleeping. He will not turn youngsters over to the police but try to use the peer group to exercise social controls.

This generally detached segment of the youth population, discussed in more detail in Chapter 11, represents only a small percentage of the total youth population, but it is important beyond its numerical strength. These youths are a heavy burden to law enforcement agencies, which try to work with them on a preventive basis, to the extent their manpower permits (Dean, 1965: 7). Many of these youths will enter the army at age 18. Some will adjust while others will be discharged for lack of social responsibility.

The national service

When youths reach the age of 18, boys are expected to report for thirty-six months' service and girls for twenty-four months. Men remain on reserve duty until the age of 55. Women are generally discharged when they marry, or before, if not needed. Every citizen is subject to call without prior notice. If he has a motor vehicle, his car may also be drafted. There are malingerers, draft evaders and an occasional deserter. No statistics are available, but a reading of the Israeli press shows that enforcement of the national service requirement occurs without much legal coercion. Many more cases of tax evasion and serious traffic violation are reported than failure to meet national service requirements.

The national service was excluded from our study. It begins at age 18 and provides a dramatic break between childhood and adulthood. It is relevant, however, as the last organizational effort to influence adolescents. Military service is a nearly universal experience, in which the impact of the youth organizations, the school and other adult-making organizations are put to a test. But it is not the only test. Life beyond the army provides other challenges to national service equal and more relevant to what the youth programs want to achieve.

Girls first train in separate units, but are then assigned to such roles as drivers, typists, cooks, nurses, administrators, social workers, youth leaders and teachers. They serve with men, except during actual combat. Their work is usually commanded by the unit (and male) officers, but female officers in each area are responsible for the personal needs of the girls. When parachutists come back to the camp from a training jump, female soldiers are likely to have a snack ready for them.

The availability of woman power in the military not only releases men for direct combat units, but also humanizes the army. While interviews with women soldiers indicate that some think they are inadequately utilized, many also responded: "I would not have wanted to miss this experience for anything."

Girls from traditional families can be on their own and make their own decisions. They often return home more self-confident and grown-up than they were before entering the service. It is here that adolescence gives way to adult status at home and in the community. Some meet their future husbands in the army.

Most Israeli institutions are responsive to "protektia," the expectation that office holders in performing their job give some weight to party politics, religious outlook, kinship and friendship. "*Who* you know" competes with "*What* you know" when it comes to speeding up the process of getting a driver's license or the determination of promotion of personnel in government and industry. Such a policy of considering personal criteria is vigorously suppressed in the army. A strong merit orientation is enforced. Able young people from underprivileged groups without contacts will generally get their chance. Over-protected middle-class youngsters of lesser ability learn to confront themselves realistically.

Zahal, the Israel Defense Army, is not a distant bureaucracy. It is an institution affecting virtually every Jewish family. It is the people's own militia and is generally above politics and patronage. Class privileges mean much less than in many other Israeli institutions, even those under the direction of socialist organizations and the Histradruth trade union. Officers are expected to lead, rather than tell others to go ahead. The "batboy" and the officers' washroom are unthinkable. Even more than in the United States Defense Forces, the power to command is kept clearly separate from social privileges.

National service also provides young Israelis with a sudden introduction to the harsh realities of existence. There is little of the romanticizing of military experience which the Israeli army has earned abroad because of its fighting capability. Quite a few officers do not conform to the ideal model of the task-oriented charismatic leader. There is red tape, boredom, neglect and other bureaucratic complications. Above all, there is the risk of injury and death. The young Israeli learns to balance his pride in being part of an organization that can defend him and his loved ones against the cost. Casualties are not reported by the numbers. They are known by name. Each loss is felt keenly.

The army has a double set of models. There are the usual military heroes who risk all in battle. But the Halutz, who measures his achievement by what is developed positively, shares some of the limelight. Zahal does much more than defend the borders. It provides transportation and communication in border areas. Its volunteer Nahal pioneer corps develops new settlements. A vast network of vocational and academic educational services are maintained, especially for immigrants. Efforts are made to have everybody leave the national service in good physical condition and enriched by social and vocational experiences that can be of value to him in meeting adult responsibilities.

For many under-privileged youths, military services can be a framework for the last chance to "make-up" education. The program is extracurricular in the sense that no one will be court-martialed for failure to take advantage of it. Boys and girls from disadvantaged segments of the population tend to enter the army deficient in work habits, social skills and motivation to succeed with educational tasks. Some of them will have an unusual success experience because of their physical courage or endurance. But towards the end of their service, many begin to worry about their future: "What will I do when I get discharged?"

Special classes are organized for the educationally handicapped throughout their two years of service, but the most intensive course comes near the end of military service. The Army Education Corps found that soldiers are then more motivated than they are at the beginning of their national service. While not all of them succeed, hundreds each year graduate from Camp Marcus School in Haifa,[20] before discharge from the army, in accordance with an order by the General Staff (Bar-On, 1966a, 1966b: 37–38).

>   (1) Every soldier who has not previously finished an elementary education must go through his basic studies during his national service, sit for a final examination and receive a graduation certificate.
>   (2) A soldier who has finished his elementary education abroad must attend a course to round off his Jewish and civic education.
>   (3) The basic studies course aims at elevating the cultural level of the soldier, deepening his attachment to the state's national values, and laying the foundations for future training and further education.

(4) Soldiers whose Hebrew has been graded by the Army authorities as 0–5 (out of a maximum of 10) must study the language before they can attend the basic-studies course.

(5) Basic studies comprise the Bible, geography and history of Israel national renaissance and independence, mathematics, general geography and history and civics.

The army reaches a good many, but not all of those for whom national service could serve as an integrative experience. As one high official explained, "Fighting is our primary mission. Welfare is a luxury. I wish we could afford more of it."

The army will not draft severely delinquent, socially maladjusted and psychologically disabled youngsters. But when the military budget permits, several hundred of such socially marginal youngsters are accepted for rehabilitative purposes. They are given special attention and conditioning under quite unmilitary permissive circumstances. Runaways are not normally court-martialed. They are more often brought back to camp by their own officers who function more like social workers than commanders.[21] About one-third of these special recruits end up doing well in the service. Another third complete their period of service, but are marginal. About one-third cannot adjust and are discharged.

In advocating a somewhat similar program of alternative military and developmental services for the United States, Sargent Shriver (Shriver, 1966), the former Director of the Peace Corps, and the Director of America's "War on Poverty" characterized Israel's example in the following concise, if somewhat oversimplified, description:

Israel has found that its program of universal national service which brings all young Israelis together for training and for either military duty or work in pioneer farm settlements, is the most effective factor it has for national integration and education. Young men and women, literate and illiterate, from fortunate families and from the most demoralized backgrounds, come together for common service to their country. And they come out of this service more productive, better educated and healthier citizens.

Leadership mapping

Youth organizations are strongly influenced by those who lead them. At policy-making levels, dozens of officials were contacted and interviewed with respect to both current and past trends. This descriptive information was supplemented by a questionnaire survey of 2,201 youth leaders who were carried on the roster of various Israeli youth programs or who were enrolled in a youth leader training course. This conglomerate group of officials included many of those responsible for their programs. Recently employed youth workers or those disinterested in their work are probably overrepresented among the nonrespondents. The principal findings are reported in Chapter 12.

Different subunits varied much in the proportion of those who were reached. Only a few were missed among the Army Gadna Youth Corps leaders, mostly persons who were ill or on vacation on the days when our staff met with them. Many permanent cadres, who did not think they were expected to take part in the questionnaire survey, also failed to participate. Our coverage was much more restricted in other leadership subcategories. Respondents could not often be assembled in one place for group administration of the questionnaire. Our data comes from those interested in replying.

There is no reliable list of youth leaders that could be used for sampling purposes. No one knows how many persons work in this profession, although their number exceeds 10,000. In part this is because the definition of youth leaders (*Madrih* in Hebrew) covers many types of youth work. The following categories were included:

Youth Work Administrators: Officials who administer a program or teach youth leaders without direct responsibility for any adolescent groups. Most of these administrators once served in direct leadership posts. They tend to be full-time personnel.

Paid Youth Leaders: Most of the direct youth leaders receive some form of compensation for their work. It may be a part- or full-time salary. More often there is a more modest compensation for expenses and maintenance from the adult sponsoring agency, a *kibbutz,* the army or the youth movement central headquarters. Some leaders are teachers who earn extra pay by serving as extracurricular youth workers.

Volunteer Youth Leaders: About seventeen percent of the youth leaders in our sample served without any form of compensation. Their actual proportion is probably greater. Volunteer leaders are not easily contacted because they must be active for a long time before they are likely to appear on a national roster of the type used in this study. Most of them were under 18 years old.

Additional information about the volunteer and very young leadership reservoir was gathered from a sample of 722 leadership trainees enrolled in the 1965 summer courses of the Gadna Youth Corps. Most of them had completed the first year of high school. All those in attendance, except for a handful who were ill or refused to take part, completed a questionnaire which was administered to groups.

Membership mapping

In addition to policy makers and youth leaders, the research team questioned several samples of adolescents about how they think and feel, with special reference to their involvement in leisure-time programs. Previously collected data from two already completed surveys of students were recoded for reanalysis in our study to determine how the "customers" of youth programs think. Most questionnaires were group administered in school classes and special programs and were supplemented by mail contact.

The interviews were at two different age levels, in the last year of elementary school (age 13–15) and during later adolescence, at the tenth-grade level. Most of these informants were 16 years old, although the range was from 15 to 18. Students do not progress through the educational system at a uniform pace, especially in an immigrant country where many young people lose a few years of schooling because they have to learn a new language.

A total of four samples was utilized:

The Sekker Sample: Twenty-five percent of a nationwide sample of more than 10,000 eighth graders in 1963 were questioned about their youth program participation. Most of them (eighty-seven percent) were between thirteen and fourteen years old.[22] The data were collected as part of a study to relate school performance to each youngster's socioeconomic background, his future and vocational plans. Each student's responses were related to scores on his Sekker comprehensive examination, which is given each year on a nationwide basis to determine access to high school programs. The examination includes items on vocabulary, reading comprehension, arithmetic, geometry and the Bible and two I.Q. tests. Evaluations of each student are also solicited from teachers.

The Holon Area Sample: In 1965 all tenth grade level adolescents in that metropolitan satellite city of Tel Aviv were asked to complete a questionnaire about their current schooling, work, future plans and youth program involvement. Included in this sample of 1,040 youngsters were 250 who previously had been interviewed in the 1963 nationwide Sekker Comprehensive Examination sample. This provides our study with a panel of youths, permitting comparisons of their 1963 and 1965 responses.

The choice of the city of Holon was advantageous in a number of ways. Holon has a diversified network of youth programs coordinated by an above-average Youth Department director, who was willing to cooperate in the study. Holon is fairly representative of Israel's urban population (Chen, 1967). With 67,250 inhabitants it is small enough so that all the adolescents in one age group could be studied, using the limited resources available.[23] But it was big enough to have a 1963 graduating class of 1,040 eighth graders who we then tried to locate in 1965. Limited demographic data about each student was available from the 1963 Sekker study. A field team of college students relocated 879 of these same subjects during 1965. They were then questioned about their youth program participation, their vocational plans and their attitudes about many personal as well as social questions.

The leisure-time survey data of a nationwide sample of 2,045 high school age students in 1963 were made available to the study staff. Youth program participation of these older adolescents had been studied within the context of their leisure-time activities, employment, and school attendance. These data provided a means of checking the national representativeness of the Holon area sample findings.

The Welfare Department Sample: The 1963 national Sekker survey as well as the 1965 Holon area study focused on youngsters graduating from Israel's regular elementary schools. This enumeration procedure makes it probable that many school drop-outs were missed. About 5 percent are given permission to leave school; roughly another 5 percent leave illegally; and perhaps another 5 percent are in parochial or special education classes. These youngsters were underrepresented in our samples. The few studies that have been made of these population segments agree that they have two characteristics: the children come from poor families and are poor students.

The inference that our survey data fails to include a representative sample of the deprived and socially inadequate segments of the population is confirmed by internal analysis of our own findings. Ninety-four percent of the good students in the 1963 Sekker study were located for a follow-up interview in 1965, as compared with only 74 percent of the poor students. Eighty-eight percent of the high socioeconomic scale students were re-enumerated, but only 74 percent of those of the lowest socioeconomic scale point.[24]

This underenumeration led to the decision to make a special survey of children of welfare department clients. Supplementary data about these largely lower-class youngsters were collected in a survey of 514 adolescents from the files of the Department of Welfare in Holon.

Arab youths were excluded from this study. While Israel is a binational state, there are almost no integrated adolescent youth groups. Youth organizations play a very minor role in Arab youth culture. Their social system is still predominantly traditional. The patriarchal family is in conflict with overt expressions of peer group power that would be generated by youth programs. Organizational efforts to influence the beliefs, expectations and voluntary activities of the next generation through youth organizations and extracurricular programs are well developed only among the Jews. In 1968 the Gadna Youth Corps was extended to incorporate boys of the Arabic speaking Druze minority who supported the Jews during the War of Independence. Druze males serve in the Israeli army, but even this group has no extensive youth programs. Girls are kept close to home until marriage. There is ambivalence about coeducation in the schools.

Participation index

Israeli youth program planners and educators tend to assume that like school attendance, youth organization affiliation is socially desirable. This view is justified by references to such facts that affiliated youths more often do well in school and express more idealistic preferences than non-joiners. This assumption was confirmed, as were a number of other variables, such as sex and school attendance.

The meaning of organizational affiliation for each youngster was not elicited directly. But in order to test if this variable might be related to the impact of youth organizations on behavior, respondents were divided into the following four categories (see Figure 2):

(1) Nonjoiners
(2) Passive participants
(3) Volunteer (non-youth movement) participants
(4) Youth movement activists

Only 6 percent of the Holon sample reported no youth program membership. They were the nonjoiners. Three-quarters of them were also poor students. They had failure scores in the eighth grade Sekker examination given two years before our survey was conducted. Many of the non-joiners came from families where the father had no education. Only 2

YOUTH ORGANIZATION PARTICIPATION OF HOLON
ADOLESCENTS IN 1965 - BY SEX

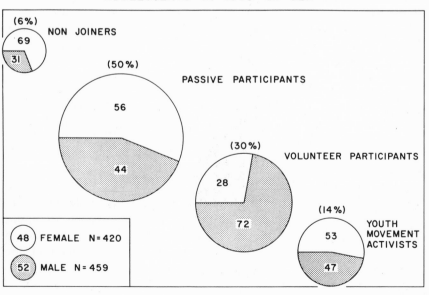

FIGURE 2.

percent of youngsters growing up in such a family were youth movement activists. Over two-thirds of the nonjoiners were girls. This reflects several cultural variables, especially the fact that Afro-Asian families are often unwilling to allow their daughters the same freedom as boys in joining organized peer groups.

About half the young people were identified as passive participants. They were enrolled in the semicompulsory activities of Gadna, those conducted in secondary schools, or they reported belonging to a Beyond School program conducted in their school buildings. They were designated as relatively passive since involvement did not require the youths to show much autonomy. They just had to "fall in line" with what was offered in their school. Also included among the passive participants were the ex-youth movement members who had resigned.

The passive participants were more often girls than boys. Relatively few expressed pioneering preferences in response to our attitude questions. Only 6 percent of these so-called passive participants—the same proportion as among those never reporting any youth program participation—expressed a preference for settling in a kibbutz, development town or rural community (see Figure 3).

PREFERENCE OF HOLON ADOLESCENTS FOR SETTLING IN A KIBBUTZ, DEVELOPMENT TOWN OR RURAL COMMUNITY

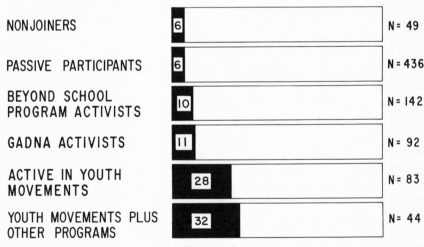

FIGURE 3.
(boxed figures are percentages)

Thirty percent of the sample can be designated as volunteer (nonyouth movement) participants. They reached out to enroll in a voluntary Gadna Youth program or a community centered Beyond School activity.

They had to be sufficiently interested in these peer group programs to join an activity that was not located in their school. But they were not members of a youth movement at the time our survey was made when they were in the tenth grade.

The volunteer participants ranged between the nonjoiners and the youth movement activists on nearly all variables, except that the girls were very much underrepresented. Few girls were interested in joining voluntary Gadna programs, many of which were devoted to target-shooting and airplane model building. One in ten volunteer participants expressed a preference for settling in a kibbutz, development town or rural community.

Fourteen percent of the Holon area sample were active members in youth movements. One-third of these were also volunteer activists in the Gadna Youth Corps and/or in a community centered Beyond School program. However, in our survey they were counted only once—as youth movement members. This was done on the assumption that youth movement membership tends to the most differentiating type of voluntary association because it requires the greatest amount of ideological commitment.

Girls were slightly more numerous than boys in this activist category with a ratio of 53 to 47. Academically able students were also overrepresented. The youth movement members ranked high in their expression of pioneering preferences. Twenty-eight percent said they would like to live in a kibbutz, a development town or rural community. The percentage was even higher (32 percent) among the very active youths, those currently taking part in a youth movement *and* in a voluntary Gadna or community Beyond School program.

The evidence is consistent with the theory that organizational affiliations tend to increase the likelihood that a youngster will grow up to assign a priority to public service needs. Idealism, as evident in readiness to be of service in a concrete national program, can be organizationally encouraged. Peer group interactions are utilized planfully and indirectly for the accomplishment of socially approved goals. Whether or not this theory works cannot be proved, but there is no doubt that idealistic attitudes are more common among youngsters who prefer to spend their leisure time with friends, a club or a youth movement than among those who prefer more solitary pursuits (see Figure 4).

Joining a youth group is not a random probability. Students in technical courses or those enrolled in a work-study plan were organizationally more active than their age mates who are working without studying. But in each category, about one-third were enrolled in a voluntary program of the Gadna Youth Corps and/or in a community centered Beyond School program. The academically oriented and brightest students were most active organizationally. They were especially overrepresented in youth move-

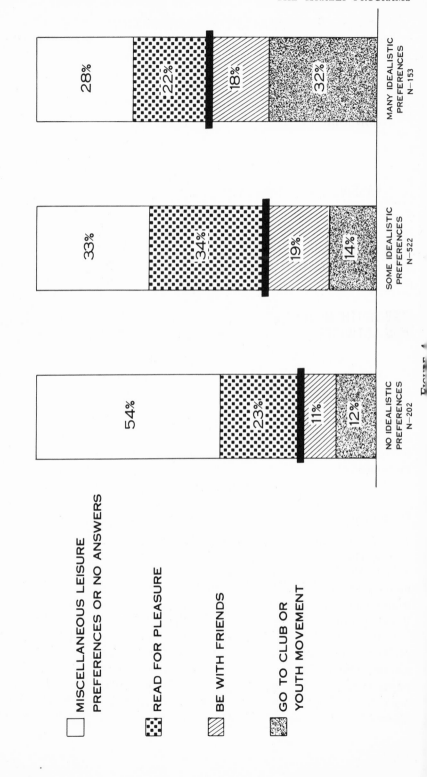

LEISURE TIMES PREFERENCES OF HOLON ADOLESCENTS
BY THEIR FREQUENCY FOR EXPRESSING IDEALISTIC ATTITUDE CHOICES

YOUTH ORGANIZATION PARTICIPATION OF HOLON ADOLESCENTS IN 1965 BY SCHOOL ATTENDANCE

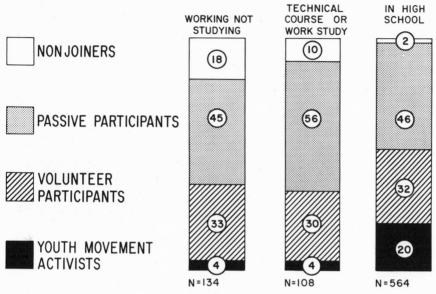

FIGURE 5.

(encircled figures are percentages)

ments. As shown in Figure 5, only a negligible proportion (2 percent) of high school students reported themselves to be nonjoiners, persons not active in any of the three programs, while one in five was active in a youth movement.

Conclusion

A youth culture is a web of interrelated institutions, folkways and mores. The concern of this study was with what can be learned by examining the organizational affiliations of young people. Their folkways and mores were observed only incidentally. Ours is a macro-study rather than a micro-analysis of how adult making agencies can plan to influence the thinking of their offspring.

It was not our intention to generalize about Israel, but to study the problems of youth culture management through adult-controlled organizations. Our staff succeeded in reaching the core of the country's growing population, even if some of the smaller subelements were inadequately represented. For instance, the demographic findings could be checked against Israeli census data. The distribution of the samples by age, sex, immigrant status, and so forth, was close, which supports the inference that the study population was representative with the previously noted exceptions.

There is no equally reassuring method for validating the attitude responses. Questionnaire responses represent what people are willing to say when asked such personal questions as: "How do you get along with your parents?" or "Where do you hope to live?" A youth who answers "in a kibbutz" at age 14 may think quite differently when he is 16 or when he enters the army and must decide whether he wishes to volunteer for a Nahai assignment. Not all kibbutz members are responding to idealism. There are other incentives for considering this way of life, the inability to decide on a career, the desire to try out something unfamiliar but safe, or the hope that one will be taken care of in a kibbutz. Attitude responses often differ from what people will actually do when the opportunity arises for them to act in accordance with their expressed opinion.

The weight of our evidence lies in the relative consistency of the data. The different samples provided response rates similar in direction and in the attitudes expressed. It is reasonable to assume that our respondents opened their thoughts and feelings to allow the investigators to explore meaningfully the questions they had come to answer.

Few of the policy makers interviewed questioned the theory that adults should help young people organize their leisure time. There is an increasing number of commercial recreation centers that one can frequent without being affiliated in any group. There are movie houses and concert halls. The country leads the world in per capita concert attendance. There are also many swimming pools, beaches, state parks, discotheques and other popular recreation facilities. All of them cater to young people. They are viewed as being supplementary to the adult-sponsored group programs. But the structure of the major youth programs is much what it was before independence.

Any consideration of social planning variables needs to take account of the fact that social research of system and institutional variables occurs in a live laboratory which will not stand still. The country has changed much since independence was attained, as have the circumstances under which young people grow up. The issue of "how a stable social structure can adapt itself to new functions" can therefore be studied well in this dynamic laboratory. During the period of data analysis, Israel confronted a military crisis that began with the closing of the Tiran Straits by Egyptian troops and the ejection of United Nations peace-making forces. When the Six Day War ended, the entire strategic position of Israel was transformed. The impact of this victory on Israel's thinking was overwhelming. Efforts were made to take this change into account in the interpretation of our findings.

The research process also affects the social system under study. For instance, the attention given by some Israeli officials to youth services often seemed to be influenced by the fact that their programs had been selected for special study. Interviews with policy makers went beyond the furnishing of information. Some were followed by a change in priorities by the officials for reviewing minor and some major organizational questions. It is probable that the conduct of the study helped to hasten the initiation of planned changes that had already been under contemplation. Such change had not been its purpose. But the vital concern of many Israeli leaders for improving the impact of their programs provided a receptive milieu for this study. It opened many doors and made people willing to talk candidly about many of the questions which they were considering.

Chapter 6

Pioneering

Peer group screening

All over Israel one can find assemblies of small groups of boys and girls without adults. In Jerusalem's Valley of the Cross, especially on Tuesday and Friday evenings and on Saturdays, the landscape is dotted with a dozen clusters of youths. They are members of youth movements that aim to inspire today's adolescent to become tomorrow's pioneer. Group activities are under guidance of a volunteer youth leader only a few years older than the members of his group.

Irrespective of their party affiliation, the different youth movements vary little in organizational structure. Now, as decades ago, youngsters can join as early as 10 years of age. The groups become coeducational after members turn about 13. Relationships are informal among equals, superiors and subordinates. Many of the organizers are unpaid or work for a subsistence salary. They are expected to rely on charisma, rather than authority, to make their influence felt.

In spite of ideological divergencies among the groups which range from theocratic to Marxian socialism, there also is much similarity in programming. Each meeting takes about two hours. Going and coming together in small cliques or boy-girl pairs adds personal meaning to the group activity. Many meetings start with group singing, followed by indoor or outdoor games. Usually there is a group discussion about a political, moral, religious or cultural topic, such as "How can we make peace with the Arabs?" or "Should one always tell the truth?" This is started by a youth leader or group member who makes a presentation, which is followed by discussion. There is much emphasis on membership participation. No authority figure can command order. A common word is *Sheket* (let's have quiet!). Members as well as the youth leader will be heard to make this demand repeatedly when the group spirit gets high and begins to interfere with the program in progress.

In addition to discussion centered meetings, there are traditional scouting activities—woodcraft, hiking and picnics. Special programs are prepared to celebrate holidays or historical events. The religious youth movements emphasize memorial and fast days, while those of the labor parties take note of May 1, the international Labor Day. All movements join in marking the Jewish festivals, especially Hanukah, Purim and Israel's Independence Day.

Vacations take on special significance. This is when groups leave home to visit archeological, historic sites and tour unpopulated or border regions. These journeys are usually full of adventure. Youngsters sleep under the open sky, live under primitive conditions and face many a test of endurance, resourcefulness and courage. They hear tales about the lives of the early Halutzim, the pioneers who developed Israel and, when need be, defended it under great odds. Members learn to care for themselves, help each other and test their limits of independence, without any parental or teacher presence. Management of each unit is characterized by a high degree of autonomy. Committees are elected which decide on budgets and expenditures, allocate jobs, enforce discipline and organize cultural and recreational programs.

Members who are 10 and 11 years old go only on overnight trips. In the 14 to 15 year old groups, trips can extend to five or six days. The older youths, aged 16 to 17, often serve as leaders. They may go as a group to work for several weeks as volunteers in a kibbutz communal farm. They try out collective living, with the view of settling in a kibbutz after their army service.

The abundance of personal reports and diaries about these hikes and work experiences in youth movement periodicals document the intense emotional meaning they have for the members. The youths are on their own and can feel grown up. They can relive the saga of Masada, where Israel made its last stand in Roman days. They can visit the cave where the Dead Sea Scrolls were found. They can bathe in the Sea of Galilee or admire how trees have grown in a hillside reforestation project.

A public service movement

Before statehood youth movements were the principal organizational instrument of the Zionist resurgence. Small local groups, most of them in Europe but federated on a worldwide basis, recruited young people to rebuild a national home for the Jews in Palestine. At first, many of the members were attracted by social activities rather than by ideology. They would discuss Jewish problems and study Jewish history, the Hebrew language and the geography of Palestine. Those who became committed would make plans for emigration. Such plans included prior vocational training, especially in agriculture and the building trades. Each local or regional group would then send a few members to Palestine to prepare the groundwork so that the rest could follow.

Unlike the contemporary schools, the Gadna Youth Corps and the Beyond School programs, the youth movements still have a loose organizational structure. They own few buildings, have few permanent employees and their appropriations are always tight and pieced together from many sources. Much more than any other youth program, they rely on what the members and the leaders contribute. In an age of bureaucracy, with high overhead costs, they remain informal. The resultant casualness can make for inefficiency, but it also allows individual members and units to innovate without much opposition. There are no forms to fill out in triplicate before a group hike can be arranged. No central office approval is needed to accept a new leader or to arrange for discussion of a controversial issue.

It is one of the ironies of history that the style of informality and voluntarism of the early Zionist youth movements was modeled in part after Germany's Wandervögel (see Lacqueur, 1962; Kanowitz, 1927; Thurnwald, 1927). This pre-World War I movement aimed to bring about a moral revival of the Vaterland by personal example. Members shunned politics; they did not demonstrate in the streets. The Wandervögel were idealistic romanticists without an action program for the larger society. They encouraged the formation of bands of young boys ("warriors") who would attach themselves to a charismatic leader-hero in a deep emotional relationship. They hiked in the mountains, sang songs around campfires and vowed to forgo the bourgeois superficialities of their parents. They advocated a pure simple life, devoted to patriotic values. The Wandervögel had no plans for socioeconomic development. Few of their leaders had a universalist outlook. Many espoused a teutonic tribalism that was later to characterize Nazism. It included a distrust of strangers bordering on hatred. World War I swallowed up this youth movement as it did much else in Europe. Many of its members died in Flanders and Verdun.

A few young Jews tried to gain acceptance in this movement but a larger number set up separate Jewish youth movements. From the very start many of them adopted a universalist and socialist platform. They copied some of the Wandervögel patterns. They organized in small groups preferably around a charismatic peer group leader. But the youth movements which had a Zionist ideology gradually federated in an large multinational organization. They also demanded more than an emotional attachment. Work was expected from each member, concretely related first to the revitalization of the Jewish community in their home towns. The most dedicated later were to make a personal commitment to build a better world in Palestine with their own hands.

The development-defense corps concept

There were no plans for an army when the early Zionist congresses convened at the dawn of the twentieth century. Not with guns, but with ploughs did the Halutzim hope to redeem Zion. The Jewish National Fund, the Jewish Agency and the Jewish Colonization Association had no budgets for the purchase of arms or even for police protection. The first Jewish watchmen's cooperative had to purchase arms and equipment from their own earnings, savings brought from abroad, and occasional gifts from sympathizers. In a novel describing the not-yet-established "old-new land," Herzl (1960: 61–62) described a utopian "new society," having a capitalist system without exploitation, a welfare state without poverty, and many social reforms in such diverse fields as penology and education. He anticipated the transformation of military conscription into a peaceful nation building force:

All the members of our New Society, whether men or women, must devote two years of their life to public service. As a rule they are the years from eighteen to twenty. . . . This two-year service provides us with an inexhaustible reserve of lower-grade personnel for all those institutions and public works which have been declared generally useful by the New Society. The upper echelons are staffed by paid personnel.
"I see," said Friedrich: "Your army consists of both regular soldiers and volunteers." "I accept the analogy," David replied. "But it is no more than an analogy—We have no standing army. . . . We are satisfied with making and keeping our youth physically fit."

In retrospect, this was a geopolitically naïve approach. The early settlers had to learn painfully that this theory would not work. They hired neighboring Arabs to guard their property, but this practice led to repeated extortion. In Palestine, as elsewhere in rural areas under Ottoman rule, trespass, anarchy and robbery were the order of the day. "They were indeed a regular source of livelihood for many desert tribes all over Arabia" (Golomb, ca. 1940: 11). Herzl's plan was too utopian in its hope that Zionists could devote themselves exclusively to the developmental tasks of building a nation.

The necessity for combining defense and development led to an organizational pattern that has characterized the pioneering youth groups since it was first improvised by the *Hashomer* (watchmen's society) in 1907. A group of eight Halutzim decided to organize a self-defense cooperative, selling its services to Jewish villagers. After several years, the society succeeded in gaining acceptance for the principle that all local defense be entrusted to Jews. By that time it had become clear that Arab watchmen could not be relied on, all the more in view of the growth in Arab national consciousness (Yaari, 1958b: 264–282).

These *military-development* units have always relied primarily on youth movements from which to recruit their members. They established the country's communal farms (kibbutzim) and cooperative villages (Moshavim Shitufim). Each follows the principle that men are most effective when they defend their own homes. Areas exposed to military conflict instead of being left a no-man's land of trenches, are settled by families, who create all the institutions required for normal living. These families are defending not an abstract location, but their homes, often between breakfast with their children and putting them to bed with a story at night.

The defense-development units have changed in name and size since they were first organized but their operating procedures have changed little. Before World War II they were called Hashomer; during the period of the British Mandate, Palmah; and since independence, Nahal (Levitas, 1967; Heymont, 1967: 314–324). Nahal is a volunteer unit that has no counterpart in other modern armies. The kernel of a Nahal group is self-selected. Boys and girls, usually from one youth movement, request induction into the national service as a unit. Assignments will be discussed by the group. Except for specialized military training given to some members, the entire group will serve together to explore their compatibility as a nucleus for establishing a new settlement. Along with rudimentary military skills, girls study agricultural, land settlement and home-making skills. Boys will be trained as parachutists, tank corps specialists or in other military specialties along with agricultural and other work skills. With the group's agreement, individuals not previously part of a Nahal group can be assigned to it in the hope of integrating new members. Aside from guard duty, Nahal units will do construction, land clearance and engage in agricultural production.

Officers and enlisted men live in the same quarters. Except in combat, orders are not issued from above. Policies for internal management are sanctioned by the group. Socially, each Nahal unit is a close knit Hevrah, or primary group. They combine national service with life goal planning. While living in an exposed, dangerous and often uncomfortable location, the members experiment with the practical details of communal living to see who is ready to satisfy his personal needs in a unit of pioneers sharing common ideals. Members must be able to adjust to group pressures, accept them and find them satisfying.

After the Six Day War of 1967, Nahal settled the Kfar Etzion compound, an area of Jewish residences that had been occupied by the Arab Legion in 1948. It also sponsored an urban cooperative of religious youths, who moved into an urban slum near the Western (Wailing) Wall in what had been old Jerusalem's Jewish section before its occupation by Jordanian troops in 1948. Nahal is establishing settlements in the Golan Heights, in selected areas of Judea and Samaria and the coast of the Sinai desert. It is readying more desert land in the Negev for permanent settlement to make this area more secure from infiltration of Arab fighters from Jordan.

Development is Nahal's most time-consuming mission. When there is no attack the members engage in the battle for production—against low income. Nahal incorporates the idea of civic action—the use of military force for peaceful purposes. But this is not a unit for pacifists, who are in any case rare in Israel. Military training and discipline are at a high level. The close tie-up of military and developmental public service objectives can be best surmised from a report (adapted from Schul, 1968: 8) of a Nahal outpost during its first few days.

The 28-year-old lieutenant in charge, received us in the room he shares with three others. He was just planning the guard and patrol roster for that night. B., from Yotvata, is a Tel Aviv-born native. He is a reservist who followed the call of his Kibbutz movement to command at Nahal Golan.

"As far as the sexes go we are a well-adjusted unit. Now wait a minute, don't misunderstand me. What I mean is that both sexes are adequately represented; half and half. They are youngsters from Haifa and its suburbs and some from the villages. They will stay at Nahal Golan for less than a year—and will then be replaced by a second unit while they, richer by the experience, will rejoin another permanent settlement they were intended to reinforce in the first place.

While we are here, we will start implementing our assigned agricultural blueprints: 'Humus' [chickpeas], which are raised much in Israel; 2,000 dunams of unirrigated grain crops; 75 dunams of irrigated vegetables; poultry; cotton; and a beef-cattle herd. No milkers."

Michal—from Kfar Ata ("I am just as old as the state!") was a typical sample of the several scores of boys and girls at Nahal Golan. Yes, she liked it, she said fiddling with her straight black hair. Michal is pretty, cooks and doesn't mind cooking. She was in a hurry. She had to finish cleaning her rifle, before inspection.

"Everybody is terribly polite about my food and if they don't like it they at least don't say so," she says. "No, there were no 'couples' here yet," she said. "But we are all terribly good friends, really." She said it was thrilling to be "an actual pioneer." There was nothing she would have liked to do more. The girls who do not like it so much are a very small minority—most of us would have volunteered for this kind of thing anyway." Michal wants to study when she gets out of the army but doesn't know what. She matriculated recently, as did, incidentally, every single member of this unit. All are graduates of secondary schools.

Reuven, 19½, wants to study economics. He does not know yet how he is going to bridge this with his equally strong desire to join a settlement nucleus. But the decision will have to wait anyway until he finishes his army service. When he came here on Thursday, his first assignment was to set up the flag pole. "We had a bit of a parade afterwards and some of the veterans from the Jordan Valley came up to greet us. The Syrians are just behind the gorge east of the settlement. The cease-fire line runs along the bottom of the wadi."

The bulk of the young people who volunteer for a Nahal assignment are attracted by a mixture of motives. The opportunity to perform a nationally recognized task is joined with a chance to live in a group of self-selected young men and women who get acquainted in a youth movement and who are testing their capacity to organize a community. For some, this preference is associated with prior ideological commitment to join a kibbutz after the end of their army service. For many more, this choice reflects uncertainty over what to do with themselves. For others, it is a means of being in an atmosphere that is more creative and less constrained than the more structured combat services.

In the choice of Nahal, as in all options of public service, idealistic incentives reinforce prosaic inducements. No large-scale and viable programs are likely to survive without a mixture of idealistic and realistic incentives. Indeed, fanatic idealists, who are intolerant of the human preference for meeting personal and family needs, are likely to create problems. No human institution that must attract large numbers and change its composition each year can restrict itself to the limited supply of single minded and purist idealists.

The relative prestige of Nahal has declined within the youth culture. Developmental projects, such as the months of back-breaking work involved in preparing the mine-infested Golan Heights for extensive cattle grazing cannot compete in glamor with the capability of the air force to insure Israel's fate within ninety minutes of actual combat. It is commanded by a 41-year-old kibbutz born officer, who chose flying in preference to kibbutz living when his time came to select a pioneering career (Ben Shaul, 1968: 133–141). About one in four of the youth movement activists in the Holon area sample expressed the preference of joining the air force or paratroop corps.

For some years now, the tactical need for Nahal settlers has exceeded the supply of youth movement volunteers. The Nahal command is now accepting individual draftees who select this option, even if they were not previously active in a youth movement. Some units have been asked to absorb youngsters from the slums who were not youth movement members to help rehabilitate them. (Fifteen percent of the tenth-grade level youths in Holon who thought they would like such service, in preference to any other, had resigned from a youth movement or never had been members.)

Ideology in transition

Public service is no longer a youth movement specialization. It has become routine and compulsory. After young men complete their three year required tour of national service and women give two years of their life to a nation-building task, they have reason to feel that a shift in their personal priorities is justified. They want to start their professional education, begin a civilian career, get married—in short, to live for themselves rather than serve as instruments of a cause. The majority of the native born Israelis are realistic rather than idealistic in their general mood. Some observers think today's youths are less collectivist in outlook than their elders, except during a period of emergency (for instance, Friedman, 1968: 117–131).

Before statehood was attained, the Halutz pioneer was often the only available manpower source for meeting urgent public requirements. There were many with a lifetime of dedication who, as volunteers, built the hundreds of new rural settlements and towns. Volunteer manpower was a critical factor in what was done or failed to get accomplished. Manpower planning has become more predictable since statehood. Leadership personnel are now recruited by offering them career incentives to fill such roles as army officer, industrial manager or civil servant.

The ten pioneering youth movements who still operate much as they did before statehood have lost their near monopoly on pioneering. They now are able to recruit members from a native born generation that faces a different challenge, of being good citizens of an already well established state. The law requires of them a period of national service. Youth movements appeal to members to render this service through the army's Nahal option and to use this experience for considering the idea of lifetime settlement in a kibbutz. But this public service option is now just one of many ways by which a young Israeli can plan to fulfill both his personal and his public priorities.

There also has been a decided reduction in partisanship. When the youth movements were founded, there were many competing ideological models of how to combine humanitarian values for a productive life, socialist principles for a nonexploitative existence, and aspirations for a Jewish cultural renaissance with the needs of every human being for self-fulfillment, in marriage and by rearing a family. Many of the doctrinal differences that could be entertained during the experimental decades have mellowed by practical experience.

It is hard to interest young people in carrying on the feud between the late Vladimir Jabotinsky and Chaim Weizman, which broke out in the 1930s over the issue of tactics of cooperation with the British Mandate authorities. Few care today why Mr. Tabenkin of the Achduth Avodah (Unity of Labor party) split with Ben Gurion many decades ago. The realities of Israeli politics, especially the existence of a stable coalition government since the inception of statehood, favor a tolerant coexistence of the different youth movements.

All the youth movements are becoming more professionalized by hiring paid youth leaders. Technical expectations for skill in group work begin to compete with ideological commitment in determining who gets hired. In rural areas there often is only one active movement. In small towns only a few of the larger movements tend to be represented.

Few youth leaders are willing to make adherence to the "party line" a criterion for membership. Most youth leaders prefer to retain a member who is active even if he does not conform in his ideology. This "organization above all" attitude is least pronounced among the more purist youth movements, both religious and socialist. For them ideology is still considered a criterion for membership. But even in these movements, expulsion or threat of expulsion is advocated only by a minority of the leaders.

All youth movements are concerned with the common problems of planning and management. The youth leaders, who try to recruit new members from among the oncoming generation, meet to discuss such common concerns as how to prepare group meetings, turn out a movement newspaper, plan for hikes and train volunteer youth leaders. In the larger cities there is a citywide coordinator for youth movements ready to assist all of them in programming. Training schools have emerged, which offer a common curriculum. Only a few lectures are given separately to discuss the particular problems of each movement and its political or religious doctrine.

There also has been a change in the meaning of joining a youth movement. Halutzim in Europe were rebelling against their parents' willingness to live in a ghetto, to endure anti-Semitism, to strive for a middle class occupation and to pray, rather than to work for the reestablishment of a Jewish home in Palestine. Their native-born children in Israel are not challenging the social system when they are recruited into the same youth movement structure. They are conforming to it. They join a program closely identified with the "establishment." Youth movement members are rarely found among the spontaneous crowds that assemble from time to time to protest a government policy. There had been fist fights in the 1930s between the nationalist Betar and some of the socialist youth movements. Such fights have not happened for many years. None of the contemporary youth movements are belligerently missionary or oppositionist. Certainly, they are opposed to illegal or revolutionary tactics, which once were espoused because the target was an unfriendly British Mandate regime.

As will be elaborated in the next chapter, the majority of all youth movement members (67 percent) belong to nominally socialist groups. But to conclude that the majority of the country's youths are led by persons with Marxist views would be erroneous. None of the movements advocate full nationalization of existing private enterprise. Israel's brand of socialism has more kinship with the Owenites and Hutterites of North America (Eaton, 1943: Ch. 27; Eaton and Weil, 1955) than with the state socialism of Yugoslavia or Soviet Union. In fact, Zionist socialism is viewed as counterrevolutionary in Russia. Its leaders have been opposed to genuine collective living by small groups, each independent of the state as well as the party. In Israel, kibbutz members make their own policies. They can and do deviate from party policy.

When dramatic changes occur, the different sectors of the social system are never affected in the same way. Independence transformed Israel overnight. The Six Day War in 1967 further changed its geopolitical condition. Elections since 1948 have led to only minor shifts in party strength, in spite of mass immigration. What has changed is the militancy of ideological controversies (Seligman, 1964: 87). All youth movements are searching for a new ideological basis for pioneering, in view of the disinterest in many of the issues that divided the parental generation.

Youths now disaffected with the status quo tend to be unaffiliated with or resign from the youth movements. The rebel of the contemporary generation may associate himself with informal groups such as a "salon dance" clique (*Hug Saloni*) or he may become active in a group like the "League Against Religious Coercion." There are small cliques of orthodox "activists" who demonstrate with stones against violations of the Sabbath by their fellow citizens. And many—indeed most—Israeli youths are too busy with their own needs to be politically active.

The youth movements must try to be relevant in a new era with different public service priorities.[25] Should kibbutz living continue as the primary goal? This way of life demands too much priority for group needs to appeal to many of the "best" young people who are ready to volunteer for other forms of public service. Also, many occupations of national significance cannot be pursued well within a kibbutz framework. The nation now needs young doctors more urgently than pioneer farmers. Not enough physicians are ready to live in the desert towns of Beersheba and Arad. Good public officials are in short supply in development towns. Cooperatives need business managers who will select staff more on their merit and less on influence. The kibbutz member, who had been the undisputed culture hero, is the occasional butt of cynic jokes—as someone who takes himself too seriously, is too self-satisfied and too provincial (Spiro, 1963). A linguist index of the change in ideological priorities is the Hebrew word for Zionism: *Ziyonuth*. The parental generation proudly identifies with it. Some of their native born children use this "sacred" term to connote "outdated sentimentality."

The next decade is, therefore, likely to see a drastic change in the program and the political orientation of the youth movements. All the socialist parties have merged. The remaining political parties are in search of new foci of identification. Their youth movements have not merged, but ideology is less and less a basis for differentiation. In the universities nonpartisan candidates have been elected to head student organizations, victorious over candidates associated with existing parties or youth movements.

The world, as defined by members of one generation, in order to deal with the issues that confront them, cannot look the same to their children. They are growing up under the much changed conditions their parents struggled to bring about.

Kibbutz viability

Verbal expression of intent to settle in a kibbutz at age 16 can involve a variety of attitudes, ranging from "I don't know what I want to be" to the romantic desire to identify with a pioneering elite that embodies universalist values which transcend Zionism. Few will take issue with the conclusion of Georges Friedman (1968: 86), "The kibbutz movement, in spite of its limitations and difficulties, is the biggest and most successful 'utopian' revolutionary experiment that has been attempted." For every person who joins a kibbutz, several try it out. This has always been the case. Most of the youth movement activists will ultimately choose a different career, often based on technical study at a university. The communal way of life provides a good deal of security, but it also calls for the willingness to conform to group expectations in many areas of life planning.

The country's national service ideology still helps to recruit new members, but the days are gone when enough people are prepared for a lifetime of pioneering in development areas, where there are many economic and cultural disadvantages without compensatory allowances. Therefore concessions are made. High schools are free for the children in border regions or newly developed towns. But there are also psychic and prestige gains that accrue to those who live according to kibbutz ideals, which are admired by many more than those who practice them. To be a *Haver Kibbutz* (member) remains a role of distinction. Of the 120 representatives of the parliament elected in 1969, 13 percent were members of kibbutzim, although these settlements contain only 3.7 percent of the population. Nowhere else in the world can one find villages of farmers and blue-collar workers, who also include among their ranks a good number of philosophers, scholars, writers, artists and otherwise creative human beings. Kibbutz children are overrepresented among the youth selected for pilot training or as army officers. They also head the casualty lists.

Kibbutz living has lost some of its priority in the country's core ideology, but this form of social organization still has ideological attractiveness. No statistics are available about the current postarmy career selection process of youth movement graduates. One clue comes from Peres' study (1967: 58–74) of 600 youngsters in the outskirts of Tel Aviv. Of the youth movement members, 76 percent in his sample said they wanted to live in a kibbutz for awhile. But only seventeen percent attached no condition to their verbal preference. Forty-three percent said they would join, but did not know for how long. Sixteen percent said they would be interested in kibbutz life for the period of army service in a Nahal unit.

For every kibbutz-born youth who at the eighth grade level in 1963 was thinking of leaving to live in a city, four city children expressed a preference of making their lives in a kibbutz. In both the Holon sample and the sample of Gadna Youth Corps leadership trainees, nine out of every hundred respondents chose kibbutz life as what they hope to do in the future. The kibbutz ideal has its greatest attraction for children born there. The majority of the graduating classes in kibbutz schools at age 14 said they intended to remain. This was true of 82 percent of the bright youngsters and 73 percent of those who were not doing well in school. City youths who are bright, especially those from European families also were overrepresented among those expressing a kibbutz preference. Such a verbal choice during adolescence certainly does not mean that all or even most of them will act out this choice when they become eligible to join. Only a minority of all youth movement members end up making their life in a kibbutz. The size of this proportion is one of the best kept secrets in Israel. Whatever the ratio of intended members and actual joiners may be for different youth movements, kibbutzim are still able to recruit among the country's oncoming generation (Eaton, 1969: 74–82). Their population increased from 47,408 in November 1947 to 77,999 in 1961 (Matras, 1965: 52). The population continued to expand slightly, reaching 80,600 in 1967 (Tamir, 1968: 4).

This population increase is in part due to immigration from overseas. The kibbutzim attract non-Jewish as well as Jewish idealists from all over the world. Many come to try this way of life for a limited time. A small proportion remain. The total population of Israel has grown much more than the kibbutzim where the pursuit of self-needs is deliberately balanced with group efforts to achieve public purposes. But they represent a significant economic and political power. They were responsible for 30 percent of Israel's total agricultural production. There were also 180 kibbutz-owned manufacturing and industrial plants in 1966. Most of them were small, but they employed 7,000 workers (Tamir, 1968: 28).

The 232 kibbutzim continue to play a leadership role in the country. Idealism remains a major asset. This is not to imply that they are composed of only dedicated men and women. But there are many of them and they tend to control each village. Twenty-two percent of the noncommissioned and commissioned officers in the draft army are kibbutz children, although they constitute only 4 percent of the population taken into the services. The proportion of kibbutz children is even higher in combat units.

They volunteer six times more frequently than do other youths for special risk units, such as the Parachute Corps, the air force and submarine units (Haaretz, October 16, 1966: 11).

Somewhat like large law firms or corporations in the United States, kibbutzim can be flexible about releasing members for public service. Men without independent resources are inclined to be careful. They cannot readily take the risk of a political career. They need a steady income. A kibbutz member, when given leave for a national assignment, remains a member in full standing. He and his family retain their home. The kibbutz allows them to keep enough from their salary to defray the extra living expenses in town. No kibbutz member needs to allow economic considerations to affect the way he functions in a public service post. When his mission is completed, he can and usually does return to an important post at home.

Conclusion

Youth movements furnished many of Israel's pioneers. They provided small cadres of self-selected idealists, who did the heavy work required to develop the institutional framework for the absorption of large masses of immigrants on a public service rather than a remunerative or coercive basis. Their origin was in Europe. Rejection of the ghetto, anti-Semitism and disillusionment with the betrayal of socialist values by European nationalists were incentives to the recruitment of youth movements. Their positive identification with the Jewish renaissance was also a source of attraction.

The youth movements have, however, been affected greatly by the social forces that had to be confronted in Palestine. Developmental priorities increasingly had to yield to military considerations, with the resultant creation of the concept of the farmer-soldier. He settled land and turned it into an economically productive enterprise, while also fortifying the area for defense purposes.

Military establishments are inherently wasteful. The Israeli Defense Forces are no exception to this rule. But to keep this inefficiency factor to a minimum, even some of the army combat units devote occasional resources to economically productive purposes. They build roads and improve communication. They have released men and women in uniform to serve as youth leaders and teachers. No senior career officer can expect to spend his life being a soldier. He is expected to acquire a skill with civilian utility, since for all but a few technical specialists, retirement in the forties is expected.

The country's capacity to raise a large army during an emergency, while maintaining a high state of defense readiness during more normal periods is a function of the merger of military with developmental functions.

Nahal is only the most explicit example of this jointure of pioneering with defense (Eaton, 1968: 129–134). It has some counterparts in the comprehensive military reserve, in which civilians are periodically called up for military service.

The high priority given in Israel to developmental rather than militaristic values may well be related to the continued vitality of the youth movements. They recruit those young people for the kibbutzim who view themselves as guardians of the utopian and universalist ideals that have always balanced the more nationalistic trends in the Zionist movement.

It is on these communal farms that many young immigrants first experience as temporary residents the culture shock of adjusting to a new environment. Many kibbutzim conduct special educational programs for problem children. They were among the first to confront the emotionally painful challenge of being hospitable to German youths who want to come to Israel to demonstrate their feeling of remorse about the outrages committed by their parents' generation against the Jews of Europe.

The diverse public needs of a rapidly developing urbanizing country seem to be less and less consistent with the single-minded stress of most youth movements on the virtues of kibbutz life with its agricultural base. Israel needs many other kinds of dedicated public servants. Some youth movement groups have reacted to this fact by organizing short-term volunteer community organization projects in a development town like Dimona. These programs have received much publicity but they have not attracted enough real support to do more than illustrate the difficulties and utilities of an urban counterpart to kibbutz living. Some Israeli leaders think that such support will have to be developed if socialist living is to retain vitality.

The youth movements and their rural emphasis retain an important but almost static influence on the expanding population. Only a minority of youth movement members end up living in a kibbutz. Some Israeli observers interpret this fact as a symptom of impending decline. This assessment is not accepted by the government, quasi-public agencies and the labor parties. They take heart from the fact that even in their present status of limited influence, the youth movements have a youth culture influence beyond their numbers. They still attract and retain the loyalty of a creative minority. Their members serve as the backbone of many Israeli pioneering ventures. They also do much to attract and inspire volunteers coming to Israel from the free countries of the West.

Chapter 7

Youth Movements

Recruitment

Public service volunteers are generally recruited from among adults and when they are needed. In the American Vista and Peace Corps programs, only mature persons are encouraged to apply. They are then screened in terms of well-identified specifications. Selection is by governmental administrators, on the basis of tests, interviews and performance during a training period. Lower-class persons with marginal achievement records are not often wanted.

In Israel screening for public service begins in the youth movements during the preadolescent period. All classes of the population are approached, although they are not reached in equal proportions. The major purpose is advocacy of the idea that the country still needs pioneers. But the day-to-day programs of the youth movements are closely related to the fun-seeking, self-searching and maturation that dominate the thinking of this age group.

Youth movements initiate novices in a solemn ceremony. Young members promise to uphold the movement's principles often before they understand them. Youngsters are organized as small groups of 10 to 25 age mates. The program includes the kind of lectures, discussions and observational experiences that convert the members to acceptance of the movement's objectives. Most Israeli youngsters join the movement for a period averaging twenty-six months. A 1963 head count survey (Chen and Ormian, 1965) of the Youth Department of the Ministry of Education showed that about one-third of the 11 to 17 year-old Jewish youths were currently members of youth movements.[26] Seventy percent of eighth grade students who were surveyed in 1963 when registering for the nationwide Sekker comprehensive examination reported themselves as having been active in a youth movement at one time.

The impact of youth movements is further enhanced by the fact that three of them operate labor branches for employed youths. Ideologically, each movement would prefer to integrate working youth with those who are in high school. But there are differences in program priorities, in outlook and in social status. Working youths (like all youngsters) like to play, hike and discuss, but they must also be concerned with wages and working conditions. Youth leaders of such groups therefore devote much of their effort to labor union activities with much less energy being given to conventional youth movement programs, such as discussions, weekend institutes, dances, hikes and national service. The 1963 census of youth movements enumerated 57,055 working youth as members (see Table 5). Nearly all of them were over the age of 14.

TABLE 5

Census of Jewish Working Youth Movement Members in Israel—1963

Youth movement	Percent of total membership (N = 57,055)	Party affiliation
Noar Oved	65	Mapai and Achduth-Avoda (Socialists)
Noar Oved Leumi	15	Herut (Nationalist)
Noar Oved Dati	20	National Religious Party
Total	100	

Youth movements are a highly probable life experience for Israeli youngsters, but most youths drift away from them. For all but a minority, the association is of short duration.[27] The *activists,* as those still members at the tenth grade level will be designated, were a minority of 16 percent. They tend to be a closely knit in-group, self-chosen from a much larger number of members. Most of these activists are busy young people, who attend high school and who strive for good grades. They tend to get along well with their parents and report fewer conflicts with the demands of the school or army than do nonmembers of youth groups. They generally come from homes where their continued membership is either approved or tolerated. They are a residue of enthusiasts who share a common sense of purpose and a common self-searching. It is from them that an even smaller self-selected group remain to join a kibbutz after army service. The weeding out process is gradual. Many of those who resign retain a loyalty to the ideals of their movement and a generalized commitment to good citizenship which makes them receptive to national service priorities.

All the youth movements, except for the nominally nonpolitical Scouts, subscribe to a partisan blueprint of how the country should be run. Three represent a socialist orientation; two have a traditional-religious outlook; and three are identified with middle class "free-enterprise" parties. There is also a very small communist movement.

Peer group autonomy

The tradition persists that the movements have autonomy from adult agencies which sponsor them. While the adults and children have different incentives for supporting youth movements, their respective priorities are not mutually exclusive. Adults have reason to favor opportunities for young people to develop self-confidence and autonomy. Often with ambivalence, parents will let their teen-age boys and girls go on a three day hike in the Negev Desert without adult chaperons. The adventure is not without risk but occurs in a socially protected setting, a group of self-selected idealistic youths.

The balance of autonomy and parental influence can be illustrated by the response of youth leaders to the question of how they would deal with parents requesting that a hike be canceled because of the threat of bad weather. Would they comply? Nearly two-thirds of all the leaders thought they would. It is apparent that adults have an influence, but they do not fully control the youth programs (see Figure 6).

Programs differed significantly in their members' preferences for autonomy. The religious youths were the most parent oriented. Tradition

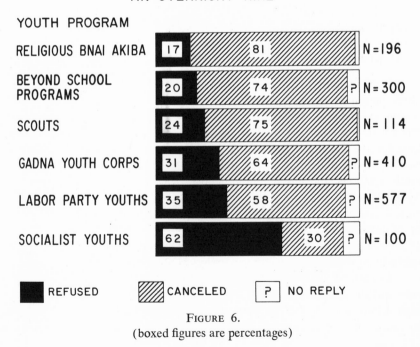

LEADER RESPONSE TO PARENTAL REQUEST TO CANCEL
AN OVERNIGHT HIKE

YOUTH PROGRAM

RELIGIOUS BNAI AKIBA	17 / 81	N = 196
BEYOND SCHOOL PROGRAMS	20 / 74 / ?	N = 300
SCOUTS	24 / 75	N = 114
GADNA YOUTH CORPS	31 / 64 / ?	N = 410
LABOR PARTY YOUTHS	35 / 58 / ?	N = 577
SOCIALIST YOUTHS	62 / 30 / ?	N = 100

■ REFUSED   ▨ CANCELED   ? NO REPLY

FIGURE 6.
(boxed figures are percentages)

tends to reinforce obedience to parents. The most autonomous programs were those of the labor parties. Among the more purist socialists, only a few, three out of ten, would humor parental objections to a scheduled hike.

In all the youth movements adolescents have more self-determination than in other adult-making institutions. Children can choose to belong or to resign, to be active or passive. This gives them a self-chosen identity as a *Herra* (member), rather than as the child of their parents or a student of the local school. There is much room for exercising initiative in planning programs, organizing a hike or in raising funds. Programs are not run by teachers, but by peers who are not much older than the members. Youth movements provide youngsters with an opportunity to search for new social ties outside the immediate family and neighborhood.

What membership entails

Fun and sociability rank high as initial incentives for getting youngsters to join. As initiates become aware of the fact that youth movements demand a commitment to certain ideals and oppose many innovations of the popular culture including social dancing, night clubs and "hanging out," there is a lessening of interest and resignation. The weeding out is progressive since expectations for a personal commitment also become more intensive. Four successive states of involvement can be distinguished:

(1) Active participation in a group (*Hevra*).
(2) Becoming a youth leader (*Hadraha*) starting at ages 14 to 16.
(3) Nahal pioneering or service in another volunteer army unit at age 18.
(4) Kibbutz membership after discharge from military service.

Participation: The initial requirement of a youth movement is active participation in the program and social life of a local subgroup, called *Hevra* in Hebrew. Members are expected to balance their awakening interest in the other sex, their worship of the local soccer team and their love for the cinema with concern for philosophical, ethical and political issues. Before and after Israel and Germany decided to establish diplomatic relations, the moral and practical aspects were heatedly discussed by the 12 to 14 year old youth movement members all over the land. The ethical issues of boy-girl relationships, of selfishness, cooperative living, or of meaningful coexistence with the Arab neighbors are live concerns at an age when in much of the world such matters would be viewed as being inappropriate for group discussion among children.

Leadership (Hadraha): The active member, unless he lacks the necessary qualifications, is expected to become a youth leader as he reaches high school and 14 and 15 years of age. Junior leaders begin by helping to recruit new members by age 16. They devote six to twelve hours a

PROPORTION OF YOUTH LEADERS UNDER 20 YEARS OLD

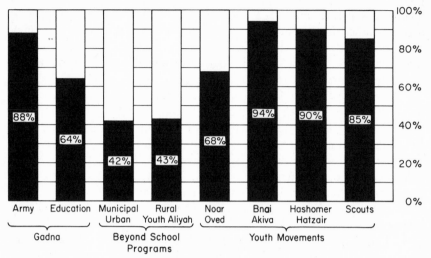

FIGURE 7.

week to this task. In our survey of youth leaders (based on national rosters), nearly one in ten were between the ages of 14 and 16. Forty percent of all enumerated youth leaders were less than 20 years of age. Only 17 percent were over 25 years of age (see Figure 7). Youth movement leaders were on the average younger than those of other extracurricular youth programs. The age difference between leaders and followers was particularly small among the Scouts and religious youth movements. About half of their leaders were less than three years older than the group being led.[28]

Voluntaristic leadership is, however, on the decline. In part, this development is a consequence of the achievement of statehood. Before 1948, youth movement leadership was a principal public service role for older adolescents. Israelis are now subject to the draft at this age. By the time they are released from service around age 21, many feel somewhat out of touch with the youth culture. They have to give priority to becoming breadwinners, husbands or wives. Most of them think they have done their share of public service.

The manpower problem has led to the recruitment of a new type of leader, one who works for a salary. For some this task may become a job, like any other job performed for the pay received. But for most of the jobholders, this is still more of a calling than a profession. Paid leaders generally earn less than in other jobs they could fill. Youth leaders are not unionized, as are all other workers in Israel including teachers. There has never been a strike of youth leaders.

Nahal Pioneering Service: As previously mentioned, youth movements prefer that members volunteer in the army Nahal Pioneer Corps, which maintains separate units for each youth movement and recruits them as a group rather than on an individual basis. Of the active youth movement members slightly more than half said they would choose Nahal service. Even among the adolescents who had never joined a youth movement or had resigned from one, 15 percent expressed a preference for Nahal.

Pioneering Occupation: Nahal units operate on the theory that members will explore the idea of establishing a communal village or of settling in a newly established development town after completing military duty. Religious youth movements also expect their members to continue learning about Jewish traditions through special courses (*Shiurim*) or study at an advanced religious seminary (*Yeshivah*). They urge members to settle in a religious kibbutz, a religious smallholder village or an urban neighborhood controlled by persons concerned with the revitalization of religious traditions.

Pioneer-type career preferences are most often voiced by youth movement activists but they also occur in the nonmember population. About one-tenth of the Holon youth said at age 16 they planned to join a kibbutz. But such preferences were three times higher, 28 to 30 percent among youth movement activists.

Among the children of Afro-Asian fathers, youth movement activism differentiated only slightly among those who voiced a preference for kibbutz life (see Table 6). Almost as many nonmembers as members voiced a

TABLE 6

Youth Movement Membership of Eighth-Grade Students
Ready to Consider a Kibbutz Career
(by Country of Birth of Father and Youth Movement Membership—1963)

Father's birth place	Youth movement participation status of kibbutz oriented students (*percentages*)		
	Members	Non-members	Ratio
Afro-Asian Countries (N = 92)	57	43	1.2 to 1
Europe (N = 230)	82	18	4.5 to 1

kibbutz preference. The ratio was 1.2 to 1. In contrast, among children of European families, 4.5 as many members of youth movements voiced a kibbutz preference as the proportion doing so among nonmembers.

Resignations

More than one quarter of all members in the 1963 nationwide comprehensive examination Sekker sample joined while enrolled in the fourth and fifth grades. They were between 9 and 11 years old (see Table 7).

TABLE 7

School Grade When First Enrolled in a Youth Movement
(N = 8191 Eighth Grade Students in 1963)

Grade Level	Percent Joining Youth Movement
4–5	26
6	18
7	14
8	8
Not members	11
No response	23
Total	100

Youth leaders were in wide agreement that the choice of which movement to join depends more on parental preference than on ideology. Proximity of meeting place, peer group composition and the personality of the group leaders were also mentioned as major variables. Three out of four in the Holon sample resigned when they reached the tenth grade. Some youths were simply too busy; others failed to find the friends they wanted or wanted to try out different leisure time activities. The average stay was found to be twenty-six months in one study, with 21 percent of all new members resigning within a year or less (Chen and Ormian, 1965).

A resignation rate of nearly 75 percent at around the age of 16 worries youth movement policy makers. It probably rises to above 90 percent by the time youths reach 18 because then they want to pursue more self-directed leisure time activities. At that time, membership entails more than willingness to spend a few hours a week with congenial and ideologically sympathetic peers. It requires a career commitment.

Resignations are also affected by poor leadership. Youth movements are often administered spasmodically. They may lack monetary resources. Some youths find their group simply boring. Not all of the 16 to 17-year-old volunteer leaders can discuss with interest a topic like "The Social Life of Animals." This is a subject youth leaders of the Hashomer Hatzair are supposed to take up with ten-year-old members to get them to accept the idea that cooperation is a *natural* trait. These and similar topics have long ceased to arouse much interest in a country which has changed much more rapidly than the youth movement programs.

The majority of Israel's youths prefer other group associations in adolescence which require less conformity and allow for more casual participation. At the tenth-grade level, youths in Holon reported themselves to be active almost five times as often in a Beyond School program or the Gadna Youth Corps than in a youth movement.

Some of the most intelligent and dedicated youths who resign from a youth movement do so because they prefer to make more individually oriented decisions about their future. They may continue to admire the

youth movement, its ideals and comradeship, but they object to its ortho-
doxy in ideology and the preference for a commitment to life in a collective
agricultural settlement. University study and professional careers can be
pursued in a kibbutz only in exceptional cases, after such a career choice
has been discussed by the group. No kibbutz could be composed of only
white collar workers and poets. Group involvement in the choice of a
career may be necessary for long-range economic planning, but it goes
beyond what most young people are willing to accept. Four times as many
youth movement activists expressed strong preferences for spending their
leisure time in peer group associations (44 percent) than those who resigned from or never joined a youth movement (11 percent) (see Figure
8). But the kibbutz idea is not always rejected by those who resign. In the

FIRST PREFERENCE FOR SPENDING LEISURE TIME

HOLON ADOLESCENTS 1965

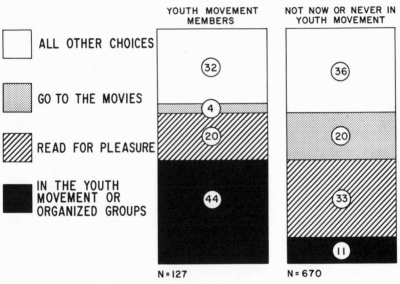

FIGURE 8.
(encircled figures are percentages)

Holon area sample, one-fifth of the 61 tenth grade level youths who said
they wanted to join a kibbutz were no longer members of a youth movement.

Those who never joined a youth movement or who resigned from
one are not social isolates. They were often active in informal groups
without adult guidance or in solitary activities. Fifteen percent thought
that they had a high peer group status as indicated by a "yes" answer to

the statement: "My friends consider my opinions," a proportion similar
to those giving this response among youth movement activists. The "not
now or never active" group seem to have less need for an ideologically
oriented organization to help them schedule their leisure time. They expressed a relatively high first preference for reading and movie attendance.
They were more likely to choose the twist than folk dancing, popular
songs than group singing.

Short-term exposure to a youth movement was not reflected in the
attitudes expressed. Youths who never joined were quite similar in their
preference for national service to those who had belonged to a youth
movement but resigned before age 16 (see Table 8). Many of the active

TABLE 8

National Service Attitudes of Tenth Graders in Holon in Relation to Their
Participation in a Youth Movement

(percentages)

Question and answer	Active members (N = 127)	Ex-members (N = 470)	Never a member (N = 200)
"Where would you like to live permanently?"			
In a rural settlement, kibbutz or development town.	30	9	5
The army demands too much of me. (yes)	1	2	2
"In which unit would you prefer to serve your army training?"			
Nahal	54	16	15
Airforce or Paratroopers	26	39	36

members were ready to have a Nahal army assignment or live in a kibbutz.
Those who never joined a youth movement and the ex-members were
much less public service oriented. But as was already seen in Table 6,
there was a minority even among the nonactivists who expressed a preference for idealistic career choices. Only a negligible proportion of all
youngsters thought the army demanded too much of them. Over one-third
of the nonyouth movement members wanted to volunteer in a high-risk
army unit, with glamour status—the air force or the paratroop corps.

The ex-members and those who never belonged tend to conform to
the conceptual model of the *realist.*[29] As *realists,* they will sacrifice little,
except during a period of national emergency, but even then they will do
so within what they view as reasonable and pragmatic limits. In our attitude

survey they were less inclined than *idealists* to express pioneering choices.

Resignations are the other side of the selective equation reflecting the progressively idealistic commitment that membership requires. Those who remain include many who sustain a high level of enthusiasm and voluntarism for public service, while keeping resources needed for personal needs close to a minimum. They are a minority of no more than one out of seven. It will diminish further as the group gets older. But they have an influence on the total youth culture that goes much beyond their numerical weight. They can count on support of many of those who left, often with some nostalgia and regret.

Partisanship

Youth services are rarely discussed in terms of their activities. One can play soccer in a sports club or a youth movement. Ethical problems will be discussed in a Beyond School program as well as in a Gadna youth leadership training session. Israelis prefer to categorize youth programs in terms of the adult institution which sponsors them—political parties, the schools, parent groups or the army. This organizational classification scheme has descriptive utility. It focuses on a clear variable: the organization which pays the bills and controls programming. It serves to pose organizational questions such as this: How does each of the adult-making agencies intend to influence the country's youth culture?

The youth movements advocate a political point of view, in contrast to the Gadna or the Beyond School programs which are more nonpartisan in their recruitment. They expect youths to be participants in an activity rather than become proponents of a cause. They espouse general patriotic virtues which call for no commitment beyond the obligation to be a solid citizen, who will obey the law, serve his country in an emergency and learn something about his country's many problems. Policy is made by appointed civil service officials.

Before Israel became a state, several of the ten movements competed actively—sometimes aggressively—with each other. They did not want to attract all comers. And they expected members to embrace the official ideology. This political exclusiveness has been modified considerably in the last twenty years. The group work aspects of the youth movements now differ much less than the political parties who sponsor them.

The official programs

Three youth movements, the Scouts (Zophim), Noar Oved Velomed and B'nai Akiva place a great deal of emphasis on such group work goals as peer group identification, self-confidence, encouragement and skill acquisition by each member. They play down ideology. They want to attract as many youngsters as possible (see Table 9). They have relatively universalist programs and enroll about 75 to 80 percent of all the young-sters in youth movements. They make a special effort to reach out to unorganized segments of the youth population, including those in immi-

TABLE 9

Survey of Youth Movements Members[a]

(percentages)

Youth movement name and political affiliation	Eighth grade national sample in 1963 (N = 4151)	Tenth grade level area sample in Holon in 1965 (N = 127)
Socialist Movements		
Noar Oved (Mapai—moderate wing)	42	42
Hashomer Hatzair (Mapam—left wing)	10	20
Machanot Olim (Achduth Avodah—center)	3	1
Religious Movements		
B'nai Akiva (National Religious Party)	17	12
Ezra (Aguda—Ultra-religious Party)	1	—
Free Enterprise Movements		
Macabi Hatsair (General Zionist)	4	1
Betar (Herut—Nationalist Party)	2	1
Noar Zionist (Progressive Party)	1	—
Non-Political Movement		
Scouts (Zophim)	20	23
Total	100	100

a. Ex-members are excluded in this tabulation.

grant housing projects and communities. This active recruitment program is facilitated by hiring youth leaders in relatively large numbers. While volunteer leaders would be preferred, their supply does not meet the requirements of an expansion-oriented program.

SCOUTS

The Scouts (*Zophim*) are non-partisan and predominantly middle-class. Their first group in Israel dates back to 1919. The Scouts emphasize general civic virtues, within a pioneering tradition. Their program can be summed as follows:

To educate on the basis of Scout values and the Scout pledge; to develop the social feelings and the individual character; to accustom its members to order, exactness, discipline, observation work and outdoor life; to strengthen love for Israel, to develop respect for tradition; and to train its members for Zionist pioneering (kibbutz membership).

The Scout movement gets much of its support from local education authorities. They also do, on occasion, use school buildings. Between 1956 and 1964, when political youth movements were banned from recruiting in the schools, the Scouts were the only program that could be active in the general trend public schools.[30] Since 1964, the Ministry of Education has shifted its policy to allow leaders of other youth movements to talk to classes in school about their points of view. Parent committees function in many localities. They help keep the Scouts going and some of them assist youth leaders in the conduct of overnight hikes.

NOAR OVED VELOMED

Quite similar in program to the Scouts, but more partisan in sponsorship is Israel's largest youth movement, the moderate socialist Noar Oved Velomed. It is backed up by the largest kibbutz federation and the country's most powerful Mapai wing of the Labor Party. For many decades Noar Oved Velomed has enjoyed the support of leading members of the Government who belong to this labor faction. Like the Social-Democratic parties of Europe, the Mapai wing is politically pragmatic. Its youth movement, although socialist in theory, subdues ideological considerations when necessary to reach nonpolitical segments of the population. Noar Oved Velomed advocates pioneering, especially through kibbutz membership. But members are not necessarily required to accept this as a life goal in order to remain active in the movement. Their members rank lower on the idealism score than those of the ideologically more "orthodox" socialist youth movements (Hashomer Hatzair and Machnoth Olim).

Political pragmatism is particularly pronounced in the Noar Oved Velomed policy of working with the children of Afro-Asian immigrants whose parents are less often supportive of socialist ideals. Few of the newcomers have been schooled in abstract political theory or in sharing with others. They have been deprived for generations. They want housing, jobs and social benefits.

Although the Mapai wing of the Labor party is secular in theory, its youth movement also tries to recruit among the more orthodox segments of the population. Religious youth leaders are hired for this purpose. This is part of a general strategy of political "ecumenism." The Mapai has acquiesced in the continuation of the Mandate Regime's practice of regulating of marriages and divorces by religious courts. There is also no public transportation on the Sabbath in most of the country. This is in spite of the fact that this policy offends many liberal sentiments. But

without such "realpolitik" concessions to the religious parties, the Mapai
leaders think they cannot remain in power.

B'NAI AKIVA AND EZRA

Both of these religious youth movements have different normative
priorities. They wish to stem the drift toward secularism. Socialist ideas
are recognized as having economic utility, but they are not an essential
part of the basic doctrine. Each of these religious youth organizations is
affiliated with kibbutzim sponsored by their respective political parties.
B'nai Akiva, the larger of the religious movements, is generally conciliatory

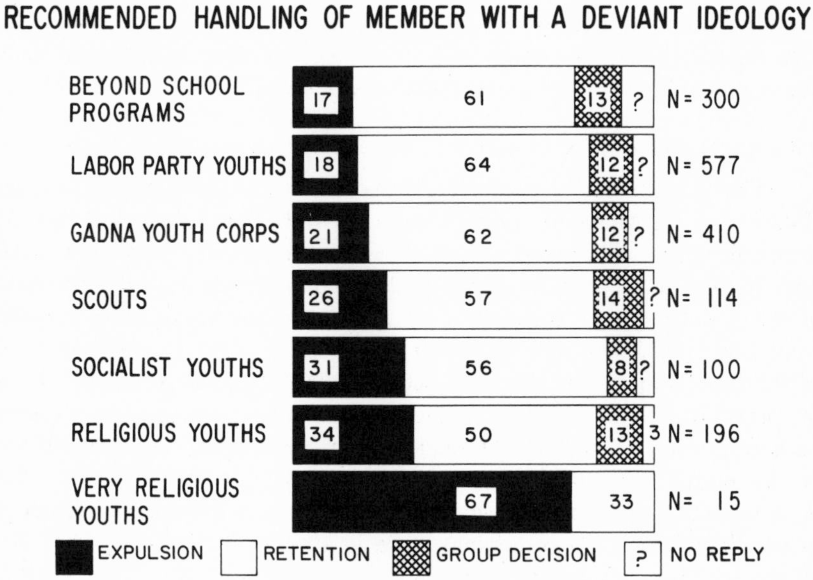

RECOMMENDED HANDLING OF MEMBER WITH A DEVIANT IDEOLOGY

FIGURE 9.
(boxed figures are percentages)

and progressive in its outlook. Recruitment in the general population is
restricted to orthodox children. This policy limits the volume of potential
recruits but also ensures the cohesiveness of each movement. Many of the
members of both movements are children whose parents were in the same
program when they were young.

The two youth organizations differ in their degree of acceptance of
secular ideas. For instance, army service by girls is more positively advocated by B'nai Akiva than by local branches of Ezra. Both of the religious
organizations could agree on the following platform:

> The education of a generation of Jews faithful and devoted to scriptures,
> the Torah, the Jewish people and their holy land. Each movement favors
> the personal realization of the ideals of "religion and labor," which find

their highest expression in the pioneering settlements. Settlement in a kibbutz, a religiously-inclined family-farm village or an urban suburb restricted to orthodox Jews is advocated.

Ezra is theocratically inclined. Its leaders tend to follow closely the political stands of its adult sponsors, the Agudath Yisrael, a party favoring strict conformity in all state and nongovernmental functions with the orthodox religious rituals. They believe themselves to be a vanguard upon whose religious fervor will depend the survival of orthodox Judaism, as it was practiced in Europe's ghettos. Ezra does not disassociate itself from the mainstream of Israeli public life, as do a number of more orthodox Jewish sects. Ezra has coeducational programs. But most of the leaders favor ejection of a member who disagrees with their movement's principles (see Figure 9).[31] Cooperation with national institutions is always on condition that religious youths are given special recognition.

HASHOMER HATZAIR AND MACHNOTH OLIM

The two smaller "left-of-center" socialist movements, the Hashomer Hatzair and the Machnoth Olim, also prefer to be selective rather than try to recruit youths who are skeptical about the movements' partisan orientation. Both of these programs favor greater expansion of the socialist sector of the country's total economy than the larger and moderately socialist Noar Oved Velomed. For the 1969 election, a merger was agreed upon of the four labor wings that had been represented as separate parties in the previous parliament. Three of them sponsor their own youth movement, each responsive to a different federation of kibbutzim. The tenuousness of this election coalition is well documented by the fact that there has been no serious talk about a merger of their youth movements, although in their day-to-day programming, there is a great deal of similarity. But all the socialist movements would in theory avow the core values stressed in the literature of the most purist—the *Hashomer Hatzair:*

> It aims to educate its members to fulfill the pioneering mission of Jewish youth in order to create a nation of workers living in an egalitarian society in Israel. The movement wants to perpetuate a national value and to develop a Zionist and Socialist consciousness as preparation for the kibbutz way of life. It wants to educate and reinforce the qualities of individuals and to train them for personal realization of these aims in a life devoted to humanism and the love of fellow man, irrespective of race or religion.

Sixty-three percent of the active members of the Hashomer Hatzair and Machnoth Olim groups in Holon age 16 said they would like to live later in a kibbutz or a development community. This proportion is more than twice as high as the incidence of such pioneering intentions expressed by the more moderately socialist Noar Oved Velomed (24 percent) and four times as high as that of members of all other youth movements (15 percent).

The high relationship of socialist education and idealistic attitude is confirmed by the small proportion of members who scored zero on a scale of idealistic attitudes. Only 6 percent of the Hashomer Hatzair members gave no idealistic responses to the questions in our attitude survey. More than three times as many low-scoring youths were active or past members of the Noar Oved Velomed. Six times as many of those never active in a youth movement (37 percent) scored zero on the idealism scale (see Figure 10).

IDEALISTIC ATTITUDE CHOICES OF PAST AND
PRESENT MEMBERS OF SELECTED YOUTH MOVEMENTS

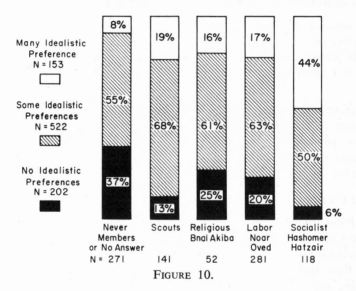

FIGURE 10.

The left socialist groups were also the most autonomous from parental influence. They were more often willing than others to schedule a hike against parental opposition. They also exceeded leaders in other youth movements in being tolerant in personal matters. For example, very few (4 percent) were willing to deprive a youth of water on a desert hike if, contrary to instructions, he drank all his own supply of water at the beginning.

FREE ENTERPRISE MOVEMENTS

The remaining three very small youth movements can be classified as "free-enterprise" in the sense that they are ideologically non-socialist. Included are the sports-oriented Maccabi Hatzair, the nationalistic Betar and the Noar Zioni movement of the Liberal Party. Their programs are hard to differentiate from those of the Scouts.

The most separatist of these small free enterprise movements is the Betar. Before Israel became a state, it had a dissident nationalist platform. Betar members were ready earlier than the majority of the pre-independence Zionist movement to oppose by means of military retaliation the British restrictions of Jewish settlement. Betar was in uncompromising opposition to the 1947 United Nations plan for the partition of Palestine between Arabs and Jews. But just before the Six Day War in June 1967, the leader of the Betar's sponsoring party joined the coalition government as a minister without portfolio.

Betar avoids taking strong stands on social or religious issues. It stresses such symbols as:

> One national flag, one national anthem, a united educational system, discipline and glory. It idealizes the characteristics of the "new Jew" who stands proudly upright and shows civic courage. It advocates pioneering for every difficult, especially military, task but does not advocate kibbutz life.

Before statehood, these movements represented a distinct political alternative to the Socialist parties. Today this is less true. The Labor party is quite pragmatic and cooperates with free enterprise to attract investment capital to Israel. The Socialist youth movements are also less doctrinaire.

COMMUNISTS

Absent from this survey of youth movements is the youth branch of the two Communist parties. Communist political activity is legal in Israel but is regarded with great suspicion by the authorities and all other parties. Fewer than 100 Jewish youths, together with somewhat larger numbers of Arabs, are estimated to be affiliated with this movement. When the field work for this study began, the party's youth secretary offered to cooperate. But just then the party broke up into two small splinter factions. Questionnaires filled out by nine of its youth leaders were not turned over to the study staff.

Post-revolutionary conservatism

The ten youth movements vary in their official programs. But they have a common style. Many of their young leaders like to think of themselves as revolutionary and change oriented. But, in fact, their acceptance of adult-making institutions, especially their parents, exceeded that of all other organized young people.[32] They are radical in tradition, but system-maintenance oriented in actuality. Joining a youth movement often was a non-conformist act for their parents. Today, except for some youngsters from non-European families, the act of joining a youth movement is eminently respectable. If anything, *nonmembership* is a form of deviance, since over 70 percent join at some time of their life.

Conservatism is the fate of every successful reform movement. Revolutionary ideas, when transmitted by parents to their children, become prescriptions for conformity. Few parents wish their children to alter again what was created with so much effort.

The readiness for conformity on the part of all segments of the youth population is also apparent in the responses of young people to the question comparing their own religious outlook to that of their parents. The great majority (84 percent) of the young people followed parental footsteps in the area of religion (see Figure 11).

COMPARISON OF RELIGIOUS ORIENTATION OF HOLON
ADOLESCENTS AND THEIR PARENTS
(IN PERCENT) N = 812

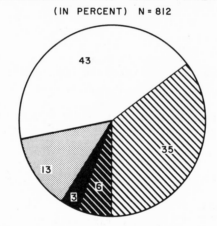

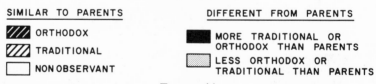

FIGURE 11.

The contemporary youth leaders are not often those who support minority factions within their respective parties. Some youth leaders reacted defensively when confronted with this evidence. They wished it were otherwise, for they sentimentalize dissent. Youth leaders are probably selected in part for their readiness to conform with the "establishment" by opposing certain youth culture innovations. Such conservatism is evident at least with respect to the current controversy regarding the propriety of social dancing. When the youth movements began, "bourgeois" ball-room dances such as the waltz were frowned on. The movements adopted folk dancing as their distinguishing mark. Most contemporary youth movement leaders continue to oppose social dancing, along with many other youth culture innovations.

The nonpolitical youth organizations, such as the Gadna Youth Corps and the urban Beyond School program, have no similar ideological past to uphold. Even though many of their leaders once belonged to youth movements, their more eclectic current orientation is reflected in greater readiness to approve of social dancing.

Popular dancing was also frowned on in Russia for a long time, denounced as "hooliganism" and, at times, punished as an offense against the state. But in Israel, a multiparty democracy, such postrevolutionary conservatism must compete in the marketplace on almost equal terms with new youth culture fads. Its youth movements are certainly not the reservoirs of rebellion that they were when their parents joined them a generation ago.

Middle-class orientation

Youth movements seem to have the highest attractiveness for the well established and the intellectually gifted segment of the population.

YOUTH ORGANIZATION PARTICIPATION OF HOLON ADOLESCENTS IN 1965 - BY EIGHTH GRADE EXAMINATION SCORES IN 1963

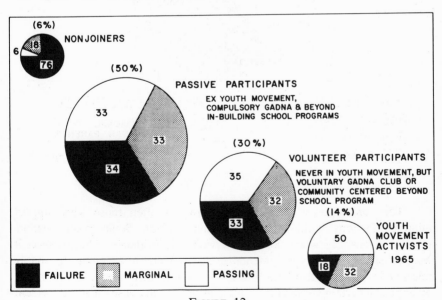

FIGURE 12.

Residents of spacious apartments, children of European-born settlers, and high achievers in school are overrepresented. Only 18 percent of the youth movement activists at age 16 had received failure scores two years earlier in the nationwide eighth grade Sekker examination. This proportion or less than one-fifth must be compared to the one-third failure score among those who had resigned from a youth movement. Among those who never belonged to any youth program, 76 percent had received failure scores (see Figure 12).

This middle class selectivity of youth movements may be related to their requirement that members submit to enforced discipline of peer groups and be concerned with idealistic values. Members must be willing to put up with primitive conditions while being on a hike or working on a national service project.

The middle class concentration of youth movement membership also confirms their postrevolutionary conservative character. When a revolution succeeds, the "underdogs" become "top dogs" (Dilas, 1963). Their children are now advantaged. This class-related selectivity must not be mistaken for exclusiveness. It is ideologically distressing to the youth movements that they are not more successful in attracting lower-class children. Sociologically, this finding is not surprising.[33]

Eighth graders from disadvantaged population segments were even more underrepresented in the youth movements in our nationwide survey in 1963 than in the Holon area sample, but they were not absent. The youth movement had succeeded in reaching some of this lower class target group.

*Socioeconomic Comparison of
Youth Movement Members and
Nonjoiners*

Youth Movement Members		*Nonjoiners*
One-third of all youth movement members live in poverty as indicated by the fact that they live under crowded conditions of more than 2½ persons per room.	*but*	Nearly 60 percent of children who are never in a youth movement live under such crowded conditions.
Nearly one-half (46 percent) of all youth movement members were academically marginal. They were below the 67th percentile in the eighth-grade qualifying examination that often is a prerequisite for admission to an academic high school.	*but*	About 60 percent of all children who never were in a youth movement made such low scores.

About one-quarter (26 percent) of all youth movement members had fathers born in Afro-Asian countries.	*but*	About 57 percent of all children who never were in youth movement came from Afro-Asian families.

Several youth movements are actively trying to recruit an even larger segment of lower class members. As future citizens their voices and votes count. Attainment of this goal of greater ethnic and class integration must overcome the divisive impact which social and class characteristic often have on informal peer group formation. It is more diffcult to reach children who are culturally educationally disadvantaged. The political sophistication necessary for embracing any ideology, including socialism, is more commonly found among middle class than lower class elements. There is a cultural gap between Europeans and persons recently immigrated from the underdeveloped countries of Asia and Africa. The gap cannot be closed in half a generation, no matter what efforts may be made, though youth movements are making such efforts.

Conclusion

A large proportion of Israeli youth are exposed to the Zionist and predominantly socialist pioneering traditions through youth movement membership. Coverage is extensive, including at least 70 percent of the total population. It is higher for the middle class youngsters who do well in school and less for those from poorer segments of the population who do not achieve well in school. The exposure begins during preadolescence, at an age before young people are ready to weigh the alternate political or religious programs which are advocated by the country's ten youth movements.

Recruitment relies heavily on natural peer group associations in schools and neighborhoods. The preadolescent proclivity for socializing with age mates is utilized by youth movement leaders to co-opt individuals and groups to join "the movement." Many of those who resign also respond to peer group, rather than ideological factors.

Ideology plays an increasingly significant part in screening the membership at older age levels. The elite who volunteer to become youth leaders, who join a Nahal unit of the army and who finally join a kibbutz are self-selected by many variables. The larger youth movements maintain their size in part by accepting readiness for participation as the primary criterion of membership. The movements which stress ideological cohesion remain relatively small but can count on much support from those youth who remain identified.

Adult-making agencies that sponsor each of the youth movements leave much of the initiative for local programming to the young leaders.

There is room for upward mobility from being a child to becoming a youth movement member and leader, who will soon be ready to take on even more responsible roles in the country's defense establishment. In each program, young people learn to make choices on their own. They are free to join or to leave, to be active or less active or to select one youth movement in preference to another. They enforce their own discipline and do much of the program planning for themselves and for others. They can practice these adult-type roles before they become adults. Through this co-optation process, youth movements have an impact not only on their active members, but on others who admire these values. This includes a much larger segment of the total youth culture. Adults who sponsor these movements can be assured that the next generation is exposed to the idea that young people are responsible for their country's future.

Planning for the youth movements is quite decentralized. This leaves much initiative to each local unit, but some supportive services are provided by the sponsoring political or religious group, plus the government and the semi-public Jewish Agency.

The youth movements have shifted from being revolutionary to becoming establishment-oriented. They retain much of the same structure and objectives that served to make them key instruments of nation building before Israel became a state. Their ideological principles, which link each of the youth movements with their sponsoring political or religious party, have changed little. But the partisan identification of young people with these programs is being overshadowed by the changing conditions under which they are confronting life, in contrast to those that were experienced by the parental generation.

One of the consequences of drafting all youths at age 18 is a perpetual shortage of older volunteer youth leaders. The movements that wish to exercise an influence throughout the country, especially among the new immigrants and the poor, have to hire more and more paid youth leaders. Paid personnel now staff the central planning and organizing jobs of nearly all youth movements. This emerging professionalization provides a degree of stability, which is counteracted by the view that such jobs are transitional and temporary for most of those who take them. More than other programs, the youth movements circulate their leadership elite. Each year there is room for the services of new people who are closer in age to the members than those who are being replaced. This circulation of elites is often paid for with organizational instability. A program will lose much of its impact when a good leader is replaced by one less competent. But there is always room for new leaders who are willing to serve the movement and who have the requisite leadership skills. The generational gap between the youth movements and the peer group culture is never allowed to become too large.

The youth movements are confronting an achievement crisis that is in store for all successful revolutionary movements: What can be the basis for their continuity? Socialist living cannot be transferred from rural kibbutzim to urban areas. Only a few new rural settlements are needed and much of this pioneering is now done by the Nahal army units. The goal of the small nationalist Betar movement for a "Greater Israel" has emerged as a realistic alternative since the Six Day War, but it is fraught with difficulty since it would involve the risk of Jews becoming outnumbered by Arabs within a generation (Shiloh, 1968).

On this and other contemporary issues, there can be division of opinion in each of the youth movements about what policy should be pursued. The youth movements are old social structures, but their historical differences have lost much meaning today. Their sponsoring political parties are forming new alliances, but so far, these mergers have not yet resulted in mergers of youth programs. Each of the youth movements is now in search of functions with enough contemporary vitality to retain or increase appeal to the youth of the country.

Chapter 8

Institution Building: The Gadna

Planning and implementation

How does a youth corps develop? There are many such organizations around the world—in Russia, in Jamaica and in Ghana. Each reflects the application of a strategy by adults to influence the emerging youth culture through an adult organization. In modern societies, innovations are less and less introduced haphazardly. They are planned. New administrative relationships and personal interactions are organized on the basis of a design to accomplish specific purposes.

The Gadna Youth Corps, organized in 1939, will be reviewed from this point of view, as a case study in institution building: *The planful establishment of a new organizational arrangement to serve purposes which are thought to require more and different resources than those which can be allocated by already existing administrative units.* This chapter presents a brief historical review of how Gadna developed, to provide a basis for suggesting explanatory hypotheses about the way this organization is linked to others in the country's extensive network of youth services. In the next chapter the contemporary operations of Gadna will be analyzed.

Little is known about the general principles of planful institution building. It must begin with estimates of how the new program can operate and its probable impact on the existing network of available services. These estimates must then be translated operationally. Such market research is almost standard when a new commercial product is introduced. It is done less often when public service modifications are being considered. The idea of a planful trial of alternate organizational arrangements is almost unheard of. In Israel the multiple network of youth programs approximates such a natural experiment which began when Gadna emerged to supplement the programs of youth organizations.

How new institutions develop

When a new function is planned, there are usually several alternatives (Esman, 1967; Taylor, 1968). It can be assigned to a new agency, specializing in the nurturance of a new service and the establishment of supportive linkages with already existing and related institutions. Or an added function can be taken on by an existing agency. A rotary club can sponsor a service project of tutoring children in a slum area to become "more related" to the key issues of the time. A small church-related school can expand to become a general university. But some new function cannot be integrated by an existing body without jeopardy to those that are already being performed. This is how Gadna became a separate program.

It began in 1939 when Jewish adolescents seemed needed for defense for lack of a supply of adult manpower sufficient to help maintain security on three different fronts:

(1) Jews were enlisting to fight against Germany.
(2) They were in active opposition to British policies in Palestine regarding immigration and land purchase.
(3) They were organizing against Arab guerilla warfare.

Before World War II was over, 33,000 adult Jews enrolled as volunteers from a community of only 465,000, including children and the aged. The volunteers served under British command to assist in such varied campaigns as the ejection of Vichy French forces from Syria, the defeat of Nazi-supported nationalists in Iraq and the battle against the Germans in Greece and in the deserts of Egypt and Libya. Jewish battalions helped to liberate Italy. At the end of the war against Germany, they remained as part of the occupation forces until the British removed them to put an end to Jewish activities to help the surviving refugees reach Palestine.

While Jews were allied with the British in the battle against the Nazis, they were opposed to them at home. In 1939, after repeated failures to get Jews and Arabs to negotiate a bi-national agreement, the British government decided to grant the principal Arab political demand: Termination of the League of Nations mandate to facilitate establishment of a Jewish national home. The British hoped to rectify what some of its leaders had come to regard as a serious political mistake, the Balfour Declaration in 1917, which committed British support to the Zionist movement. Independence was promised to Palestine after a ten year transition period. Except for a final quota of 75,000 persons, the British would subject further Jewish immigration to Arab agreement. Purchase of additional land by Jews was immediately forbidden in 95 percent of the country.

A majority of members of the League of Nations, which had originally mandated Palestine to Britain for the express purpose of implementing the Balfour Declaration, disapproved of the new British policy. But the

League had no power to enforce this judgment. If the British policy was to be stymied, the Jews would have to do it on their own. And it had to be done by passive resistance along with selectively applied force, even while a large proportion of the young men and several thousand women were away from Palestine, participating in the allied effort to defeat Germany. Under circumstances such as these, adolescents were badly needed for para-military purposes.

Even later, when the Jewish soldiers returned home, there was an acute manpower shortage. After the United Nations had voted in 1947 that Palestine be divided into an Arab and a Jewish state, the British government refused to assist in implementing the decision. Empire troops, which at times exceeded 100,000, were often used to stop Jewish military efforts to defend themselves against Arab guerilla warfare. The Jewish army had to function clandestinely. The underground Hagana could maintain a full time force of no more than 400 men who performed mostly general staff, planning and training functions. It could count on support from a small Palmah striking force, most of whom worked as farmers in kibbutzim. It included 2,100 men and women plus 1,000 in the active reserve. They were backed up by 32,000 in the Hagana civilian reserve. Other adults could be called up in case of need, but they had no military training (Lorch, 1961: 45–46). Adolescent manpower could make a difference in such an emergency.

The small clandestine Jewish force had to protect settlements against Arab guerilla actions in a civil war without a solid front. Jews and Arabs in Palestine lived in close proximity. Help was also needed to smuggle more Jewish immigrants into the country than the British quota allowed and to establish new Jewish settlements on land purchased for this purpose.

No existing organization could take on the task of training adolescents for participation in these activities without many risks. There was a Jewish settlement police force but it was commanded by British officers and was not allowed to train reserve forces. The clandestine Hagana could not muster adolescents without exposing them and their recruiters to punishment in case of discovery (Mardor, 1957; Dekel, 1959). This led to the decision to establish a "physical education" program (*Hagam*) to serve as a legal cover for what was proscribed activity, a youth corps in the high schools.[34]

Through their high school affiliation, Hagana agents could reach all qualified students as a group. Para-military training could begin during gymnasium periods and on school hikes. Sticks took the place of guns and whistles simulated bullets. Youngsters learned about military discipline, self-defense, leadership, the geography of the country, and moving about the country at night. Those with proper capabilities were then allowed to graduate into the secret Palmah shock troops of the Hagana.

A marriage of convenience: education and para-military service

Before 1939, the Hagana occasionally recruited a few youngsters as runners, to put up posters and perform other noncombat tasks. Those selected were generally associated with youth movements. Older members were invited to undergo premilitary conditioning under the guise of scouting. The curriculum included physical training, group living, learning to live off the country in isolated places, desert warfare, the use of small arms, jujitsu and the experience of moving through the country at night.

This clandestine organizational arrangement was inefficient. Each boy and girl had to be recruited separately. A different administrative umbrella was needed to recruit and train larger numbers of youths more openly without opposition from the British authorities or the risk of protest from parents who did not want their adolescent children to be part of an underground army. This is how an administrative merger of the school and youth corps came into being.

The program was first known as Hagam, an abbreviation in Hebrew of "Expanded Physical Education." It was administered within the framework of the high schools. While there were British inspectors who had to approve this curriculum idea, as they did all other general policies, Hagam could be justified as an application of the British public school emphasis on physical fitness and the ideals of the ancient Greeks who are reported to have stressed the utility of combining intellect and sports (Barclay, 1950: 49–77).

In its origin and subsequent development, the Gadna also parallels the Boy Scout movement. Both began as para-military forces. Both were later transformed with official sponsorship into permanent peacetime "character-building" agencies. Both avow such nonpartisan objectives as "endurance, resourcefulness, self-control, defense of honor and trustfulness" (Baden-Powell, 1931: 26). But unlike the Boy Scout movement in Europe and America, Gadna still retains a close linkage to the country's defense establishment. It also includes boys and girls within the same organization. This coeducational policy was consistent with the ideology and practice of youth movements, which stress the spirit of equality and comradeship of all members. Girls were not expected to equal boys in the rigor of the exercises, but they were needed to meet the severe manpower shortage. Many enjoyed this opportunity in Hagam to play a new role, hitherto not generally open to women. Their presence also added much to the morale of the units.

For working youths and those not enrolled in a high school, an administrative arrangement other than Hagam was needed. Therefore, the clandestine Hagana assigned a few men who could be spared to recruit adolescents into what they began to designate as Gadna. The Gadna and Hagam never focused exclusively on military training. Few of their officers were professional soldiers; many had an interest in education. Nearly all of them were graduates of youth movements. There were many students and Halutzim who had come to Palestine trained in developmental skills. They viewed military activities as an unfortunate but necessary deviation from pioneering. They therefore combined para-military exercises with exposure to hard work.

Many city children had no prior experience with either developmental or military skills. They were, therefore, taken on hikes where they learned to ford streams, survive in the desert on berries and snakes, and move at night without fear of "spirits." The emphasis was on acquisition of self-confidence derived from a knowledge that as part of an elite corps they could endure hardship and would be ready to help their country, as workers in time of peace, and as fighters if the need arose.

A prestigious institution

Youth corps all over the world are organized by adult-making institutions (parents, the school and the state) for two purposes which differ drastically in their consequences. A youth corps can function as an elite selector or can serve a welfare function. Participation can serve as a rite of passage from childhood to adulthood.

An *elite* youth corps is quite different from a *welfare*-oriented program such as the United States Civilian Conservation Corps of the 1930s, or the current United States Youth Corps. Both are designed for impoverished youngsters. They provide social services for the marginal. They are virtually without members from the more influential segments of the population.

In Israel, as in the Boy Scouts or the American Peace Corps, the elitist theory predominates. Middle class elements set the tone from the very beginning. The Hagam trainees in high schools outnumbered the few who were recruited outside the schools through Gadna. The status of a new institution within the total network of related agencies was very much influenced by the high status of those involved in its initial development.

Organizational linkages

The Gadna Youth Corps began as a legal cover for an illegal program. It developed gradually into a permanent administrative organization that combined educational with military requirements and was linked closely to two major adult-making institutions: The schools and the army. Their cooperative relationships were symbolized by the linkage of the chief architects of this program: Dr. Arthur Biram, a school principal in Haifa, and General Yaakov Dori, one of his many illustrious students. They developed a dual-focused organizational pattern that still persists today.

In their lifetime Biram and Dori both spanned the era of Jewish history when the idea of Jewish statehood became transformed from improbable romanticism into a political reality. Biram started out as a reform rabbi in Berlin, but this calling did not suit him for long. He decided to study classics, especially Greek and Latin, and obtained a degree from a secular university. This qualified him for a teaching post in one of Berlin's high schools. But in 1914 at the age of 36, he left a promising career in the German Civil Service to settle in Palestine and became headmaster at the Reali High School in Haifa. He was a man in search of himself, whose identity was a mirror of the conflicts of his generation of early Zionist leaders.

Dori (Dostrovsky) was one of Biram's first students. He had been born in Haifa of Russian parents. After graduation, Dori joined the Hagana to become the Haifa Commander. For many years he was one of its few full time military experts. He had a strong interest in education. After his retirement as chief of staff, he became the president of the Technion in Haifa, Israel's center for high technical studies. He served in this second career until his retirement in 1965.

The outbreak of World War I interrupted the relationship between Biram, the school principal, and Dori, his soldier-student. Both were Zionists, devoted to the same cause, but they served different armies. Biram decided to return to his German fatherland to do military service. He reappeared in Palestine in 1916 as a German officer in the Turkish Army. Young Dori joined the Jewish Legion in Egypt. He reentered Palestine in the service of the British Army, which conquered the country from the Turks.

When students had to be recruited for clandestine service, Dori and Biram could work together. Neither liked the politically partisan spirit of most youth movements. Some students, far from being old enough to understand the complexities of politics, would barely talk to fellow students enrolled in a competing youth movement. Biram actually banned them from operating in his high school. Nor did he relish the idea that the underground Hagana might directly recruit students in his school. He wanted educators to retain exclusive administrative responsibility for all students, including their military preparation. He was first and foremost an educator, but with a classical Greek regard for the importance of fitness and defense.

Dori had a similar outlook. He thought the army should have an educational aspect. He did not mind if his officers were appointed to the faculty when directing a voluntary and clandestine military program. They could then turn to school authorities to enforce discipline.

This cooperative arrangement between the clandestine Jewish army and the Jewish high schools worked well in part because this arrangement supported certain key values of leaders of both institutions, as follows:

(1) Defense conditioning should be conducted under a nonpartisan umbrella, within which youngsters from youth movements of different parties and those not affiliated could participate together.
(2) Teachers and students should be united in support of the cause of independence. This helped develop a spirit of comradeship that affected the total milieu of a school.
(3) Educationally oriented leaders could counteract an excessively militaristic spirit, which might develop more easily if military training were to be conducted outside the school system.

When World War II broke out, Expanded Physical Education became a "course" in most Jewish high schools. Few youths refused to participate. Training officers of the underground army could function as high school faculty members, thus reducing their isolation, helping to broaden their perspectives and their social prestige. The schools provided office space and other services. In some cases, they also gave financial aid because the clandestine training officers did not have a regular source of income.

Gadna survives success

When the Independence War began, Hagam-Gadna trained youths were among those who fought, died, and helped win the country's independence on the field of battle. In Jerusalem, under siege for many months, manpower became so short that Gadna units were assigned to battle stations (Lorch, 1961: 121). But after the establishment of a Jewish state, the necessity for a clandestine youth corps disappeared. Not even during the Six Day War in June 1967 did the Gadna Youth Corps have to be mobilized for military tasks. The fighting was done by the regular reserve, which yielded a force of more than 300,000,[35] although through the school and the Gadna youths were organized in many localities to help in distributing mail, newspapers, and milk and for aiding such civilian defense activities as filling sandbags. Approximately 14,000 Gadnaists worked temporarily in ordnance factories, the aircraft industry, in making camouflage nets, in hospitals and as farm helpers in border villages (Alcalay and Nurock, 1968: 121).

When an institution attains its goals, why should it continue? The certainty which united those who worked together tends to be displaced by uncertainty about what priority to give to new objectives, if indeed such new goals can be agreed on. The idea of Gadna's dissolution was entertained in 1948, but rejected. The issue of its future was resolved at the highest level by former Prime Minister David Ben Gurion. Independence had brought sovereignty, but not peace. Neither the High Command of the Israel Defense Force nor the political leaders of the country wanted to disband the Gadna.

Successful organizations generally tend to exert pressure for their continuity. In this instance, what had begun as a military emergency program became a permanent organization in which para-military objectives were supplemented by social welfare, educational and developmental goals.

In Israel, as elsewhere, serious outside threats have had a tendency to unify divergent streams in the nationalist movements. In politics and religion, Israelis disagree in many ways. But there is an overwhelming consensus that the shaping of youthful minds is too important to be entrusted to any single program. The Gadna Youth Corps was designed as a survival oriented nonpolitical youth program in an otherwise zealously partisan community.[36]

Although under government sponsorship, the Gadna has remained nonpolitical. Unlike the Hitler Youth of Germany, China's Red Pioneers, Russia's Komsomol and the youth corps in several newly emerging countries, Gadna has never been used to stage "spontaneous" protests and riots. Its leaders neither have the power nor seem to aspire to control their participants. Disciplinary infractions, of which there are few, are turned over by the Gadna commander to the school principal. There is no legislation to make Gadna compulsory and permanent. Each school can decide whether or not to have a Gadna program. Few principals refuse. Gadna offers them an enrichment and physical education program without cost. All instructors are paid by the army or the Ministry of Education.

The rehabilitation mission

Gadna has shifted its program priorities a number of times since statehood. After the Independence War, premilitary activities were reduced in favor of new developmental challenges. The organization was mobilized and greatly expanded to help meet a new "emergency," mass immigration.

Before independence, Israel had been a predominantly European community. In 1968, over 70 percent of the children in primary grades had parents born in the underdeveloped countries of Asia and Africa. The biblical prophecy of Jews being gathered from the four corners of the earth came true. The entire Jewish community of Yemen made their way to Aden, to be flown to Israel. From every other Arab country, Jews came by plane or ship, often having to leave behind all their belongings. Europe's displaced persons camps were emptied of their Jews. From the Americas and South Africa, as well as the democracies of Europe, came smaller groups to cast their fate with the new nation. Israel's Jewish population doubled in thirty months and quadrupled by 1969.

An influx so large and fast taxed the country's resources to the limit.

During the first few years, strict rationing had to be introduced. Many immigrants had to be housed in tents and asbestos huts. There were shortages of teachers, social workers and other public servants to help integrate the newcomers. The Ministries of Education and Social Welfare did what they could. But their manpower and budget were sufficient only to meet the most urgent needs. Gadna was given a new mandate to give "social first aid" to help decrease the gap in educational and welfare services.

This emergency national service mission was launched with eleven people, two rooms and a bicycle. It was soon given more funds and manpower, released largely from the Defense Ministry budget. With it, the Youth Corps established over 200 youth centers in immigrant towns and slum sections. They offered recreation and supplementary education. In a few locations Gadna also helped in hospitals and crèches, in fire-fighting and in building new roads. Several youth villages provided shelters for poorly housed adolescents. Many had been living with their families in hurriedly put up tent cities. Some of them lacked the rudiments of knowledge about twentieth century living. They had to learn the use of flush toilets, tooth brushes and the care of their new clothing. Nearly all needed instruction in Hebrew. Gadna also organized summer camps, where thousands of youngsters from poor homes were given a chance to spend a few weeks under healthy conditions. They received good food, medical care and free clothing, along with a chance to mix with Israeli children from more established sections of the population. Trips were organized to different parts of the country to acquaint youngsters with the new land to which they had come.

The challenge of helping new immigrants attracted some adolescent volunteers from the more settled families of the country. Helping to integrate the refugees was a new cause, with powerful youth culture appeal. For some of the immigrant youths, Gadna had glamour. What could be more inviting to a recent immigrant, living in a leaky tent, than to be taken to an Israeli army camp? There his rags were exchanged for an army uniform. He ceased being a poor refugee. He became part of a prestigious organization.

The education-welfare emphasis was reflected in the outlook of Colonel Akiba Azmon, the first commander of the Gadna after independence. His military career began in the Engineering Corps. He came to the prime minister's attention during the war with a plan to employ border village housing for defense purposes. Living quarters were built so that they could be used as fortified positions. He was a charismatic pioneer personality, with direct access to David Ben Gurion, then the Prime Minister, who was also the defense minister. Azmon sometimes used this power to circumvent normal military channels. He was no organization man. He was the kind of person who would smile and thumb his nose in response to a salute when entering a room of junior officers, to whom he was to lecture.

When Azmon was appointed as Gadna commander, he decided on a program with just enough military drill to make youngsters feel part of a military unit—which has prestige value. Most of the attention was devoted to the welfare and character development aspects of the program. He recruited a staff of educators and youth movement enthusiasts rather than persons who had a military orientation.

An "elite" image is projected by the symbolic recognition given to Gadna by the prime minister and many leading persons. Gadna is highly visible in ceremonial celebrations. Its units, *without arms,* participated in every Independence Day parade. In 1969, the military aspect of the festivities was cancelled. Public celebrations to mark Independence Day were focussed around Gadna activities as a deliberate move to tone down the previous military emphasis of this national anniversary.

Gadna also sponsors an international march to Jerusalem lasting two to four days for different participants who walk from the coast to Jerusalem before the Passover season. This march also includes youth movement units, foreign visitors, golden-age club members and, in many years, a small unit of the United States military who are stationed in the country as embassy guards.

Gadna entertains the participants with mass gymnastics, singing and acrobatic spectaculars in an open air auditorium, located on the hills outside Jerusalem. Gadna also sponsors other mass hikes, track and swimming meets. Each involves large numbers of youths, usually entire school classes. They are conducted to give the students a sense of participating in a national program of considerable visibility. There is only limited emphasis of individual competition. Most prizes are given for group performance.

The significance of this civilian transformation of what was supposedly a para-military youth corps is heightened if one keeps in mind that the Israeli government had no money for "extras" in 1952. Instruments for the Gadna orchestra had to be imported. There was severe austerity including food rationing. Some army officers raised their eyebrows: "Is it army business to maintain a music education program," they asked, "when funds are also badly needed for strictly military purposes?" There were also staff recruitment problems. Well qualified youth leaders were in short supply. Among recruits with qualifications for Gadna leadership, most preferred a truly military assignment to being a youth leader.

These substantive issues about budgetary and manpower priorities were complicated by organizational "politics." Some staff officers envied the personal prestige of the Gadna Commander in the prime minister's office. Azmon acted more like a civilian in uniform, than a soldier. The integration of immigrants rather than para-military training seemed to be his priority concern. In 1954 he was asked to leave his post, immediately after Ben Gurion first resigned from the government. With his protector out of power, the army's High Command preferred a Gadna commander with a more military orientation. Most staff officers, whom Azmon had brought into Gadna, gradually left as the Youth Corps shifted policies and, to a degree, reasserted the priority of its para-military objectives.

Stabilization

In the 1960s the need for Gadna's recreational, informal education and welfare programs began to decline. Attendance at voluntary Gadna youth centers dropped markedly in many towns and villages. The Ministry of Education was rapidly expanding more varied and hobby-oriented leisure time activities. Gadna had to use army personnel who were draftees and were changed each year while the school and youth movements could employ youth leaders for longer periods. By 1968, all the centers had been liquidated except for a few youth clubs in Druze Arab villages in response to Druze demands for fuller integration in the Israeli military establishments (Weigert, 1968: 19).

The phasing-out of most of Gadna's welfare programs did not affect its para-military and national service programs. They have become stabilized, encompassing an increasing proportion of the country's adolescent population. Officials estimate that their program reaches 60 percent of the country's adolescent population. This participation rate is likely to increase soon, since the government is extending compulsory education through the tenth year and most secondary schools have a Gadna program.

Gadna is today the largest youth program in Israel. It has more members than at any time in its over twenty-five years of existence. It enjoys financial and logistic support from two administrative units, the Ministries of Defense and Education. For the army, it is a nondefense activity; for the schools, it falls into the "nonschool" category. This gives the program a diffuseness which allows for highly flexible content. The Ministry of Education pays for Gadna instructors in academic high schools and full time vocational schools. The army furnishes leaders to agricultural, kibbutz and other rural schools, to part-time vocational training programs, and to welfare institutions, including those for juvenile delinquents.

The army Gadna is headed by a Colonel, who did not have prior experience in the Youth Corps. The post is not a step toward a power position. It usually is the last military assignment for a man reaching his early forties, the conventional "retirement" age for command officers. The first commander during the survey period, after completing his tour of duty, entered the Foreign Service as a military attaché. The next commander retired to enter the field of education.

Day-by-day programming is by a more permanent career cadre of education oriented officers. They enter Gadna as young officers and remain to train and supervise successive cadres of draftees who are assigned each year by the army to direct youth corps programs in vocational schools, youth centers, apprenticeship classes, agricultural settlements, and welfare and reformatory institutions.

General policy and budgeting of the Youth Corps are supervised by a civilian "Department of Youth and Nahal" of the Ministry of Defense, in line with the overall Israeli policy of civilian control over military affairs.

The Ministry of Education branch is headed by the director of sports and physical education. He hires civilian youth corps instructors who are paid by the ministry. They are assigned to function as Gadna teachers in local schools. Their program supplements what is being taught in physical education classes, which are staffed by teachers who have to complete a university or teachers college curriculum. Gadna instructors who perform much of the same tasks can be hired with lower academic credentials. This overlapping in function was organizationally reflected by a shift of the Gadna director in the Ministry of Education to be a subordinate to the director of physical education. In previous years, the two posts had enjoyed equal organizational status.

As shown in the attached organization chart (Figure 13), neither the Defense Ministry or Ministry of Education controls the program. Funds must be allocated each year by both ministries from a tight budget. These allocations occur in spite of the fact that the army has military units that are understaffed. The Ministry of Education is unable as yet to provide free high school level education for all. But it finances Gadna Youth Corps teachers in most academic and vocational schools.

The Gadna Youth Corps, much like the Reserve Officers Training Corps in the United States, forges a link between the country's armed forces and its schools. In the view of many army officers, Gadna is uneconomical if judged by purely military criteria. Gadna trainees may not be outperforming non-members with equivalent qualifications. Adolescents are certainly no longer needed for military service, but strategists want to maintain Gadna as a conditioning program. It is a convenient organizational framework for reaching youngsters of all social classes. The most publicized Gadna activities are not those involving para-military training, like target practice. The Gadna orchestra, which plays on many state occasions and gives excellent concerts both at home and abroad, the Bible Quiz and Gadna's many work projects are emphasized, as if to symbolize the symbiotic liaison that Israel's civilian militia wishes to maintain with

GADNA ORGANIZATION CHART

National Gadna Advisory Committee

Defense Ministry GADNA COMMANDER (Tel Aviv)

LIAISON OFFICE of Defense Ministry for Budgeting relations with civilian groups and local government

Education Ministry DIRECTOR OF PHYSICAL EDUCATION & GADNA (Jerusalem)

REGIONAL OFFICES
SOUTH   CENTRAL   NORTH
Supervision of Gadna Teachers in Local Schools

REGIONAL OFFICES
SOUTH   CENTRAL   NORTH
Supervision of officers and enlisted youth leaders

PROGRAMS in Academic High Schools, Vocational High Schools, Evening High Schools

Training sites, cooperative agricultural settlements, youth hostels, national forests, miscellaneous school facilities.

PROGRAMS in Agricultural settlements, Youth Aliyah Institutions, vocational training centers, welfare and reformatory institutions, apprenticeship training courses

Municipal sharp-shooting ranges.

Military Training Bases, Nurit, Beer Ora, Sde Boker Djelil, others.

Gadna Clubs
Sharpshooting
Air Clubs
Marine Clubs
Slum recreation clubs

EXTERNAL NON-SCHOOL PROGRAMS
Overnight hikes, forestation, harvesting help, archaeological expeditions, other national service volunteer work, youth leadership courses (domestic and foreign) Bible quiz, Independence Day Parade, 4-day march to Jerusalem, Gadna youth orchestra, theatre groups.

----- Cooperative relations
——— Command relations

the civilian sector. Gadna wants to be identified with both the military *and* the development accomplishments of Zionism. Pioneering, along with defense, are key organizational values.

Replanning

When Gadna-Hagam was set up in 1939, no existing agency could offer illegal para-military training without endangering its other functions. What emerged was a new institution, closely linked to both the school and the clandestine Hagana. Gadna still functions cooperatively as a program run by two separate and different bureaucracies. Its structure has changed little, although much else has changed. Gadna is now a legal youth corps. It is less needed militarily.

Social planning cannot be a one-time activity. It must be continuous so that changes in social functions can be reflected in the organization's structure and its goals. The unequivocal support of Gadna by most school and army officials has given way to the consideration of new policy issues. For instance, should premilitary training receive quite as much priority in 1970 as seemed justifiable in 1939? Israel can today maintain a military deterrent force without reliance on adolescent manpower. Why should the process of training for national security begin at age 14 when only four years later, all Israeli citizens are subject to military conscription? There also have been discussions of whether Gadna should be made an elective subject in high schools for those vitally interested. Other issues up for consideration involve the qualification of youth leaders. Is it feasible to attract young officers who want to leave the army to enter the field of education?

These and other questions illustrate the fact that in any planned program there is a need for periodic reassessment. When such a reassessment is made, planners must confront conditions different from those that pertained originally. Before a program is set up, many more options tend to exist than when a stable organizational structure has been in operation. It can be altered; it can grow or decline. It can even be abolished, but all these alternatives first have to answer the question: Is the change better than the condition it is designed to replace?

These policy considerations provide the background of an ongoing reassessment of Gadna by its administrative leadership. New programs, such as first aid clubs, are being set up to fit the desire of many young Israelis (especially girls) to acquire technical skills that have personal as well as public utility. Gadna has become a comprehensive internal tourism enterprise, offering young people a chance to see their country under circumstances that also offer tests of endurance and the opportunity for peer group companionship. It facilitates volunteering by adolescents for adult-like roles, whenever such help is needed.

Conclusion

Gadna originated during Israel's struggle for independence as a seemingly temporary program of clandestine para-military training. It became a permanent institution after the country's independence, although this event outdated its original functions. Israel's defense requirements can now be satisfied without reliance on adolescent manpower.

Over the nearly three decades of its existence, Gadna has maintained a stable organizational structure. But this has not meant a freezing of its functions, which have shifted repeatedly, in response to different public priorities. Without abandoning its para-military training objectives, an educational and social welfare dimension was added. This organizational flexibility may also be related to the fact that Gadna regularly rotates its top leadership.

Gadna does not compete with but supports and uses other youth serving institutions, especially the schools and the youth movements. Most Gadna instructors have had experience in youth movements. They provide high schools with a nationally planned supplementary education program, rendered without charge to the local taxpayers. This budgetary fact is particularly important in immigrant quarters and rural areas, where the local educational authorities lack resources and manpower to provide them enough leaders to organize hikes or to maintain an orchestra. Gadna confers prestige on those who participate in its program. Although efforts are made to enroll youngsters from disadvantaged families and those not enrolled in secondary schools, the tone is set by youths who are achievement oriented.

Gadna is compulsory for all those enrolled in a post-primary school with a Gadna instructor. In addition there are voluntary programs with an elite appeal. The curriculum includes physical toughening, volunteering for developmental pioneering, and visits to historic sites, natural wonders and other points of interest. The Youth Corps espouses only very general civil and patriotic objectives consistent with the country's core ideology, such as defense readiness, the ingathering of exiles, and a Jewish cultural renaissance. Its leaders are selected on a merit basis. Gadna avoids many of the devisive controversies, such as religion versus secularism, socialism versus free enterprise and others. This ideological neutrality is re-inforced through Gadna's linkage with two of the country's other major non-political institutions—the army and the school system.

Barnard (1950: 29) once observed: "An organization must disintegrate if it cannot accomplish its purpose. It also destroys itself by accomplishing its purpose." This contingency has been avoided by adding new functions. Gadna devotes a proportion of its resources to sponsoring developmental rather than military activities. This combination of para-military training with education and recreation gives the program a high degree of public acceptability in conformity to the predisposition in Israeli society that the civilian sector gain ascendancy when there is a close working relationship between civilian and military authorities (Perlmutter, 1968: 606–643). Gadna's history represents an instructive case study of the capabilities and limitation of operating a nonpartisan governmental youth program in a democratic political system. It is within the framework of this generalization that its contemporary functions will be examined in detail in the next chapter.

Chapter 9

Gadna Today

Program

Gadna is a youth corps specializing in para-military training within the context of Israel's civic action tradition. Any weekday, groups of boys and girls can be seen drilling in school yards or assembling in suburban firing ranges to practice sharpshooting. Youngsters come together to hear lectures and to discuss issues of military strategy. This part of Gadna is compulsory for all students registered in a postprimary school that has agreed to include it in its curriculum.

What gives Gadna most of its lustre and favorable public image are its elective programs. They include a variety of local after-school Gadna clubs. Their members build airplane models, marine-scout, target shoot, and hold discussions. Each year Gadna sponsors an International Bible Quiz. Dramatic groups are sponsored in several parts of the country, as well as soccer teams that play in an amateur league.

Gadna exposes young people to the idea of national service labor. In the eleventh grade, entire school classes spend a week or two in Gadna-sponsored reforestation projects, farming, harvesting or archeological digging. Participation is voluntary, but it is rare for any youngster to remain home. Working youths, who attend evening schools or apprenticeship classes only one day a week, go for shorter periods of time, since in order to go on these trips, their employers must release them from work.

These field trips provide opportunities for youths to test their capacity to work. They learn to respect the people who live in border areas and who bring up families within reach of a rifle bullet. Unfriendly soldiers on the other side could—and sometimes do—fire without notice. Each Gadna unit posts guards every night. Physically and emotionally they experience what it means to have borders without peace. In the words of one military reporter (Heiman, 1964: 44–45):

The Gadna provides useful training in marching, outdoor camping, sharp-shooting, night reconnaissance, first aid and communications. More important, Gadna inspires a sense of comradeship which makes the participants ripe for the next stage when they are inducted into the Israeli armed forces.

The descendants of those who were slaughtered in pogroms throughout their long history want to have children who will never face extermination for the lack of ability to defend themselves. The range of physical conditioning is indicated by the following annual events:

Event	*Number of participants in 1967*
The Kinnereth Lake (Lake Tiberias) mass swim	9000
The desert hike in the Negev	6200
The Jerusalem hike	6000
The spring track meet	4000
The Galilee hike	3600
The Lake Kinnereth (Lake Tiberias) hike	3400
The picnic hike	3260
The Mount Tabor hike	3000
The Mount Gilboa hike	2700
Samarian area hike	2200
Ashkelon beach and antiquity park hike	1900
Tel Katzir track meet[37]	1732
Hehadar track meet	1700
Sinai Desert track meet	1200
Frontier hike	512
Hefer beach swim	314
Eilat bay crossing	220
Yona swim meet	220
Public bicycle track	212
Nakruth swim meet	115
Bat Yam swim meet	105

Many Israeli adolescents have been to Mount Herzl with its two memorials: *Yad Vashem,* with its speechless message of how six million Jews were exterminated under Hitler and the National Cemetery, where many who helped found the Jewish state are buried. Survival remains a very personal issue. All youths at eighteen must face it. Few will shirk their turn in taking the risks of military service.

Gadna advocates universalist as well as Jewish renaissance values, along with training and military and civic skills. This combination is the essence of the Zionist core ideology, which is also sponsored by other of the country's public service organizations, such as the Nahal pioneer corps and the youth movements.

Universalist values:	Honor, unaffectedness, self-control striving for faultlessness, comradeship and forbearance.
Jewish Renaissance values:	Knowledge of Jewish history, the Bible and historic sites throughout the country.
Military attitudes:	Patriotism, discipline and obedience, fieldcraft (scouting); water discipline for desert living, punctuality, secrecy and capacity to live normally near the borders, even if danger lurks there.
Civic skills:	Love of work, protection of property, getting along with people of all walks of life and capacity to accept physical hardships graciously.

The Youth Corps gives special attention to youngsters with leadership ability. Over one thousand are invited each year to participate in summer camps conducted under army auspices. Military vehicles transport school children to the sites where the leadership training courses are held. While in attendance, the youngsters wear army uniforms. Their mail goes through military channels. Nevertheless, civilian values in character building are emphasized. If this were otherwise, there might be considerable opposition to the Gadna program.

Much of the discipline in the field is enforced by the peer group, as is the practice in the more autonomous youth movements. The Gadna instructor tries to limit himself to directing para-military exercises. He is helped by assistants (*Makim*), who are members of the class and who have attended a course to train for such leadership during previous summers and other vacation periods.

The course includes group living under hardship conditions, physical toughening, survival skills, premilitary training akin to army basic training, calisthenics and group games and lectures about patriotic subjects. The aim is to build up the leadership skills of each boy or girl who participates, to be applied when they are employed as assistant leaders in their Gadna class.

The curriculum is mirrored well in the content of the agency's monthly journal, "In the Gadna Camp" which has a circulation of over 10,000 copies. It has a full staff of youthful reporters, photographers and graphic artists. Its articles deal with military subjects which appeal to young people, scientific topics, news items on the youth culture and organizational announcements. The December, 1967 issue, for instance, included the following stories:

Military Subjects:

Aryeh Katz, a tourist guide. Since 1930, he served in six armies. He began as a British village auxiliary policeman. Later he also served in the clandestine Haganah, the Jewish Brigade during World War II (under British auspices) and the Independence War. He also was called to serve in the Sinai Campaign of 1956 and the Six Day War in 1967.

The new and the old Chief of Staff of the Israel Defense Forces.

Egyptian prisoners of war and their life while awaiting repatriation.

Scientific and Cultural Topics:

Feature story about astronomy.

The Gadna orchestra's trip to 11 countries in Europe, the United States and South America, under the baton of comedian Danny Kaye and conductor Shalom Ronelli Riklis.

Stories and poems contributed by youngsters.

Music, theater and movie reviews.

Visit to a historic site in East Jerusalem by the director of the Ministry of Religion.

Local history: The Jewish pharmacy in the old city of Jerusalem before independence.

A story about Israel's foreign aid program: Youth leadership training course No. 7 for emerging nations with students from ten countries.

Youth Culture News:

The Olympic Stadium in Mexico City.

Biography of the late James Dean, U.S. movie star.

Stamp collector's corner.

Crossword puzzle.

Cartoons and jokes.

Organizational News:

The Sinai Desert hike.

Letters to the editor, including members complaints.

Sharpshooting Club news.

Membership

Gadna's present coverage of about 60 percent of the adolescent population is likely to increase further when compulsory education will be extended through the tenth grade over the next few years. No precise data are available on the relative importance of the compulsory and voluntary Gadna programs. In the suburb of Holon, near Tel Aviv, where tenth grade level adolescents were surveyed in 1965, one-third of the Gadna members were also *activists,* in the sense that they were members of one or more voluntary Gadna clubs.

Gadna tries to reach the educationally disadvantaged. Gadna instructors conduct programs in evening schools, apprenticeship courses, and

institutions for neglected children. They also teach in vocational training
courses for socially marginal youths, who are not in school nor in a job.
Gadna does not exclude youngsters with minor physical handicaps. There
is a unit in the country's reformatory at Tel Mond.

The children of poverty in Israel are not excluded, but they are
underrepresented. Among the marginal segments of the population, adolescents are often expected to go to work early or, in the case of girls, to
help out at home. Others are too undisciplined to feel comfortable in any
organized program, where peer group discipline plays an important part.
Only 36 percent of the eligible youths in our area sample of a Tel Aviv
suburb, Holon, who were Welfare Department clients or whose families
were on its rolls, reported themselves to be Gadna participants.[38] Like
the youth movements, Gadna tends to have the greatest impact on youth
in academic secondary schools. But the Youth Corps does reach 61 percent of the adolescents who were never in any youth movement.[39]

TABLE 10

Gadna Youth Corps Membership of Adolescents in Holon
Who Were Never Enrolled in a Youth Movement
(N = 194, 10th Grade Age Levels)

	Percent
Activists in one of the Gadna voluntary clubs	18
In a compulsory Gadna school-sponsored program only	43
Not a member of Gadna	39
Total	100

The existence of several organizations, each with the aim of instilling national service values does provide a somewhat better coverage than if only
one of them were to be functioning.

The Gadna Youth Corps has difficulty in reaching orthodox youths.
Some of the religious schools, though state financed, refuse to allocate
time for Gadna training in their curricula. They give a higher priority to
the study of religious subjects. Sixty-one percent of those ever enrolled
in the religious B'nai Akiva Youth Movement in Holon, were not in
Gadna. The proportion of nonparticipants was even higher for girls. Among
orthodox families, the belief is widespread that women should be educated
exclusively for feminine roles, such as housewives, teachers and nurses.
They should stay close to parental control until marriage. Extremely orthodox elements are even unsympathetic to the idea that boys engaged in
religious studies do military service. They certainly object to attendance
at a Gadna camp where boys and girls mix with no more than the routine
controls maintained in any coeducational setting.

Gadna leaders try to overcome this resistance in orthodox circles by
co-optation, through the establishment of an administratively separate re-

ligious section. Its director and all of its youth leaders are orthodox Jews. A special Gadna training center for orthodox youngsters has been established. The usual camp program is supplemented by regular religious services and daily *Shiurim* (Study Groups). No data are available on how much impact this procedure has had on reducing the resistance of orthodox educators to Gadna, but the officer responsible believes he is "making progress."

There also is an under-representation of orthodox religious youths among the youth-leader trainees. Only 10 percent of the 1965 sample of 721 Gadna trainees said they were orthodox. Most of them were boys. An additional 3 percent, whose parents were not orthodox or traditional, said they were more religiously observant than their parents. This proportion is a measure of how far Gadna has succeeded in reaching the traditional elements of Israel who represent a much larger proportion of the society. Their underrepresentation also shows how far Gadna has to go before it is to have a uniform impact on the total population.

Among the *activists,* the participants who join voluntary after-school programs, girls represent only 13 percent of the membership (see Figure 14). Few of the adolescent girls are interested in sharpshooting. A higher ratio of participation by girls is anticipated when Gadna implements a new plan to offer first aid and nursing education through the voluntary clubs. But there are quite a few women Gadna leaders, about 40 percent of the army instructors and 22 percent of the Ministry of Gadna Education teachers. Gadna duty is one of the noncombat roles for which women are

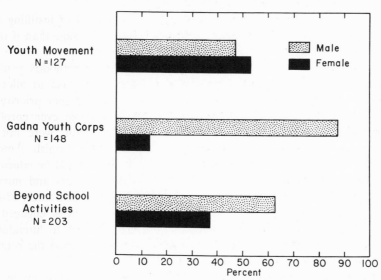

SEX OF YOUTH PROGRAM ACTIVISTS, HOLON 1965

FIGURE 14.

eligible. The coeducational makeup of Gadna prepares women for such supportive roles and reinforces the idea that national defense affects everybody. As future mothers, girls should know what will be required of their husbands and sons. Their presence also keeps the program from becoming a male subculture, in which soldiers' slang might replace ordinary language or the courtesies of normal social life would be downgraded. While women can claim exemption from military service for religious reasons, the majority take their defense-related responsibilities seriously. There are few "Amazons," however, who care to invest a great deal of their time in a para-military program.

Even with the exceptions noted, Gadna reaches a somewhat wider population of adolescents than other programs at an age when youth movements decline in influence. The number of youths who join Gadna is high, but the movement does not have the kind of meaningful impact on its members that occurs in the youth movement involving older adolescents. Few of those interviewed identified Gadna as a major focus of their interest. For most, it is just an added school course. Gadna is not a program with which students identify deeply. It is not a center of social life or peer group interaction. Its activities are often perceived as fun and of educational significance, but they are not essential. There is disinterest in Gadna. About 40 percent of the adolescents do not now participate.

Militarism and education

Most armies train men to think of battle. They pay less attention to the requirements of peace, the hoped for aftermath of war. The fatalist idea so well expressed by the Prophet Isaiah "Let us eat and drink, for tomorrow we shall die," competes with the values of civilization building. Peace as a key objective of national policy is commonly stressed in the Israel Defense Forces. Gadna programs counteract rather than incite hatred of the enemy. Military roles are stressed as being necessary but not primary.

Israel's militia has no militaristic traditions. There is no Prussian type of military elite (Ben Shaul, 1968; Heymont, 1968: 13–19). Civilians control national policy. There is discipline in battle or on maneuvers, but officers are taught to lead by persuasion and to rely on co-optation for their power to command. More is expected of Israeli soldiers than obedience. They must think. Developmental technical skills are often utilized. Military habits are a poor preparation for life in a modern society and its demands for productivity. As Hebrew University Professor Ernest Simon (1961: 431) points out, "In some armies, one of the preconditions of training for discipline is to get the soldier to accept meaninglessness: he must learn to wait passively until an order is received.[40]

After the first thrill of wearing a uniform or holding a gun wears off, adolescent fantasies about the possible glories of military life tend to be corrected by the reality of carrying a heavy pack in the hot sun. They are all too often chastened further by personal confrontation of injury or death of a comrade, or of an enemy soldier. One of the best-selling books about the Six Day War is *Fighters' Conversations* (1968), a realistic account of the horrible realities of battle and the moral dilemmas of soldiers brought up on the idea, "Thou shalt not kill."

An educational orientation to youth work can be inferred from the choices made by the Gadna leaders for organizing a discussion program. From a list of twelve topics, including one that was military, the army Gadna leaders made first choices that were similar to those of political youth movement leaders. They gave top priority to the topics, "Should one always tell the truth even if it causes harm?" and "Wildcat strikes: Their causes and how to prevent them." The military topic included in the listing ranked third (see Figure 15).

Gadna leaders who serve as draftees on assignment by the Ministry of Defense, give a somewhat higher priority to the educational objectives of Gadna than do those hired as civilian instructors by the Ministry of Education. This inference is further confirmed from their ranking of the three "most important" youth work occupations from a list of six occupa-

FIRST CHOICE OF YOUTH LEADERS FROM A LIST OF TOPICS FOR INCLUSION IN A DISCUSSION PROGRAM

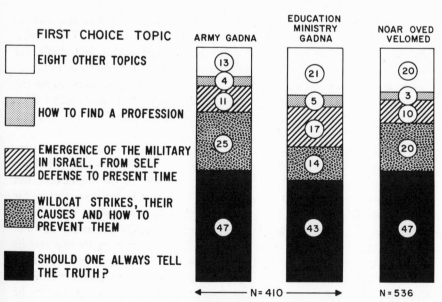

FIGURE 15.
(encircled figures are percentages)

tions. Army Gadna leaders more often ranked teaching in a frontier area above being an army officer than did the civilian Gadna instructors, who were hired by the Ministry of Education after their army service. But in both categories of Gadna leaders, the majority expressed considerable interest in the pioneering and developmental objectives of their work. Youth leadership courses, work programs, the youth orchestras, the International Bible Quiz, the Gadna's international aid program to emerging countries were more often mentioned in interviews as representing the Gadna "spirit" than is the core program of drilling and sharpshooting.

Although Gadna originated as a para-military unit, pioneering values share the limelight with military heroism. The idea of the *dignity of physical labor* is given a good deal of stress. There is a general agreement that no one in Israel should grow up to think that he is "too good" for hard work. Only a few youths in the Holon sample wanted to make careers in the army—a proportion equal to those who are thinking of choosing social work. Certainly there were few Spartan youngsters among the sample of 703 Gadna leadership trainees. This is evident by the following education-oriented responses to certain forced-choice questions:

TABLE 11

Gadna Leadership Trainee Responses (N = 703) To The Question
"Which Quality Is Most Necessary For A Leader To Be Successful
In This Task?"
(percentages)

Military Choice			*Education oriented choices*	
Courage	= 9	or	Understanding of child's personality	= 91
Physical Fitness	= 7	or	Talent of speaking and discussing	= 93

Public service orientation

Young people seem to be more willing to favor an extension of Gadna Youth Corps activities than those who are responsible for making its policies. The majority of youths who are enrolled think that basic Gadna training should be made more compulsory. Only about one in ten think the program should be entirely voluntary. Activists who are enrolled in voluntary Gadna programs do not differ markedly in their attitudes from those whose involvement is restricted to programs that are compulsory because they are part of the regular curriculum of many schools. As might be expected, youths who had never been in Gadna were much less interested in it. Many of these nonparticipants were girls who did not attend school or who were in a religious school where Gadna programs are often rejected by the school authorities. But in general, as shown in Table 12, Gadna enjoys considerable youth culture support:

TABLE 12

Attitude Toward Extension of Gadna Youth Corps
by Gadna Membership
Holon Tenth Grade Level Adolescents

(percentages)

	GADNA ACTIVITY STATUS		
	Never participated (N = 199)	*In required activities only* (N = 407)	*Volunteer activities* (N = 198)
"Youth corps activities should be extended and be made compulsory."	31	63	63
"The present situation should be continued" and "No answer."	56	29	24
"Gadna participation should be made voluntary."	13	8	13
Total	100	100	100

This high degree of youth culture acceptance may be related to the fact that Gadna requires only participation—not an ideological commitment. This is confirmed by the analysis of the responses to the questions that attempt to differentiate between the more and less idealistic youths. Gadna members did not differ from the total adolescent group in their readiness to join a kibbutz or in their choice of idealistic responses to attitude questions. Those who were activists (and who joined in voluntary Gadna programs) were more idealistic than those whose participation was restricted to required activities. But neither reached the level of commitment attained by activists in youth movements.

Nonpartisanship

A governmentally controlled youth corps can easily be turned into a propaganda agency to support the existing power elite. This is what happened to the Ghana Workers Brigade under the leadership of Nkrumah. Certainly this is the case of the Komsomol in the Soviet Union and the Red Guards in China. Gadna has shown no signs of becoming such a coercive youth-culture control agency. Gadna personnel are recruited on the basis of technical qualifications, including high intelligence and an interest in education. Lecturers are expected to avoid issues outside the area of national consensus, the widely shared core-culture values, especially

TABLE 13

Youth Movement Membership of Gadna Leaders

(percentages)

Youth movement membership	Army section of Gadna[a]	Education section of Gadna[a]	Adolescent youth leader trainees (N = 679)
Noar Oved Velomed (Moderate socialist)	15	35[c]	25
Scouts (nonpartisan)	17	14	26
B'nai Akiva (National Religious Party)	21[b]	14	9
Hashomer Hatzair (Left wing socialist)	13	14	8
Beitar (Nationalist Opposition Groups)	3	3	5
Other Youth Movements	9	10	9
None or No Answer	22	10	18
Total	100	100	100

a. N is large in both sections; total for both is 410.
b. The over-representation of B'nai Akiva leaders (National Religious Party) in the Army Gadna reflects a deliberate policy. Religious schools have refused to take part in the Youth Corps program unless the instructors are also religious.
c. The overrepresentation of Noar Oved Velomed (Labor Party) youths among the Ministry of Education is more difficult to explain. It may reflect the fact that this movement includes many youths who did not quite complete the minimum educational requirements for teaching jobs. Also, there may be an element of political influence, since the Ministry of Education has been headed for many years by a member of the moderately socialist Mapai Labor Party.

defense conditioning and the Jewish renaissance. There is an explicit prohibition against political action on the part of the Gadna staff. As shown in Table 13 they belonged to youth movements with varying political orientations.

TABLE 14

Gadna Leaders Designating as "Very Important" a Youth Program in Which They Had Been a Member When Younger

(percentages)

Youth program	Number	Army section of Gadna	Education section of Gadna
Gadna	(348)	20	31
Youth Movement	(342)	26	42
Beyond School activities	(107)	36	40

GADNA LEADERS EXPRESSING CRITICAL VIEWS ABOUT A
YOUTH PROGRAM IN WHICH THEY HAD BEEN A MEMBER

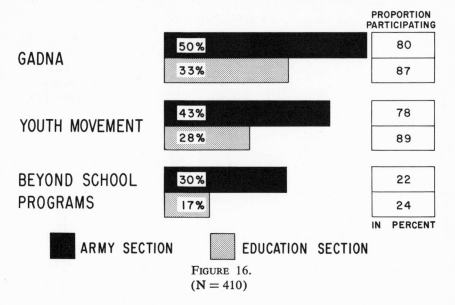

FIGURE 16.
(N = 410)

Relatively few rated Gadna as having been a "very important" influence in their life (see Table 14).[41] Gadna leaders expressed a more critical view of Gadna than of the other youth programs in which some of them had been members (see Figure 16). The model Gadna youth leader would not seem to be a pliant "organization man." They seem to include a high proportion of personnel who balance their service with objectivity about the program's limited impact on them and their peers.

Manpower utilization

The military and civilian Gadna leaders conduct identical programs. An assessment of the organizational capabilities of the two branches for doing the same job reveals a number of differences in the respective qualifications of the leaders, their concern for education and their public service perspectives.

Both the army and Ministry of Education suffer from a high rate of personnel turnover. During their normal tour of duty, army Gadna leaders are available for less than two years before their discharge. They tend to be young, with 44 percent being under 20 years of age and only 1 percent over 25 years of age. Nearly all of them are single. They are predominantly civilian in outlook. Twenty-five percent want to be youth workers or teachers. Only one of the youth leaders in the sample wanted to have a military career.

In the Israel Defense Forces, Gadna leaders are selected and assigned from the total manpower reservoir of the country. Selection is on the basis of high personal qualifications and leadership skills. Since such persons are also needed in every branch of the army, many male Gadna leaders tend to be youths with minor health defects disqualifying them for combat duty. Gadna duty is recognized as being important. It provides leaders with an opportunity to gain experience in working with youths. But most male Gadna leaders would have preferred a combat assignment which has more prestige in the army as well as in the youth culture. The attitude tends to be different among girls. For them, Gadna leadership is a choice assignment among the noncombat duties now open to women.

The army Gadna leaders generally are from middle class and well established families. Ninety percent of their fathers finished an elementary school, more than twice the proportion of the fathers of Ministry of Education Gadna leaders. One in five army leaders came from a family who had immigrated from North Africa or an Asian country. This was true of about twice the number of Gadna leaders hired by the Ministry of Education. Fewer of the Ministry of Education Gadna leaders came from the prestigious collective farms (kibbutzim) than was true of army Youth Corps leaders. The army leaders also ranked high in their ideological readiness for kibbutz life. More than twice as many (14 percent) planned to live in such a settlement than did the Education Ministry leaders (6 percent).

The army leaders also had higher vocational aspirations. Nearly twice as many Army leaders (29 percent) as Ministry of Education instructors (16 percent) hoped to enter the professions. Over half (55 percent) of the military Gadna personnel completed a high school or teachers' seminary and passed the matriculation examination, qualifying them for admission to a university. Only a minority of the Ministry of Education Gadna personnel had reached a similar educational level.

The Ministry of Education policies have, in the past, defined Gadna leadership posts as jobs requiring less education than is needed for academic teaching. Gadna teachers in secondary schools, unlike the physical education instructors, require no certification. Gadna salaries are lower than those for certified teachers. Few of the Gadna instructors completed the minimum training required to teach any other high school subject.

In the Ministry of Education, Gadna teaching has low organizational status. Gadna leaders must have military experience as noncommissioned officers. None were under 20 years of age. Sixty-two percent were between 20 and 24 years, and over one-third (38 percent) were over 25 years old. Only 4 percent had been educated beyond the high school level. They are not in line for promotion to school administrative posts. Such jobs are, therefore, most likely to appeal to persons who are poorly prepared academically who want to teach but cannot meet the requirements. Some are studying at a university to correct their deficiency in training. They see Gadna teaching as a part-time temporary job to finance their studies.

Those who are not studying and who do not intend to qualify for better jobs are more likely to see Gadna as a career, as the best job they can get.

Consideration is being given to upgrading the requirements for Gadna teaching in the Ministry of Education. If this were to occur, it might affect the impact of the programs in the school. But it would cost more money. It would also reduce the upward mobility function of the Ministry of Education Gadna jobs now open to people who do not have the credentials for being regular teachers.

Even now, only a few of the leaders are of lower-class origin. While 10 percent of the army leaders had fathers who did not finish elementary school, this applied to 21 percent of those hired by the Ministry of Education.

Of the adolescent youth leadership trainees—a voluntary program for youngsters beginning at age 14 to 15—only four percent were from the clearly lower class segment of the youth population who are already working or who did not report themselves to be in any school. Over half (57 percent) were attending an academic high school or teachers' seminary. Only six percent of the trainees came from the approximately 50 percent of Israel's disadvantaged families that had a father who never attended school or had not completed the eighth grade.

This proportion of lower class trainees is regarded as "woefully inadequate" by those identified with Gadna's objectives in social rehabilitation. But for those who are in leadership jobs and trainee courses, Gadna represents an opportunity structure for upward mobility.

Conclusion

Gadna is a youth corps that specializes in para-military training within the context of Israel's pioneering tradition. Its leaders are full time employees, most of them with a youth movement background. In Gadna hikes and work programs there is some overlap with what the youth movements are doing, except that the Youth Corps is nonpartisan and demands no intensive commitment from its participants. Adolescent volunteers are utilized as assistant leaders, but they enjoy less of the peer group autonomy than in the youth movements. While the Gadna program is planned more directly at the top, peer group solidarity is primarily relied on in the enforcement of discipline. Leaders co-opt rather than command obedience. Only rarely does any youngster have to be sent home from the Gadna for failure to behave within a range of what is acceptable.

By the late 1960s, the Gadna Youth Corps had become firmly institutionalized. Its premilitary conditioning and public service experiences have become a part of the educational preparation of a majority of Israeli adolescents. The program is closely linked to high schools as well as the curriculum of part-time courses for adolescents. Within each school, the principal has final administrative power over the program. Only field exercises and outside school Gadna programs are under army auspices.

Few of those who participate in the program view it as having extraordinary significance for their personal development. They accept it as a necessary activity. It is just a specialized program of a few hours a month, plus a way of seeing interesting parts of the country and offering occasional public service. It can be a source of fun and novelty, physical challenge and sight seeing, but it is not an activity that gives rise to strong emotional identification.

In spite of military sponsorship, the use of uniforms, rifle practice, and use of army installations, the Youth Corps is no militarist lobby. Equally strong expression is given to developmental values and the idea of self-discipline. Ministry of Education Gadna teachers were slightly more identified with their military functions, but few leaders want to have an army career. Gadna teaching tends to be a temporary job for most of them.

The majority of the leaders and members tend to be more realistic than idealistic in their outlook. They transmit the attitude that defense must be taken seriously, but it should be no more than one of the many roles citizens may have to perform. Military education is seen as a specialized preparation for life in embattled Israel. Most of the youth leaders wish to keep the program this way. The majority oppose the idea that Gadna should take more of the student's time. But they also do not want it to take less time or become entirely elective. It is rare to find anyone who romanticizes Gadna as a cause around which young people should rally. It is a program to give concrete expression to certain pioneering values and the idea of self-discipline. In this, Gadna has something in common with Outward Bound schools.[42]

Gadna would like to but cannot now reach many of the lower class youngsters for whom participation would be an opportunity for better integration in the dominant youth culture. But a proportion are reached. They are primarily those who attend high school and part-time vocational training programs.

In contrast to the American Youth Corps, the Ghana Workers Brigade, or the Kenya Youth Service, the Gadna carries no lower class stigma. It has youth culture prestige. Members can identify with the Israel Defense Forces, whose uniforms they are allowed to wear. They can discover that physical labor is dignified, not degrading. They become acquainted with middle class youngsters, some of whom are willing to get their hands dirty in the cause of nonmilitary development—helping to build a new village, harvesting the crops or building a border road (Hanning, 1967: 119–131).

But Gadna is no "big cause" that makes the heart beat faster. It plays a circumscribed part in the strategy of Israeli adult-making agencies to influence the ongoing generation to identify with the future of their country.

Chapter 10

The Beyond School Programs

Professionalized youth work

There is a third major organizational framework for youth programming, the Beyond School programs. There is limited planning at the national level. Administration is through local schools and the municipal Departments of Youth and Sports. The designation, Beyond School programs, was selected to call attention to one of their distinguishing characteristics: Informal education and recreation are primary rather than ancillary objectives.

Of the participants, nothing is required other than an interest in regular attendance of a program. Each offers enrichment education without requiring a normative commitment. The Beyond School programmers are inclined to stress "What can be done for our participants" rather than "What can young people do for the organization?"

Youth movements or the Gadna sometimes sponsor an amateur skit, which the group decides to put on. But in a drama club of a Beyond School program, the coach is likely to be a drama specialist. He will be interested in the theater. He is not concerned with infusing a patriotic or political attitude. His first priority is to help youngsters acquire professional understanding of the art.

This is not to suggest that the public service element is absent in the Beyond School programs. No youthful peer group program in Israel can remain immune to idealistic values. There is a "Youth-to-Youth" helping program. It is not based on a political ideology. It springs from the more simple and fundamental belief in mutual aid—that young people help those less fortunate through tutoring or visiting the sick.

Beyond School programs are largely a post-independence development and have grown much in the last decade. Many are conducted in school buildings after school hours. Informal and voluntary youth services can be organized in such facilities with little extra overhead or administrative costs. It is largely a matter of budgeting for overtime pay for some officials, for extra janitorial services, and for the employment of youth

YOUTH LEADER INTENTIONS TO WORK FOR MANY YEARS

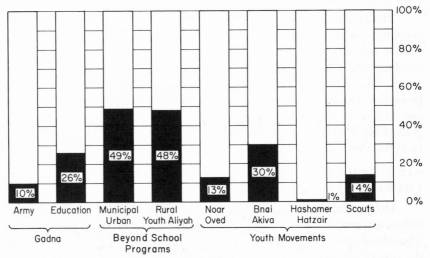

FIGURE 17.

leaders. The extension of services by educational agencies to develop leisure-time programs fits the general proclivity of all organizations to expand their jurisdiction.

Other programs take place in neighborhood and community centers, catering to both youths and adults. They are nonpolitical and have much in common with those conducted in community centers in the United States. The Ministry of Education does much to encourage the scheduling of group work and recreational and other extracurricular activities, especially in development towns, new communities and urban slums in cooperation with local youths and sports departments. There are also a few independent nonprofit agencies, like the YMHA and YMCA in Jerusalem and Beth Rothschild in Haifa. But there is no single national administrative structure.

Beyond School activities are consumer oriented. Youngsters can select a few or many activities. Reduction of activity or dropping out is not viewed as letting down a cause. Each activity—be it a sports team or a radio hobby class—stands on its own capacity to keep youngsters interested. Youth leaders are hired primarily on the basis of technical qualifications, such as a skill in radio work, carpentry, sports, or group work. Nearly one-half of them thought of youth work as a career. They were planning to remain a paid youth leader for many years, a proportion very much higher than youth leaders in either of the youth movements of Gadna (see Figure 17).

Beyond School programs vary considerably. They are not centrally directed as are the Gadna Youth Corps or the youth movements. But some nationwide patterns exist because of fiscal subsidies and program guidelines from the Ministry of Education and Culture to local authorities encouraging the organization of such programs as the following:

GRADE SCHOOL — AFTER SCHOOL CLUBS
(BATEI TALMID)

Tutors are hired in selected schools in the afternoon, to supervise youngsters who wish to remain to complete their homework. They are usually teachers who work on an overtime basis or part-time teachers hired especially for this program. The tutors also conduct enrichment programs, hikes, and rhythmic dance, or drama groups; they sponsor visits to movies, theaters and concerts, and supervise athletic programs. Nearly one in five of the youngsters in our nationwide 1963 survey of eighth graders reported himself as participating in such a Beyond School program. In 1967–1968, the same proportion was reported to be participating.

HIGH SCHOOL SOCIAL EDUCATION
(HINUH HEVRATI)

Hobby classes, music, current events, sports and other voluntary activities are conducted in many high schools under this administrative label. The school sponsors attendance at theater performances and concerts with the cost of the tickets subsidized by the Ministry of Education. Internship experiences for high school seniors in local government offices are occasionally arranged to give practical experience in civic affairs. Social education programs are a local responsibility. They are encouraged by a small subsidy fund from the Ministry of Education of about 300,000 Israeli pounds a year. Local matching funds are probably ten times as large. The programs are more intensive in academic than in vocational high schools. The curriculum of the latter tends to be crowded by technical requirements. Direction is by part-time specialists or teachers working for extra pay after their regular hours.

Academic high schools and a few vocational schools also have organized social work services. Some students give tutorial help to others who need it. Elderly persons who could otherwise be left alone are visited. Students also collect clothing, toys, and other necessities for persons in need.

School administrators provide administrative encouragement and supervision, but most of the initiative for particular activities of the Youth-to-Youth programs comes from the students. Some of the leaders are ex-members of youth movements.

COMMUNITY CENTER PROGRAMS

School-centered programs have a ready-made "consumer market" among the pupils who are enrolled. However, they cannot organize school drop-outs or youths from different schools with similar interests. Schools also have physical limitations to extending the focus of peer group organization. If they are left open at night, they have to be cleaned for the arrival of students the next morning. Furthermore few school buildings have the proper equipment for hobby programs. Therefore more and more extra-curricular, informal education and recreational services are being organized in special buildings. Four principal types can be distinguished: neighborhood centers (*Moadonim*), youth centers (*Batei Noar*), social clubs (*Havuroth Noar*), and technical clubs.

Neighborhood centers are maintained by voluntary organizations, local governmental units, public housing authorities and the Children's Fund sponsored by the Ministry of Religion. Some are housed in wooden huts. Often they function with part-time paid youth leaders. Overhead costs are kept low. In the late afternoon the facility is often reserved for youngsters under the age of 14. In the evening, the premises remain open for the older age groups. This double programming sometimes leads to conflict and gives rise to demands for more spacious community centers. There have been rashes of arson in such centers reflecting tensions among different groups in the neighborhood.

Youth centers (*Batei Noar*). Communitywide programs of recreational sports, hobby and informal educational activities can be more conveniently housed in permanent quarters. There were 247 such youth centers at the beginning of 1968, many with a full-time director and a diversified part-time staff of specialists.[43] The youth centers are open to anyone willing to come and, therefore, tend to draw their clients from the entire community. Their number is expanding rapidly in response to the high priority that the Ministry of Education and Culture gives to their development. Educational programs have been organized to train the necessary staff. Salaries are offered to induce a career rather than a transitional job outlook.

Social clubs (*Havuroth Noar*) constitute another community program. Many youngsters leave youth movements to form informal cliques. The pattern of having a group identity is so pronounced in the Israeli youth culture that many of these friendship circles prefer to function like a club. In the larger cities, the municipality hires youth leaders to approach some of the spontaneous clubs to meet in a youth center instead of the street or the beach. Space is furnished free of charge. The only condition is the group's acceptance of a youth leader paid by the center.

This co-optation program is designed to bring more of the lower middle class peer groups under the influence of adults. In a few cities group workers in slum districts are seeking out social clubs and trying to gain the confidence of the members. The worker meets them in the streets and cafes and uses group work methods to prevent them from becoming the nucleus of dangerously antisocial gangs (Leissner, 1965, 1967).

Technical clubs are included among the community centers. They were introduced under the leadership of Colonel David Wortman in the late 1950s. Col. Wortman had served as a liaison officer for the British Army in Soviet Russia during World War II. There he was impressed with a centrally planned program for encouraging youngsters to pursue technical hobbies.

Participation in these technical clubs, although voluntary, requires a readiness on the part of the youngsters to attend regularly. The curriculum is carefully organized to teach youths about electricity, metal work, the building of model boats, the telephone, radio and other arts and crafts. It is planned for a three-year period with increasing levels of difficulty. Equipment, models, blueprints and other teaching aids are carefully designed for each level of skill. A total of 7,000 members were enrolled in forty such clubs in 1969, most of them located in urban areas. One-third of the participants are girls.[44] Teams of twelve to fifteen youths work under the direction of a technically competent instructor. He need not be an educator; he can be an electrician or sheet metal worker who enjoys teaching.

Financing is provided from modest private contributions plus grants-in-aid from local authorities. The Ministries of Labor and Education and the National Labor Federation also give subsidies. A central office, directed by a volunteer board of directors, helps in establishing new programs. Its executive provides program consultation, helps locate teachers and sells mass-produced hobby equipment at cost. The office prepares training manuals and sponsors nationwide competition among the various clubs.

The Beyond School network of youth services in Israel is even more diversified than suggested by the brief description of its major components. At the lower end of the age range are *Mesiboth,* meetings arranged by third and fourth graders in some schools. They hold occasional meetings in their homes or organize class parties. Particularly in middle class areas, these spontaneous groups need little help from teachers and only supportive aid from parents.

The Department of Information of the Prime Minister's Office sponsors selected activities for older youths in the large cities. University students are organized and have a national federation with local chapters. Each chapter functions somewhat like a student labor union, negotiating for lower fees, easier examinations, and better employment prospects. The local chapters also publish a university newspaper. They alone among the youth programs are independent of adults. The university authorities exercise no direct influence on them.

Taken together, the Beyond School programs in the streets, in community centers and in school buildings are Israel's most rapidly growing network of youth services. They can be viewed as a supplementary education program. Most youngsters start school before 8 a.m. and some get home as early as noon, especially in the lower grades. Even the high school ends at 2 p.m. Quite a few children then come to a home without parents: 30 percent of the married Jewish women age 18 to 54 are working (Central Bureau of Statistics, 1967: Table K/8, p. 266).

The Ministry of Education, the Ministry of Religion, the Prime Minister's office and the Ministry of Labor and Welfare provide some of the leadership and fiscal subsidies. Each agency aims to influence the emerging youth culture by organizing programs which can command the enthusiasm of young people. Except for the more voluntaristic Youth-to-Youth activities, the Havuroth Noar cliques and the younger age Mesiboth, where much of the leadership is exercised by students, a directive strategy is employed in the other Beyond School programs. Experts rather than youth leaders do most of the planning of these supplementary education or leisure-time programs on the basis of technical and professional proficiency.

Participation patterns

The diversity of program content, fiscal sponsorship and location is considerable. No simple analytic scheme can adequately guide the analysis of how youngsters participate in Beyond School programs. For purposes of estimating their relationship to the different adult-making institutions which aim to influence the youth culture, the following classification scheme was adopted.

Elementary School activists. Fourteen percent of the Holon area tenth grade sample were enrolled in a Beyond School program located in their school. They were not members of a community center or high school program. Nearly all these elementary school activists also joined some other youth program. Except for a small minority of 4 percent, they reported to have been in a youth movement, a sports club or in the Gadna youth corps.

High School activists. They accounted for 25 percent of the Holon sample population since high school is elective and attendance is limited to academically qualified students. This category tends to include a high proportion of good students and youths from middle class homes. They tend to try out many organized peer group programs. Only one percent had never enrolled in another youth program.

Community-centered activists. Twenty-three percent attended programs in special buildings, where there is no restriction to participation on the basis of school attendance. Thirty-five percent came from families of Afro-Asian origin as against 23 percent of the high school activists. Membership rolls in the community-center programs are not inflated by pro forma participation of those mostly middle class youths, who passively "fall in" with school peers by enrolling in a conveniently located and well-staffed leisure-time program.

Community-center programs reach farther down the social scale than the school-centered programs. More than twice as many members in community centers were thinking of a technical career than were the youths in high-school-centered programs; 37 percent of those enrolled in community centers were ambitious to enter professions or wanted to do youth work, in contrast to over half of the youths in Beyond School programs in high school.

The nonjoiners. More than other organized youth programs, the Beyond School activities were reaching all ethnic segments of the Israeli population. Those not in any Beyond School program comprised 38 percent of the Holon sample. But as shown in Figure 18, the children of Afro-Asian parentage were only slightly overrepresented among them. Nonparticipants in the Beyond School program had an ethnic distribution similar to that of youths in elementary school sponsored and community youth programs. Only the youths in high school centered Beyond School programs showed a sizable overrepresentation of youths from European families.

Noninvolvement in Beyond School programs, while somewhat more often characteristic of youngsters with Afro-Asian fathers and those who were underachieving in their formal schooling, was not a good predictor of the way young people would relate to other youth serving agencies. Half of the nonjoiners were attending a high school of an academic or technical nature. Being disinterested in Beyond School programs was certainly not restricted to marginal students or to those generally disinterested in youth organizations.

Growth potential

The Beyond School programs are the most flexible of the three major youth frameworks. Participation is possible without an ideological commitment, as in a youth movement. Youngsters can be active in a community center without being in a school, which is now a requirement for enrollment in Gadna. Expansion of Beyond School programs, especially in slum sections and immigrant areas, is possible by providing whatever may be of most interest to the youngsters, be it sports, informal games or hobbies.

As was already indicated, the disadvantaged among Israel's youths are touched by youth movements and by Gadna, but activism is much lower than with adolescents, whose families have attained middle class status. This discrepancy is least true for the Beyond School programs. This was demonstrated by a special survey made of a sample of adolescents whose families are known to the Ministry of Social Welfare because they receive some of its services owing to such factors as unemployment, absence of a wage earner, or presence of a mentally retarded child, severely ill person or a delinquent. Youngsters whose families received welfare services were less involved than the general population, but the difference was least pronounced for the Beyond School programs. Although 62 percent of the general Holon area sample reported they participated in them, so did 45 percent of the sample of welfare youth.

Coverage of the population is lowest at younger age groups. In the nationwide survey of eighth graders, most of them 14 years old, only 44 percent reported that they had been active in a Beyond School program at some time.[45]

The majority of the Beyond School participants also reported involvement in other organized group activities. But a noteworthy minority

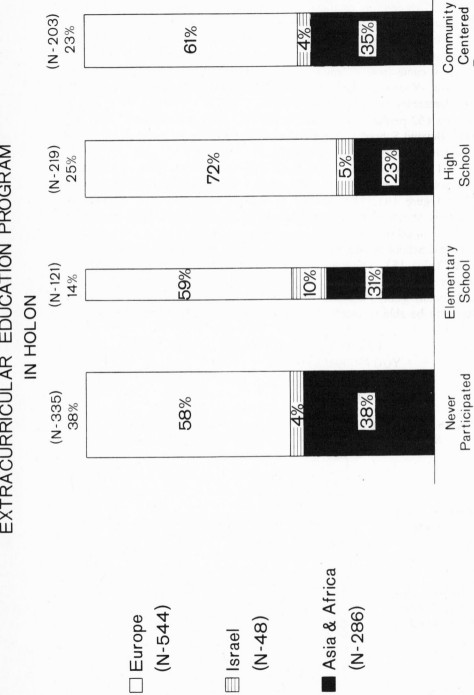

FATHER'S BIRTHPLACE OF PARTICIPANTS OF
EXTRACURRICULAR EDUCATION PROGRAM
IN HOLON

□ Europe
(N-544)

▥ Israel
(N-48)

■ Asia & Africa
(N-286)

(N-335)
38%

Never
Participated

58%

4%

38%

(N-121)
14%

Elementary
School
Sponsored

59%

10%

31%

(N-219)
25%

High
School
Sponsored

72%

5%

23%

(N-203)
23%

Community
Centered
Programs

61%

4%

35%

178

(11 percent) took part in no other organized youth program. This group included three-fifths of those who reported no participation in Gadna or in youth movements. Disadvantaged youngsters were over-represented in this group. Sixty percent were doing very poorly in school. They had sub-standard scores (below 67) in the eighth grade examination. Fifty-seven percent came from a family in which the father had been born in Africa or Asia. Youngsters active exclusively in Beyond School programs located in elementary schools included a much higher proportion from crowded homes (62 percent) than those active in a youth movement (33 percent). The Beyond School programs, therefore, reach a key target category: The majority of the otherwise unorganized.

The Beyond School programs exceed the Gadna Youth Corps and the youth movements in attracting lower class youths on a voluntary basis (see Figure 19). The children of recent immigrants who do not learn Hebrew at home, those from Afro-Asian families and those who under-achieve in school are more active voluntarily in the highly adult-controlled Beyond School programs than in the more autonomous youth movements (see Table 15). The youth movements require less conformity but make heavy demands upon their members for idealistic commitments. Youth movement leaders are predominantly of the volunteer type. They do not seem to be able to reach out to the underprivileged as much as the more

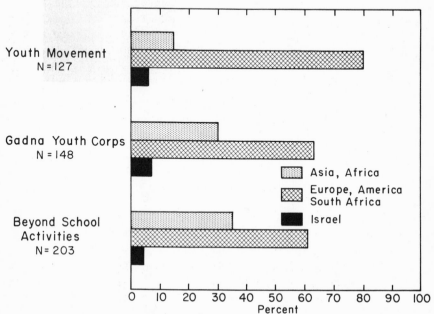

FATHER'S COUNTRY OF ORIGIN OF
YOUTH PROGRAM ACTIVISTS, HOLON 1965

FIGURE 19.

TABLE 15

Capacity of Youth Programs
To Attract Disadvantaged Tenth Graders in Holon—1965

(percentages)

	Community-center Beyond School programs (N = 142)	Volunteer Youth Corps activities[a] (N = 125)	Still active in youth movements[b] (N = 127)
No Hebrew spoken in home	12	10	9
Father born in Afro-Asian land	39	32	14
Failed 8th Grade Comprehensive Examination	37	29	18

a. Not currently active in a youth movement; some of them were also in a Beyond School program.
b. Some were also active in a Beyond School program or the Gadna.

professional, and more often, full-time paid youth workers. This is in spite of the ideological expectation of socialist youth that they reach the working classes.

Impact data

Skeptics of education through autonomous peer groups theorize that there will be an overemphasis on peer-group loyalties. This would lead to the development of excessive cliques based on social or ideological considerations, at a time when young people should explore their world with an open mind.

This danger does not seem to materialize. There is a great deal of multiple participation. No single youth program meets all the needs of young people for structured leisure time. Ninety-five percent of the Holon tenth-grade adolescents had joined at least one major program at some time. But half of those belonged to all three, a youth movement, the Gadna and one or more Beyond School programs. Membership in one was correlated with participation in all the others, although youngsters were not necessarily active in all of them at the same time. The different adult-managed programs are not competitive. This is not to suggest that they could be expanded indefinitely. The amount of leisure time is limited.

The readiness for multiple participation was as great among the political as among the nonpolitical groups. Two-thirds of the youths active in the radical socialist Hashomer Hatzair and Dror youth movements also reported to be in one or more Beyond School programs. Members of the less socialist Noar Oved Velomed movement were even more active. Only one in four reported no participation in extracurricular programs.

Youngsters who had never been in a youth movement had a nonparticipation rate (forty-eight percent) that was nearly twice as great (see Table 16). Youth movement members are not antiestablishment as Chen (1967:

TABLE 16

Beyond School Program Participation of Tenth Grade Holon Youths
by Youth Movement Affiliation

(percentages)

Beyond School participation	Socialist: Hashomer Hatzair and Dror activists[a] (N = 53)	Labor Party: Noar Oved Velomed activists[a] (N = 53)	Never a member of any youth movement (N = 200)
None reported	33	25	47
In elementary school programs	37	11	16
In high school programs	19	34	17
In community programs	11	30	20
Total	100	100	100

a. Active member only. Ex-members of these youth movements who had resigned when our survey was made were excluded.

123) concludes on the basis of a more extensive analysis of these data: Youth movements "even when they advocate a radical ideology do not lead to a reduction of social contacts."

Like all other organized youth services, the Beyond School programs were somewhat more successful in reaching those who felt positively identified with their country and were aware of what was needed so that it could survive. This is apparent from the analysis of preferences expressed by youngsters about where they would like to live permanently. Only 8 percent of the uninvolved as against 14 percent of those active in a community-centered program said they wanted to live in a kibbutz, a development town or a rural community (see Table 17). The uninvolved also were overrepresented among those who expected to be exempt from military service for religious or health reasons. Fewer expected to volunteer in the Nahal Pioneer Corps, the Air Force, or the Parachute Corps. One-third of the entirely uninvolved answered their questionnaire without a single idealistic reply, a proportion twice as high as youths enrolled in community-centered, Beyond School programs.

The youth programs share with other adult-making institutions the objective of encouraging a patriotic identification. The Israeli society seems to succeed considerably in reaching this objective. Few youths expressed cynicism about the Israeli goal of being an open society. Only fifteen of 878 respondents thought there is ethnic discrimination. Around election

TABLE 17

Where Beyond School Program Participants in Holon
Hope to Live Permanently

(percentages)

Where I want to live permanently	Never participated (N = 335)	Elementary school sponsored (N = 121)	High school sponsored (N = 219)	Community centered programs (N = 203)
In Holon (N = 362)	35	53	42	44
In a kibbutz or development area (N = 95)	8	13	11	14
Other choices (N = 421)	57	34	47	42
Total	100	100	100	100

time, much is said by some opposition parties about the allegedly discriminatory policies of the government in favor of new immigrants and
against Jews of Afro-Asian origin, who occupy few leadership posts. Their
ranks include a high proportion of persons with a low income and little
education. But only a minority of the children who thought there was
ethnic discrimination viewed this reality as a barrier to upward mobility.
In answering the question, "Who can advance and succeed in the State of
Israel?" few checked as their reply: Being an "European" (*Ashkenazi*),
or being an "old-timer" (*Vatik*).[46]

A larger group of all eighth graders in our sample, nearly 12 percent,
thought that advancement is related to economic and social advantages.
They checked "having pull" or "coming from a wealthy family," as the
most important reason for success in Israel. Uninvolved youths, those
never enrolled in any Beyond School program, were over-represented
among those who explained success in terms of having "pull."

But the largest proportion of the Holon respondents thought the
Israeli social system is an open opportunity structure. Over half (53 percent) checked "education," "having a profession" or "being an industrious
worker" as their primary explanation of social mobility. Another 18 percent checked being "strong willed."

Israel does not now have a revolutionary climate. The establishment
is strongly oriented towards welfare. Much is being done by the government, the Histadruth Labor Federation and the Jewish Agency to integrate
newcomers. Some criticize the pace as being too slow. Many think the
programs could be more effective. There are deviant cliques and delinquents. Street worker programs (not included in our study) try to reach
them. Most of the young people now growing up, however, are willing to
be identified with publicly sponsored enrichment programs. Even a fair
proportion of the underprivileged attend community centers and other

Beyond School programs during their leisure time. Except for a small proportion who keep the police busy, Israeli youths are not roaming the streets, they are not "dropping out."

Conclusion

Schools have carefully defined and crowded curricula. The three "R's" (reading, writing and arithmetic) are stressed plus cultural subjects. Hobbies, personal interests, sports and other "luxury" topics cannot find much room within the regular course requirements. The Beyond School programs try to provide for some of these special interests. They cater to hobbies, the arts and the mind, from soccer teams to running an amateur radio station. Many are administered by school officials. Full-time leaders are recruited, trained and certified nationally. Beyond School programs represent the most highly professionalized segment of the network of Israeli youth organizations. Some of the planning is done by Ministry of Education officials, but there is no coordinated program or central control of policy. There is room for local innovation.

Neither Gadna nor the youth movements are primarily concerned with education: both have service-oriented missions. The personal needs and interests of the members are of secondary importance. Beyond School programs are more consumer oriented. They are publicly organized to provide enrichment education.

The Beyond School programs reach over three-fifths of their target population in middle adolescence and somewhat less than half of those during the earlier years. The highest proportion of participants is among those who are also in a youth movement. Members of these relatively autonomous peer group programs find no conflict in taking part in the much more adult directed Beyond School activities.

Eleven percent of the participants in the Beyond School program were working or studying in a vocational, commercial, nursing or a part-time postprimary school. The programs are relatively successful in attracting the children of underprivileged "other Israel" newcomers. But they fall short, although less so than other youth programs, in being able to attract all the children of the poor, the uneducated and the immigrants from Afro-Asian lands.

The Beyond School programs have a good potential for organizational expansion. They are less costly than schools. There is still a shortage of high school and technical education programs at the postprimary level. Leisure time programs fill this void, to some extent. Financing comes from local authorities, the central Government as well as voluntary groups. The programs can utilize part-time sports leaders, teachers, musicians, dance teachers, artisans and other hobby specialists. They also are more able to offer a career possibility to professional youth leaders than the other peer-group agencies. This gives them an organizational capacity for long range planning and the resources for implementing of such plans.

Chapter 11

The Hard-to-Reach

The welfare challenge

In Israel the territorial therapy theory was applied on a large scale. After the establishment of the state, 1,290,000 refugees came who could not continue to live decently in the lands of their birth (Jewish Agency, 1968). Many more had arrived earlier and helped found the state.

Before World War II the manpower influx was primarily development oriented. Many of the immigrants came after a period of *Hahschara*, of technical study in nation-building skills and/or with investment capital. Skilled adults, persons with capital, unattached adolescents or members of Halutz-oriented youth movements were favored by the immigration policy of both the British government and the Jewish Agency.

A high proportion of them were strongly identified with Zionist and socialist ideals. They generally suffered from only one social handicap: they were Jews in an environment where this status led to discrimination and worse. They felt outcast socially, but not necessarily personally disadvantaged. Indeed, a disproportionate number of highly gifted and technically skilled persons were among the pre-World War II settlers in Israel. Pre-independence Israel was oversupplied with physicians, writers, poets, engineers, lawyers and other professionals.

This positive manpower selection policy had to be modified during World War II. All of Europe's Jews faced death. Migration could no longer be planful. Any Jew who could find a way to reach Palestine, even without permission of the British government, was welcomed by the Jewish community. Selective immigration ended completely after Israel attained statehood. Complete Jewish communities were evacuated from Arab countries. Many of them had lived there under primitive conditions; some showed the scars of having lived in a low-caste status for many generations. No one was excluded from the right to "return to Zion." The poor, the blind, and the sick generally were sent out first. Many youths came too late to fit well into the country's educational system. The result: the illiteracy rate of Jewish persons over 14 years of age doubled from 6 percent in 1948 to 12 percent in 1961. Even in 1963 when educational conditions had made great strides, 43 percent of the boys and 50 percent of the girls scored very low on their eighth grade qualifying examination. About 10 percent of the youths cannot meet eighth grade minimum standards when examined for entry into the army. Most of them are culturally deprived. Only two out of five have a low level of intelligence to help explain their academic deficits. Delinquency and crime had been minor problems during the pre-World War II era. But in 1966 there were 10,588 children in need of probation services (Burg, 1968).

A large proportion of these immigrants have struck personal and economic roots. But for a variety of reasons, one in ten families in Israel is in need of welfare assistance. Most of them live in slums. The majority are from families of Afro-Asian origin. Over 70 percent of Israel's Jewish children in the 1970s will be from non-Western families who were reared in a traditional culture and can give, at best, very limited guidance to their children in finding their way in a rapidly modernizing country.

Israelis openly discuss the question: will our land become a Levantine state controlled by the power of those not yet ready to live in a modern state? Or will the "other Israel" be acculturated to the twentieth century traditions of the early settlers? Can our land continue to have the highest volume of book and newspaper readership in the world? Or will our nearly quarter million illiterate voters gain more influence?[47]

Israel is experiencing the limitations of the Zionist theory that territorial therapy can cure the ills of persecuted Jews. Migration from a politically unstable or even untenable situation to a land where Jews can live by right rather than sufferance does make a difference. Not many of the welfare clients in Israel would like to return to their countries of origin. But there are those who brought or newly acquired problems that made them clients in need of education, medical, casework and other types of personal intervention.

The uninvolved

In a country with several well-organized peer group programs, non-participation cannot be casual or accidental. It reflects a deliberate policy on the part of the youngster and/or his parents. Repeated invitations for joining must be resisted. This population segment will be referred to as the *uninvolved* or *hard to reach*.

Not all of them are poor and disadvantaged. Some are chronically ill, mentally retarded, unusually introverted or isolated in homes where parents actively oppose participation of their children in an organized extracurricular program. But the majority of these organizationally non-involved adolescents are the children of poor and uneducated parents.

TABLE 18

Low Status Characteristics of Holon Youths by Self-Estimates
of Peer Group Standing—1965

(percentages)

	SELF-ESTIMATES		
Characteristics	Leaders (N = 124)	Ordinary members (N = 655)	Social isolates (N = 21)
Youth Program Participation			
Never belonged to a youth movement	21	24	55
Never in a Beyond School program	27	35	33
Socioeconomic Status			
Crowded living quarters (four or more persons per room)	7	14	17
Father born in an Afro-Asian country	26	33	57
Low socioeconomic level	33	39	52
Father had only elementary school or less education	45	51	52
Aspiration Level			
Plans to work now full or part time	3	8	24
Does not think he can achieve his goal	2	2	6
Peer Group Standing			
Low Comprehensive Examination (Sekker) score (67 or less)	25	30	43
All friends are of the same sex	18	32	47
National Service Orientation			
Thinks he will not serve in army for religious or health reasons	10	14	25

Uninvolved youths are overrepresented among the approximately 12 percent who drop out of school before the eighth grade in a country where education is compulsory and highly valued. Only 22 percent of the non-joiners in youth programs were in an academic high school. Very few were bent on achieving much academically. Many did not know what they were going to do in the future, work or go to school.

The lower class relatedness of organizational uninvolvement in youth organizations is also confirmed when it is defined in more social-psychological terms. The adolescents in our Holon area sample who described themselves as social isolates, were much more deprived and socially marginal than those who thought that they were "ordinary members" of their peer groups, not to speak of those who designated themselves as leaders when replying to the question: "What is your status among your friends?"

As shown in Table 18, the social isolates, a mere 3 percent of the tenth grade level adolescents, came predominantly from families of lower socioeconomic standing. They were substandard in school achievement and had low vocational aspirations. A fairly high proportion were organizationally uninvolved in youth movements, but more of them did relate themselves to the more professionally directed Beyond School programs.

Social stratification is universal. Classes and castes develop often on the basis of centuries-long generational transmission of privileges or disadvantages. Not so in Israel. Its status system was recently "imported." Its class disparities are not "home-made" and are ideologically inconsistent with both Zionist and Socialists' theories. But they exist, nevertheless.

The unevenness of this heritage is colossal. Most immigrants from Europe were educated and had marketable skills; those from Asia and Africa often had neither. This discrepancy has consequences that are transmitted to the next generation. Boys whose fathers came from an underdeveloped country had three times as many failure scores in the eighth grade and only about one third as many passing scores as those who were born into families from developed countries. For girls from Afro-Asian families the differences were even more pronounced. Girls from European families tended to outperform boys academically. The opposite was true for the children of Afro-Asian families. Boys outperformed girls in school work.

The cumulative impact of the existing differences in environmental supports for education stand out glaringly when Israeli youths are drafted into the army. As shown in Table 19 below one finds in Israel many of the gross variations among ethnic groups in the proportion of those who can meet requirements for officers training and service in technical units as are reported in the United States armed forces (National Advisory Commission on Selective Service, 1967: 17–26).

If these ethnic and cultural differences were to be perpetuated for a generation, Israel might well become a divided land, like so many countries

TABLE 19

Formal Education of Male Soldiers in Israel, 1960–61
by Their Father's Area of Origin

(percentages)[a]

Highest level of education	Afro-Asian country	Occidental country
Seven years or less	15	1
Completed primary grades	49	13
Partial secondary school attendance	28	39
Completed high school	10	45

a. Adapted from Mordechai Bar-On, *Educational Processes in Israel Defense Forces,* Tel Aviv, Israel, Israel Press, Ltd., 1966: 14. The percentages here as in the original source do not add up to 100.

where a privileged few command power over a disadvantaged many. Today one can find instances of political agitation in which those with status are accused of being responsible for the inequalities that immigrants have brought with them. But in all public services, the youth organizations included, there is much concern with the bridging of East and West. There are some who think that not enough is being done, but few will deny that the merger of Europeans with Afro-Asians, many with dark skins, is one of the most challenging aspects of the Israeli effort. Special school programs exist for the disadvantaged. The proportion of pupils above normal age for their grade dropped from 37 percent in 1951/52 to 17 percent in 1966/67 (Central Bureau of Statistics, 1968: 535, Table T/14). Youth programs play a key role in this strategy for reaching the children of those who are poverty stricken. Furthermore, there is widespread satisfaction in the fact that inter-marriage between these two components is rising.[48]

The lower classes are less organization minded

No youth program excludes the lower classes. All make an effort and all succeed to a degree in reaching "the hard-to-reach." But as shown in Figure 20 adolescents from the less advantaged segment of the community were overrepresented among the nonjoiners. The highest intensity of coverage is in the Beyond School programs which reach more of the welfare population than all the other programs.

School drop-outs, even more than those who attend only evening classes, constitute a special challenge. Five percent of the working youths in our sample (who were not studying), were active members of youth movements. In contrast, of those enrolled in a high school, 21 percent were active members. Similarly, children whose fathers never attended school were more often nonjoiners and much less often youth movement activists

NON-PARTICIPATION IN YOUTH PROGRAMS
ADOLESCENTS IN HOLON—1965
(IN PERCENT)

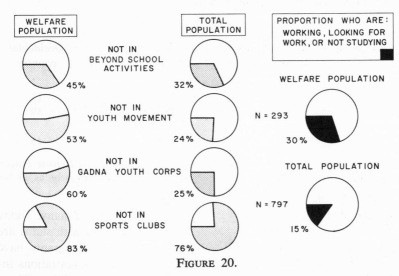

FIGURE 20.

than those whose fathers had some education (see Figure 21). In all societies, there is a tendency for class differences to be transmitted from generation to generation. The youth services of Israel represent one of several attempts to counteract this tendency.

YOUTH ORGANIZATION PARTICIPATION OF HOLON ADOLESCENTS IN 1965 BY FATHER'S EDUCATION

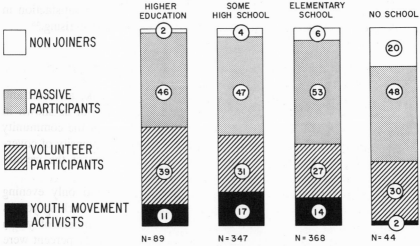

FIGURE 21.
(encircled figures are percentages)

Nonparticipation in the country's extensive network of youth services is related to a variety of other indices of underachievement and low status in the youth culture (see Table 20). A disproportionate number (69

TABLE 20

Achievement-Related Characteristics of Tenth Grade Adolescents and Their Relationship to Youth Organization Participation

(percentages)

| | YOUTH ORGANIZATION PARTICIPATION | | | |
Achievement related characteristics	Uninvolved[c] (N = 49)	Only in Beyond School program (N = 141)	Only in youth movement (N = 83)	Active in all three programs (N = 44)
Eighth grade failure score (below 69th percentile)[a]	76	37	21	14
Eighth grade success score (80th percentile or above)[a]	6	30	51	61
Low amiability index[b]	43	26	30	18
Youths much older than their class (18 years old or more)	10	2	None	None

a. Scores of the nationwide Sekker examination, administered in the eighth grade.
b. A composite of nonselection of several precoded questionnaire responses showing little interest in friends.
c. Belonged to none of the major youth programs, but five reported membership in a sports club.

percent) of the totally uninvolved are girls. This reflects the reluctance of traditionalist parents, who are much more often, but not exclusively from Afro-Asian countries, to let their adolescent daughters attend school or take part in peer group programs. Girls, more often than their brothers, are expected to remain close to home and help their parents. Irrespective of sex, underachievement and social isolation are most pronounced among the nonjoiners of youth programs.

Few will doubt the prediction that those untouched by the youth programs will later be among those who will be socially and economically disadvantaged. It is one of a web of interrelated symptoms of being unable to achieve in terms of prevailing social expectations. No amount of voluntaristic organizational effort can reach all adolescents, especially those of lower class origin whose families are not well integrated in the ongoing social system. Quite a few are active, nevertheless, if one considers the fact that many of the children in the Welfare department sample (Central Bureau of Statistics, 1968: 561, Table U/3) cannot take part in organized peer groups because they are chronically ill, mentally ill, mentally retarded or otherwise severely handicapped.[49] The hard-to-reach population who are not in school rank highest in the proportion who are unorganized (57 percent). Those attending school are being reached in larger numbers by the organized youth programs. Seventy-five percent were in a youth movement and in the Gadna Youth Corps. Sixty-three percent reported having been active in a Beyond School program and 17 percent were in a sports club. Even among those *not in school*, 43 percent are in some youth program and a noteworthy minority (25 percent of those responding to our questionnaire) reported having been in both the Gadna Youth Corps and the youth movements.

TABLE 21

Youth Program Participation of Holon Adolescents Known
to the Department of Welfare by School Attendance[a]

(percentages)

Youth organization participation	*Not in school*	*In school*
In no programs (N = 58)	57	43
In Beyond School programs only (N = 41)	37	63
Youth movements only[b] (N = 63)	30	70
Gadna only[b] (N = 34)	26	74
In both youth movements and Gadna[a] (N = 53)	25	75

a. There were 265 non-respondents to this question in the total of 514 adolescents.
b. Some are also enrolled in Beyond School programs.

Preferential treatment

Mass frustration is likely to arise when the channels of upward mobility are blocked by regulations or customs regarded as inequitable. The Israeli government does much to avoid such reactions, even resorting to discrimination-in-reverse (Eaton and Gilbert, 1969: 79–88). Being in the highest 20 percent of those taking the examination, a score of 80 (Norm A) is usually required to qualify for high school scholarship aid on the basis of the nationwide Sekker eighth-grade screening test. Children with parents from Islamic countries, however, will be accepted if their

score is 70. The importance of the policy is indicated by the fact that in
1961 two-thirds of the children of Afro-Asian families who reached high
school did so through preferential treatment because of the existence of
a "Norm B" entry route.

Even with this added help, among those finishing the fourth year of
high school in 1964 only 13 percent were of Afro-Asian origin, although
they represented 40 percent of the relevant age group. At the university
level, they comprised only about 5 percent of all the students. The "Norm
B" can open up a channel of educational mobility for "new Israel" youths
from the emerging countries. But it is not able to equalize the underlying
inequality in cultural conditioning and parental support between children
of the European and Afro-Asian origin. Preferential admission into high
schools does not guarantee graduation. Those who qualified on the basis
of Norm A were more than 3.5 times more likely to graduate than those
who had been admitted on a Norm B basis.[50]

TABLE 22

Follow-Up Study of Eighth Graders Who Passed
the 1957 Sekker Screening Test[a]

(percentages)

	Comprehensive screening test scores	
	Norm A	*Norm B*
School success level	*(Scores of 80 or more)*	*(Score of 70–79)*
Entrance into an academic high school	74	38
Graduation from high school	81	38
Earning matriculation certificates	76	21

a. Aryeh Rubinstein, "Norm B Trebles the Chance of High School for Deprived
   Child," *Jerusalem Post,* December 9, 1965: 5. No actual frequencies were given in
   the report cited.

The class lines in Israel are fluid. Social integration is more than just
a slogan. Young people who grow up in disadvantaged families are not
excluded from youth programs, but they appear to be less responsive to
the country's pioneering values. Few of the uninvolved made idealistic
choices in their attitude questions. This is evident if their answers are
compared to the idealism scores of activists in each of the youth programs
(see Tables 23 and 24). The differences are relative, not absolute. Even
among the organizationally uninvolved, 17 percent wanted to join the national service-oriented Nahal Pioneer Corps and 5 percent expressed the
hope of joining a kibbutz as shown in Table 24.

TABLE 23

Respondents Making No Idealistic Statements
in the Holon Adolescent Survey—1965

	Respondents making no idealistic statements	
Degree of activity	*Number*	*Percentage*
Never active in any of the programs	(49)	30
In community-center Beyond School programs[a]	(142)	18
In voluntary Gadna Youth Corps activities	(125)	16
In youth movement activities	(127)	7

a. Many Beyond School and Gadna Youth Corps programs are sponsored by a high school. The comparisons made here are therefore restricted to adolescents who expressed a clearly voluntary interest in these activities by enrollment in a community-centered Beyond School program or by participation in a Gadna club meeting after normal school hours.

TABLE 24

Idealistic Attitudes of Holon Adolescents and Their
Relationship to Participation in Youth Organizations

(percentages)

	YOUTH PROGRAM INVOLVEMENT			
Idealism indices	*Totally uninvolved* [a] (N = 49)	*Only in Beyond School program* (N = 83)	*Only in youth movement* (N = 83)	*Active in all three programs* (N = 44)
High idealism score	None	None	1	5
Hopes to join Kibbutz	5	5	26	26
Expects army deferment	44	12	10	7
Intends joining air force or parachute service	20	27	18 [a]	37 [a]
Intends joining Nahal Pioneer Service[a]	17	20	56 [a]	36 [a]

a. A good index of ideological commitment for youth movements. The youth movements prefer that members volunteer for Nahal service rather than any other branch.

The organizationally uninvolved were not only more detached ideologically, but also felt less self-confident. Nearly one in five of the uninvolved declined to make a self-estimate of their peer status, as compared
to less than 3 percent of those who were enrolled in Beyond School programs and even fewer among the youth movement members. Only 10
percent of the uninvolved thought they had leadership status among their
friends and that their "opinion was being respected." This finding must be
contrasted with leadership self-designations by 17 percent of those youths
who enrolled in a community center Beyond School program, 29 percent
who joined a youth movement before the age of 11, and 34 percent who
lived in a kibbutz.

Manpower utilization

In many public service fields, the most difficult cases are assigned to
the least qualified. For example, in the field of education, the most highly
trained teachers are hired by universities, where there also are the most
motivated students. Rural schools, where children often lack motivation
for serious study, are likely to have untrained teachers. In psychiatry, the
most qualified physicians tend to enter private practice. The sickest and
poorest patients have to go to a public mental hospital or a prison. Top-
flight professionals are not likely to be available to them there. No such
simple inverse relationship between the level of qualification and difficulty
of the job is to be found in Israeli youth work.

Leaders with a career commitment, who work for full time wages,
were highly likely to be working with groups in which Afro-Asian youths
represent over 80 percent of the membership (see Figure 22). Full-time
and more career minded leaders are not necessarily technically superior
than are the less career oriented youth leaders who may be working
temporarily on assignments made by a kibbutz or their political party. But
if one assumes that the allocation of personnel with a long range career
objective reflects deliberate organizational priorities, the tendency for
Israeli programs to assign the most professional youth leaders to the "hard-
to-reach" suggests how important youth programs are considered to be in
the country's strategy for reaching the difficult segments of the population.

The most active among the youth movements in the endeavor to reach
the hard-to-reach is the Noar Oved Velomed movement of the middle-class
Mapai Labor Party faction. With financial help from the Labor Federation
and the Labor Party, over 200 full-time youth workers are employed.
Nearly one-third (31 percent) were seven or more years older than their
members. This cadre of paid leaders represents definite evidence of
emerging professionalization. Fifteen percent had not even been members
of the movement when they were young.

There is a preference for hiring paid leaders who have completed high school, but many of the jobs have to be filled with those who did not. Special efforts are made to select those with a capacity to relate meaningfully to lower class youngsters. But the volunteers still tend to be better educated than the paid professionals. On the other hand, volunteers usually can invest only a limited amount of their energy in youth work. Some are unable to reach out to youths with a cultural background different from their own. Also, over three-fifths of the unpaid volunteers and kibbutz leaders were unsupervised. Full-time, part-time and army youth leaders,

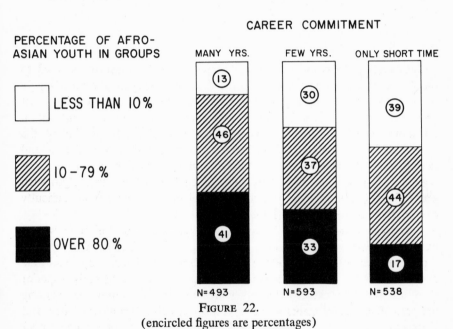

WHO GETS THE CAREER YOUTH LEADERS ?

FIGURE 22.
(encircled figures are percentages)

who were most often working with youngsters whose parents came from underdeveloped countries, were given more supervisory and administrative support than the youth leaders.

The heavily staffed and professionally supervised street club worker programs also address themselves to the hard-to-reach. Organizationally similar to those in the United States, these programs do more than reduce delinquent actions (Leissner, 1969). As much as possible, youngsters are encouraged to become an integral part in a socially approved youth service. In a small-scale experiment in a suburban slum near Tel Aviv, a youth leader seminar was conducted for adolescents from disadvantaged families. A young instructor assigned by the Ministry of Education was able to attract 25 teenagers who had dropped out of school. He could hold out the prospect of employment as an indigenous youth worker in the Municipal Youth Department after trainees completed their studies. This incentive proved strong enough to "change their attitude to their surroundings" (Levitas, 1966: 20).

A follow-up study of 97 delinquent boys who had been released from Tel Mond reformatory showed a relationship between youth organization of youth club membership ($r = 0.67$). "The longer the boy's membership, the higher his chances for success" (Shoham et al.: n.d.). Youth programs are probably more attractive to youngsters with much self-control to avoid new crimes than to those with weak superegos. But the youth-serving agencies have an effective delivery system of their values that may help to bring about a change in adjustment on the part of some of the reformatory alumni in the direction of conformity to social norms.

Conclusion

Territorial therapy can provide a geographic framework for resolving intergroup problems, but it will not make people equal in capacity, opportunity or class mobility. In Israel, immigration saved many Jews from persecution elsewhere, but residential change alone is no panacea. Many economic and psychological problems will stay with them. There are hard-to-reach families who require the bulk of the public welfare services. Their children are under-represented in peer group programs, which are intended to provide enrichment experience and do attract most middle class children. Such underrepresentation could lead to an intergenerational transmission of disadvantage.

In any study of a social program, one way of evaluating its impact is to examine its limits. Youth organizations want to serve the total population. The educationally marginal and the children of recent immigrants are not excluded. The question of how underprivileged young people will mature and what they will do with their lives and for their country are actually given priority. The disadvantaged are more likely to have a full-time and trained youth leader, who is administratively supervised, than is the average Israeli youngster. Nevertheless, lower class children are underrepresented in all programs.

Two alternate explanations of this underrepresentation are plausible. The participation gap suggests that *insufficient* effort is being expended for special programs and services to counteract the disadvantages from which lower class children suffer. Many theoretically promising youth programs in Israel are only experimental and for limited numbers, rather than countrywide. National income is always limited. Every welfare or youth program has to compete with other public priorities.

But even if youth work efforts were to be increased many times, it is highly likely that significant differences between advantaged and less advantaged children would remain. In a free society, parents exercise considerable authority over how their children are to be brought up. Their outlook and values will be transmitted to the next generation, at least in part. Youth program participation is much more likely among children whose parents were born in Europe, where patriarchal traditions are modified by child-centeredness than among the children of Afro-Asian families, some of whose parents oppose participation in youth programs.

Organizational devices and social mobility oriented welfare planning do not reach all of those who might benefit from them. Indeed, one of the consequences of being socially disadvantaged is that lack of self-confidence, parental support and other assets make it difficult to become involved in the socially approved youth culture programs. Although special efforts and preferential attention probably contribute much to the opening up of opportunities for youth program involvement to those who are brought up in disadvantaged families, they cannot be expected to wipe out, as rapidly as social planners might wish, cumulative differences in culturally transmitted skills useful in a competitive and achievement oriented modern society.

Social planning for the abolition of marginality and poverty must proceed from the fact that many people are positively identified with the perpetuation of cultural differences. They have an investment in cultural continuity as a basis for their ethnic identity, even if this means the encouragement of values that handicap their capacity to compete equitably in school, in youth organizations or in the job market. This inference is strongly suggested by the findings of an ex post facto experiment of American school children whose background is close to that of the population of Israel.

Gross (1967) found that in spite of many similarities, Jewish children, whose ancestral roots had been in Europe (*Ashkenazim*) out-performed the descendants of Jewish families of Syrian origin (*Sefardim*) on a variety of tests. The study involved data on school readiness of two well-matched groups of these ethnic subcultures in Brooklyn, New York. All data were collected by the same interviewer. All the mothers were native born. None of the children had major handicaps. All the families lived in the same neighborhood, and spoke English as their mother tongue. All of the families were tradition conscious, in that they preferred to incur the financial burden of sending their children to a parochial school, although a good public school was also located in the area.

A battery of tests was given to the children, including the Stanford-Binet, a nonverbal reasoning test and others. Their score differences, while not large, were consistently higher for the Ashkenazi children. As Seeley (1967: 4) points out: "What is clearly implied in these findings is both the virtually invisible persistence of cultural traditions ("ethnic differences") for very long periods even under ostensibly-like social conditions, and the depth to which such differences reach, right into something so profound in the ontogenetic process as "measured intelligence" or readiness for school—which comes close to readiness for eventual "successful participation in the society."

In Israel, where Sefardim are overrepresented among the slum dwellers, the new immigrants, the poor and the uneducated, a "cumulative deficit" hypothesis is often offered to account for differences between this Afro-Asian ethnic subgroup and the European Ashkenazim. As in the United States, the children of these groups do not participate in schools and youth programs in the same way. But since in the American study, the Jews of Syrian origin were no more deprived than those whose grandparents lived in a European ghetto, the theory is highly tenable that even if these ethnic subgroups achieve similar social class levels in Israel, some residual differences will remain, at least for a generation.

A society can open the doors to its members to take equal advantage of available means of social participation. But in their choice of what is the "good life" people will build on their cultural heritage to make choices in priority on how to participate in the larger society.

Chapter 12

Leadership

Peer group leaders

There are no legal prerequisites for being a parent. A license is needed to get married, but none is necessary to have children or to exercise parental rights. Being a youth leader is in the same category. Anyone so inclined can be a youth leader. He need only be acknowledged by a group. Leadership is a social role without a standardized set of behavior patterns. Expectations vary with each group and the circumstances in which they operate (Eaton, 1950: 616). But what leaders think and do has important consequences for the groups to which they are affiliated. Youth leaders mirror the culture of which they are a part and which they, in turn, influence.

Role uncertainty is common among adolescents. It is not surprising that nearly three-quarters of the youths in the Holon area sample characterized themselves as ordinary members of peer groups. In describing their own social status, they checked "my friends like me and are considerate of me, but I am not particularly important" or "I am an ordinary member of the group and am no different from the others." Very few designated

TABLE 25

Replies of Israeli Adolescents to the Question:
"What is your status among your friends?"

(percentages)

	Holon sample (N = 877)	Gadna youth leader trainees (N = 722)
Leaders[a]	14	24
Ordinary member	74	71
Few social ties	3	2
No answer	9	3

a. Youths self-defined as leaders answered the question by checking: "I have an important status among my friends and they consider my opinions."

TABLE 26

High Status Characteristics of Holon Youths by Self-Estimates of
Peer Group Standing—1965

(percentages)

		Self-estimates	
		Ordinary	Social
	Leaders	members	isolates
Characteristic	(N = 124)	(N = 655)	(N = 21)
Youth Program Participation			
Participation in four organized programs at some time in his life	48	41	19
Active Youth Movement member at the 10th grade level	19	13	4
Active in a Voluntary Gadna Program	25	17	None
Socioeconomic Status			
Spacious living quarters (less than two persons per room)	20	15	5
Father born in Europe	67	62	38
High socioeconomic level	32	23	16
Aspiration Level			
Plans to continue studies after 10th grade	52	45	32
Plans to attend a university	50	39	25
Definitely thinks he can achieve his goals	40	25	19
Achievement Indices			
High Comprehensive Examination (Sekker) score (80 or more)	41	28	33
National Service Orientation			
Plans to live in a kibbutz	9	8	None
Chose national service as *the most* important youth movement activity from many alternate choices	8	5	None

themselves as social isolates by checking: "I don't like groups of people" or "I stay away from groups of people and from friends." But one in seven (14 percent) thought they had leadership standing among their friends (see Table 25).

These self-defined leaders (61 percent of whom were male) often had their confidence reinforced by social status. Most of them had friends of both sexes. They ranked above average in socioeconomic status, aspiration level, school achievement, participation in organized youth programs and readiness for national service. Self-designated leaders were more active organizationally than those who viewed themselves as ordinary members. The Gadna youth leadership training courses enrolled a relatively high proportion of self-defined leaders (24 percent), when compared to the general prevalence of such peer group leaders in the Holon area sample.

The differences between leaders and ordinary members were moderate but consistent. But both were very dissimilar to those few who had characterized themselves as social isolates. Of the latter, only five percent lived in spacious homes, one-third of the proportion in the population as a whole. None wanted to live in a kibbutz. On all other indices, the social isolates were highly disadvantaged (see Table 26).

The advantaged and well endowed are overrepresented among the self-defined leaders. But one out of four did poorly in school, never belonged to a Beyond School program and came from an Afro-Asian family.

Role expectations

There are well-institutionalized roles for achieving formal leadership status within ready reach of young people. Leaders are usually selected by adults from a pool of eligible adolescents. As leaders they serve many functions, including those of a teacher, friend, disciplinarian and social worker. In each case there are personal variations in style within patterns of organizational preferences for what is expected.

In the youth movements, leaders are expected to serve as an ideological and moral example rather than to enforce their will by outright command. Command roles are more acceptable in the Gadna Youth Corps. In the Beyond School program, being an educator is paramount. The focus is on serving the needs of the group and on teaching skills rather than on leading a peer group. Technical standards vary considerably. The Gadna Youth Corps requires military experience. Beyond School programs hire persons skilled in carpentry to lead a technical club or in music to direct a choir.

Charismatic persons are preferred (when they can be found) to fit the role model of being a Madrih, the Hebrew word for youth worker. He should be able to guide rather than command. The Madrih is expected to act more like an older brother or sister than like an authority figure. He must be able to attract new members by virtue of his personality and retain the loyalty of those who are already active. He should be capable of understanding psychological issues so that members will be ready to discuss personal problems with him (Israeli, 1965: 7–18).

Youth leaders vary in readiness to let the group decide controversial issues. In the socialist Hashomer Hatzair youth movement, a large proportion favored a group decision about how to handle a hiker who has violated the discipline of water rationing. This is an important lesson in Israel where young people are expected to learn how to live in the desert. Even among Gadna leaders who direct a paramilitary program, there were as many as among the voluntaristic Scouts who were willing to have the group decide how discipline should be enforced (see Table 27).

TABLE 27

Youth Leaders' Answers to Question:
"Should a Youngster Be Left Thirsty if He Prematurely Drank All the Water Ration?" By Youth Organization

(percentages)

Organization	Number leaders	Leave the decision to the group	Yes—Leave member thirsty to teach him lesson	Other decisions
Gadna Army	⎱(410)	21	21	67
Gadna Ministry of Education	⎰	18	21	61
Beyond School Program	(569)	33	12	55
Hashomer Hatzair (Socialists)	(74)	41	4	55
B'nai Akiba (religious youth movement)	(196)	25	41	34
Scouts	(114)	18	27	55
Noar Oved Velomed	(536)	28	15	57

The role expectations of a Madrih appear in clear contrast to those of a teacher. Although both are expected to influence young people, teaching is a profession, while youth leadership is a calling. Madrihim can be volunteers. They can start work without passing a course of training, nor do they need a certificate. Teachers must complete formally designated training programs before they are eligible to do their work, except under emergency conditions. The volunteer Madrih can rise to the top of his program on the basis of experience and his ideological identification with the movement's objectives. Even when youth leaders are paid, they regard the job most often as a transitional one whereas teaching is thought to be a lifetime occupation.

Perhaps most distinctive of all is the difference between them in their enforcement of authority. Teachers are appointed authority figures whose powers are reinforced by the administrative hierarchy of the school system. Youth leaders, by contrast, are expected to rely for their power primarily on persuasion and charisma (see Table 28).

TABLE 28

Comparison of Teachers and Youth Leaders

Characteristics	Teacher	Youth leader
Requirements for Practice	State Board certification	Volunteer or hired on basis of each agency's standards
Educational Requirements	Formal, technical	Ideological, informal, highly variable
Age Requirements	Open to adults only	Open to youths and young adults
Source of Authority	Legal	Charismatic
Enforcement Techniques	Voluntary compliance or legal coercion under school law	Voluntary compliance or threat of expulsion, no legal powers
Pay	According to professional standards	Work often is voluntary. If paid, a reimbursement often is nominal, barely enough to meet expenses[a]
Career Possibilities	Lifetime career	Transitional career

a. This is not true of professionals employed as technical specialists or administrators. They earn pay at professional salary scales.

There is overlapping in this dichotomy. Progressive schools demand that their teachers act like youth leaders. Even in the Gadna there are leaders, many of them women, who act more like youth movement leaders than army officers.

While youth workers of different programs function within a variety of administrative settings, their respective organizational expectations are filtered through a common prism: youth movement experience. Only a minority, even fewer than in the general population, report no experience in youth movements (see Table 29).

TABLE 29

Youth Leaders Not Reporting
Prior Youth Movement Participation

(percentages)

Leaders	Number	Never a member
Youth Movements leaders	1060	3
Gadna Squad Leaders (Makim)	721	18
Gadna Teachers (Ministry Education)	410	11
Gadna Leaders (Army)		23
Beyond School Program leaders	596	16

Volunteering

Youth movements were established by self-selected volunteers. Each in turn recruited younger members, also volunteers, who were ready to lead peer groups. University students and young adults, at the threshhold of starting their own families, form the core. They rely on youths in the 16 to 18 year old age range. And whenever possible, they recruit still younger boys and girls as leadership trainees. This pyramid structure now, as before, remains the model of the youth movements. Training begins in the year or the summer before responsibility for a group is assigned. Anyone who wants to try is likely to be welcome, unless his personal conduct or belief system is at variance with the principles of the youth movement.

Youth movement leadership serves a double function. The hoped-for outcome is a more enthusiastic member and someone who can inspire younger peers. Leadership is an esteemed role, the exercise of which will provide much personal challenge to someone finishing the eighth grade or in the first year of high school. Organizational stability and a degree of predictability are provided by a small number of full time organizers who generally serve for a few years. Their support, often at no more than a subsistence level, is underwritten by a political party, a kibbutz movement and contributions from interested older persons, many of whom were youth movement members.

Youth movement leadership offers the opportunity to a minority of activists and enthusiasts to identify with an esteemed social role (Coleman, 1965: 171–175). The choice requires a personal assessment of priorities by each youngster. Organizational leadership requires ten to twenty hours a week, time which must be found from the routine of schoolwork and family obligations. On many a Tuesday or Friday evening, the leader has to prepare a program for presentation to younger members. On Saturday morning he often must attend a training session.

In the youth movements, more than priorities regarding the utilization of leisure time is involved. An increasingly firm commitment regarding one's personal conduct is expected. The majority of youths in Israel, as elsewhere, wish to test out alternatives, including being part of a self-selected social clique. No youth movement leader could openly attend a modern party, like the one described below, without criticism by his organization.[51]

> A total of 25 kids were in a room, boys mostly on one side. Songs played on a record player could be split into three categories: American new pop, like the Rolling Stones, Old Pop, like Elvis Presley and French singers and folkish pop. Although I was told there were three couples among the 25 who were present, this was not apparent. They did nothing but dance all evening.

Persistent interest in such "salon group" activities would result in expulsion. The most puritan are the Socialist Hashomer Hatzair. Twenty-one percent of their leaders would ask a member to leave if he belonged to a popular dance club. The Scouts would request resignation 17 percent of the time; and 14 percent in the religious B'nai Akiva. The Noar Oved Velomed, the country's largest youth movement, is more ready to accept popular culture. Only 7.5 percent of its leaders would eject a member, but none of them said they would encourage membership in a dance club.

Volunteer leaders are a screened residual of the much larger group who at one time were youth movement members. They view themselves as elite and they are so regarded by many people, including some of their friends who left the youth movements with ambivalence. But the majority of the country's youths seek out other channels for achievement. They want different social role experiences, with more emphasis on the popular culture, commercial recreation and participation in social cliques. Also among the non-leaders are some youth movement loyalists who are too shy or who are too interested in their schoolwork, hobbies, or sports to have time for carrying organizational responsibilities.

Volunteer leaders are an answer to any program that must operate on a tight budget. But they have their price. They tend to be independent. Their readiness to serve free of charge usually means that they have convictions about what they are doing. This makes them unrewarding targets for bureaucratic controls. To dismiss them is hard. Two-thirds of the volunteer youth leaders and those assigned to such a function by their kibbutz reported themselves to be without supervision (see Figure 23). The resulting casualness in function makes it difficult to enforce good technical standards. Many resignations from youth movements were explained by the respondents to be the result of boredom and lack of effective

ABSENCE OF SUPERVISION OF YOUTH LEADERS BY
RECRUITMENT CHANNEL

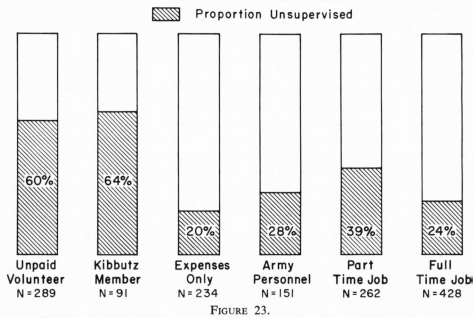

FIGURE 23.

leadership. But the youth movements would also lose an important attribute
if they adopted the controlled, more professional and better supervised
staff pattern of the Beyond School and Gadna programs.

In both the Beyond School and the Gadna programs, instructors are
appointed and paid by the Ministry of Education or the army. But volunteers are used as Gadna squad leaders after completing a training course.
Many of them rely on youth movement patterns of group leadership which
has an impact on Gadna, in spite of its paramilitary function. Observation
of squads in the field show a consistent picture of a preference for discipline by co-optation rather than command. Youth movement activists
were overrepresented among those selected for Gadna leadership training
course.

Co-optative conformity

No youth organization can tolerate leaders who oppose its expectations. Program materials are prescribed and basic materials are prepared
on a countrywide basis. Many policies set down centrally can be changed
only after much deliberation at the national level. But youth leaders have
a less precise curriculum than teachers. In schools, teachers can be assessed
by how well their students perform in nationally administered final examinations. But in youth organizations, styles of leadership can and do vary

considerably. The sense of humor, the capacity to sing, intellectual interests and the many other qualities that make up the social character of each person are at least as relevant as technical skill. Many youth leaders exercise a good deal of operational autonomy. This flexibility is reinforced by the power of leaders to resign without much, if any, loss of status. Organizational discipline from above is, therefore, maintained largely by means of co-optation.

The process can best be described by the concept of *co-optative conformity*. If there is little organized anti-adult rebellion in Israel, it may have much to do with this way of relating youth programs to the youth culture. Co-optative conformity guarantees organizational continuity and predictability without preventing changes from being introduced by those actually performing youth leadership roles. There is room for innovation, variation and non-compliance with the expectations of central headquarters, even in the paid leaderships post of the Gadna and the Beyond School programs.

Israel is a multiparty state where the arts of compromise and coalition are highly developed. The government relies a good deal on co-optation of diverse interest groups. In such a setting, a national youth "kommissar" would be unthinkable. This flexibility is further facilitated by the high turnover of youth leaders. Most volunteers work part-time; two-thirds of them work for fewer than ten hours a week. Especially in the youth movements, a volunteer leader rarely does the kind of career planning that turns so many professionals into organization men, who think first and foremost of how to please their supervisors and fellow employees, and less and less about their constituency.

Even less common is the rebellious leader who wants to ignore program guidelines, reject official training programs and introduce radical changes. The youth programs are sufficiently well controlled to make it difficult for a youngster to achieve a leadership post without showing a readiness to accept a co-optative relationship to his movement. Many fanatics were reported to have been among the youth leaders in pre-independence days. They defied parents and other authority figures to enter a clandestine program. Such persons are not now welcome in any of the larger youth organizations. Youth leaders in charge of a local program can innovate, provided they do not support highly controversial causes or run so "tight" a shop for their subordinates that suggestions or innovations from lower echelons are squelched.

The most bureaucratic outlook was observed among career youth workers. They held such posts as community center director, training school teacher, or civil service jobs in the government, the Jewish Agency, or a municipal youth department. As career officials, they were under pressure to maintain stable and long-range personal relationships throughout the establishment in order to get their work done. They have their annual fights for a budget. They want to earn an occasional promotion. But the very nature of youth work keeps even those professionalized structures from becoming too rigid. The consumers of services are adolescents who can react to dissatisfactions by resigning. Career youth workers also are dependent for help on volunteers and many temporary leaders who think of their work as transitional. This fact accounts for a good deal of careless preparation and underinvestment on the part of some youth workers. But it also helps to keep the whole field fluid, relatively informal and resistant to centralized control.

Informal training

A social role as flexible as youth leadership cannot have well-defined qualifications and still utilize untrained volunteers within the same organizational framework. Formal study, other than on-the-job instruction, is not now a requirement. But there is an increasing disposition to view role training as useful.

The most informal training programs are those of the youth movements. In most larger localities high school age members begin to serve as leaders on an apprenticeship basis. "They learn, or teach each other such skills as folk dancing, camping, scouting, games, singing, story telling, giving lectures (or what they call leading a discussion), crafts and the like" (Israeli, 1965: 72). The Scouts have regular Saturday morning sessions. In the socialist youth movement, all first year high school students are exposed to the course. In the nationalist Betar, training is limited to those who pass tests at the end of the elementary school. All movements conduct weekend vacation and summer courses. Nearly anyone attending a high school can participate in the training sessions and then test out his capabilities in practice as a Madrih.

Most of the in-service training is done by non-professionals, older leaders who once went through such a course when they were 13 to 15 years of age. This is supplemented by special lectures by the local head leader or members of the national executive. It is also customary for V.I.P.'s—the Prime Minister, members of parliament, professors and other famous personalities—to lecture to such groups. Their presence helps symbolize the status which youth movements wish to ascribe to their leaders.

Training must be brief—a matter of days or weeks. Volunteer leaders do not have much time. Forty-one percent of those who intend to serve for many years have only had an in-service training course, 17 percent were untrained (see Figure 24). In the three large cities—Jerusalem, Tel Aviv and Haifa—the Jewish Agency has for years financed an office with a small library and a mimeograph machine. These offices are directed by mature youth leaders whose duty is to assist leaders in all of the youth

INTENSITY OF YOUTH LEADERSHIP TRAINING BY CAREER COMMITMENT

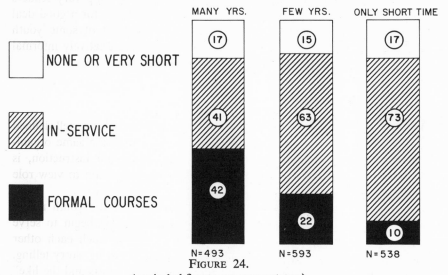

FIGURE 24.

(encircled figures are percentages)

movements in preparing their programs, irrespective of party ideology. They hold weekly seminars for senior leaders.

Each movement publishes a journal, for which members can write program material on such varied topics as Jewish and Israeli history, the movement's ideology, kibbutz life, important personalities, Jewish holidays, literature, ethics, nature study and administration information (e.g., the collection of membership fees, group diaries and reports). These and other techniques are designed to enable the young Madrih to attract and hold a group of younger members.

Leadership role training can be an important educational and maturation experience. As the childhood begins to end, adolescents can be part of an organization where the assumption exists that they must care for others, younger than themselves. They study leadership in small local groups of peers. On special occasions, they can participate in a meeting with older leaders who are finishing high school or have been released from the army.

Formal training

The tradition of voluntarism in youth work has been so strong that for many decades there was no professional training. Apprenticeship is now viewed less and less as sufficient preparation especially for persons responsible for administration and teaching. As youth programs have grown in size and importance, officials concerned with the staffing of youth organizations wish to upgrade the level of technical skills and their own professional standing. Salaries are being raised. Minimum educational qualifications are being introduced, along with formal training sequences for employees who administer youth centers, prepare budgets, deal with parents and supervise volunteer leaders. Professionalization is affecting the youth movements, but much less than the Gadna Youth Corps and the Beyond School programs.

Nundi Israeli's survey of training programs in 1965 showed that all of them offer diversified enrichment education. One such program is a three and one-half month training program conducted by one of the kibbutz movements for those of its young members who are selected to "give a year" to youth leadership outside of the kibbutz, after they complete their army service. The leadership assignment comes on top of three years of full-time army service, required of all Israeli boys since the Six Day War and thus extends the national service to four years. While this extra year forces a postponement of other vocational plans, it is not without benefits for the leader. It broadens his knowledge base, his ideological sophistication, his social skills and his capacity to influence younger persons. The following material (adapted from Israeli, 1965: 74) is included in the course:

(1) Israeli Society: Sessions on class and cultural groups and their development; Israeli youth; the school and programs of education; the Arabs in the state; the Israeli Army and national security; immigration absorption and integration; Israel's system of government; religious institutions and their role; and the economy of Israel.

(2) The Kibbutz: The *Weltanschauung* of the person living in a kibbutz; the kibbutz in the state; the kibbutz as a goal for youth; community life in the kibbutz; and child rearing practices in the kibbutz.

(3) Youth Movement: The youth movement as meeting the needs of youth; the history of the youth movements in Israel; institutionalization and the youth movement education for kibbutz; youth movements sexual education; and youth in high school.

(4) Literature and Art: The crisis of man in modern society from a literary perspective; the literature and poetry of the younger generation; Buber and his teachings; literature as an educational tool; and the arts as an educational tool.

(5) Programming: Training objectives; the movement camp; operating the center; the younger groups; the role and image of the Madrih; working in new immigrant areas; talks with graduates of youth movements; talks with children reared in kibbutzim; and Research.

(6) Methods: Group dynamics; methodolgy and didactics; and movement songs, culture, decoration and handicrafts.

Growing dissatisfaction with the absence of professional standards led to the appointment of a parliamentary commission headed by Aharon Yadlin, a young member of Parliament and a kibbutz member, who is now the deputy minister of education. He has an ideological commitment to youth movements as a means for inspiring young people. In a report issued in August 1962 (reported in Israeli, 1965), this commission recommended the adoption of a three-level civil service classification system. The certificates for each level would be issued by the Ministry of Education and Culture (Israeli, 1965: 105). The system would apply to all professional youth leaders hired for pay by youth movements, the Beyond School programs and the Gadna Department of the Ministry of Education. The three levels are:

(1) Beginner Level: A youth leader who has graduated from a basic leadership training course or has the equivalent scholastic training and experience.

(2) Experienced Leader: A beginner becomes an experienced youth leader after he has at least one year of experience. He must also advance academically from the minimum level of two years of high school and be recommended for promotion by the agency which employs him.

(3) Certified Leader: A leader is certified when he has at least two years of working experience, has been asked to stay in his job, and has successfully completed his high school matriculation examinations or a special examination for advanced youth leaders. Certification can also be obtained by graduating from a special course organized for this purpose.

This classification system has been adopted in principle. Its objective is to recruit more youth leaders who are ready to make a career commitment to youth work. But this civil service reform does not resolve the dilemma expressed in the following questions: How far can one go in formalizing an informal program, without transforming it into just another career program? Can youth movements retain their flexibility and peer group autonomy if technical criteria are adopted that would constitute a barrier to the recruitment of volunteer leaders? Are the youth programs at the threshold of bureaucratization—with more directiveness and less co-optation?

An emerging profession?

Reliance on volunteer leaders has become difficult, ever since compulsory military service at age 18 was introduced. The army cooperates somewhat to reduce this leadership drain by releasing about 10 percent of all Nahal personnel to their respective youth movements to serve as full-time leaders. However, their number is insufficient to meet the increasing demand for youth services. Youth leadership is in a transitional phase.

This led to efforts to attract career youth leaders. Schools and institutes have been established to train them, often while being paid, by the Rutenberg Foundation in Haifa, the Jewish Agency, the Municipality of Tel Aviv, the larger youth movements, Gadna, Youth Aliyah, and the Ministry of Education. Courses range from three months to two years. Their resources are limited and there is little specialization. They tend to be an improvised form of in-service training. There is usually a full-time administrator with a largely part-time faculty. Teaching materials have to be borrowed and adapted; few texts written for the training courses. Students are issued a certificate upon completion but credits cannot be applied to any university level program or even be transferred from one to the other certificate program, although there is much overlap in what is being taught. The courses tend to be at one of three levels: basic, advanced and post-graduate.

Basic training: Consists of full-time courses that last from three months to one year. They are conducted by special institutes set up for this purpose by the army Gadna, the city of Tel Aviv (Machon L'Hadracha), the Labor Federation (Beth Berl), the Rutenberg Foundation in Haifa (Beth Rutenberg) and others. Candidates can be admitted without being high school graduates. Indeed, at times they were admitted with as little as ten years of formal schooling. Upon graduation, they are certified as youth leaders, eligible for beginner-level responsibilities.

Advanced training courses require a two-year period of study, part of which is devoted to field practice. Candidates are sometimes recruited without their having finished high school, but admission standards are now approaching this minimum level, as the available number of applicants increases. Upon completion of this course, the candidates become professional youth leaders, eligible for higher pay and greater administrative responsibility than those who took only a basic course.

Post-Graduate Youth Work: In 1966 the School of Education at the University of Tel Aviv began to provide training for ten youth workers a year, to serve as teachers and high-level administrators. They are carefully screened from a large pool of applicants. The minimum requirement is graduation from of a university and a diploma from a part-time extension course.

Career Problems: All training programs tend to be classroom centered. There is almost no supervised field practice. After six months of study in the youth leader seminar in Tel Aviv, nineteen to twenty-two year old men and women are often given difficult assignments to develop programs in isolated immigrant centers. Their administrative supervisors are not accessible for day-to-day consultation. Being a youth leader requires availability during evenings, weekends and vacations. Some of the young leaders simply cannot cope with the difficulties on their first job. Personnel turnover is considerable. Only one-third of the student leaders in 1965 expected to work in the field for "many years," i.e., more than two years.

CAREER COMMITMENT AND WORK SATISFACTION
OF ISRAELI YOUTH LEADERS

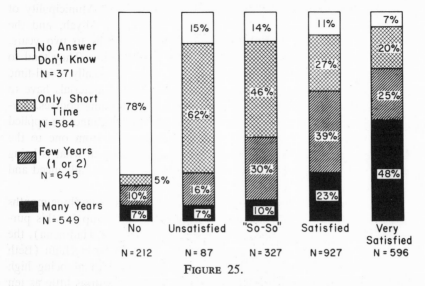

FIGURE 25.

The leadership training programs, irrespective of their level, address themselves to a number of common manpower-planning issues. There is a chronic shortage of qualified personnel. Career lines are just beginning to develop.

In the past, youth leader seminars were largely composed of candidates with academic credentials insufficient to qualify them for teacher education. This had the effect of turning leadership courses into an opportunity for personable and socially skilled youths who failed to complete high school. The courses provided are a *second chance* to enter a professional field. Steps have recently been taken by the government to set up multi-professional leadership training courses, in conjunction with teaching and social work. Such courses would make it easier for the youth leaders to do additional academic work and acquire qualifications to enter closely related fields. Many of the qualified volunteer leaders are not interested in full time youth leadership training. They prefer to prepare for entry into better established professional fields. There is a relationship between work satisfaction and career commitment, but even among the most satisfied youth leaders, not quite half expect to remain in this field for "many years" (see Figure 25). About three in ten of the leaders reported themselves as not too satisfied with their work. It is probably fortunate for the field that few of these malcontents, less than 10 percent, plan to make their career in the field of youth leadership.

It stands to reason that an occupation with only middle range status and modest economic rewards would have to rely considerably on psychic and prestige satisfaction to recruit and to retain their cadre of committed leaders. Not quite a third think they will stay in the field for more than a year or two even among the students enrolled in formal training courses. As shown in Figure 26 less than half (43 percent) of those who are organ-

CAREER INTENTION OF YOUTH LEADERS BY
LEVEL OF RESPONSIBILITY

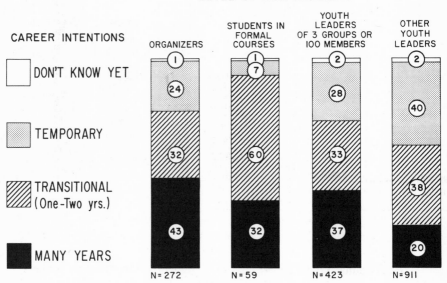

FIGURE 26.
(encircled figures are percentages)

izers are thinking of remaining in the field for "many years." There are persons who are committed to a career in the field, but the supply is far from sufficient to endow the vocation of youth leaders with careerist values of most other occupations. There is much room for upward mobility for youth leaders who are willing to stay in this field.

How much professionalization?

The transition of youth work from an avocation by volunteers to a transitional career is occurring most rapidly in the Beyond School programs. These programs are almost totally staffed by paid employees, selected largely on the basis of their technical proficiency. Steps in a career ladder have been identified. After an initial period as a direct group leader, workers can look forward to becoming program supervisors, teachers of untrained personnel and managers of youth centers. At a national level, they can look forward to an appointment as district supervisor, local program director or to a headquarters post in Jerusalem. Differences among the major youth programs in the degree of their preference for volunteer paid personnel are shown in Figure 27.

PROPORTION OF VOLUNTEER YOUTH LEADERS
■ Unpaid Volunteers or Expenses Only

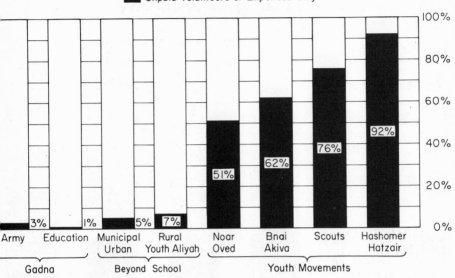

FIGURE 27.

Few Gadna Youth Corps leaders, assigned to their role as soldiers, are career minded. Most of them view their job as transitional. Some feel that they are volunteers although they receive army pay. The job will yield to different occupations after army discharge. Even many of the Ministry of Education Gadna teachers serve in their posts only while preparing themselves for what they regard as a more permanent career.

Personnel planning has to be done in terms of the following contradictory organizational realities. If there is too little professionalization, youth programs cannot maintain their present impact on the youth culture, let alone increase numerically. If there is too much professionalization, the youth programs will become like the schools. The balance between formality and informality, administrative leadership and freedom from bureaucratic control, responsible adult guidance and opportunities for adolescents to be influential has to be maintained. The issue is dramatized by two generalizations:

(1) Professionals have more staying power than volunteers. Professionals tend to move into the important posts in any organization where a large proportion of youth workers see their jobs as temporary

(2) As youth leaders get older they have increasing difficulty in interacting with young people as peers. Age leads to social distance. Many senior

youth leaders wish to exercise more control and rely less on co-optation of peer groups.

The degree of professionalization is reflected by the age difference between leaders and members. In the puritanical socialist Hashomer Hatzair, where most leaders are volunteers, only 10 percent of the leaders were seven or more years older than their groups. Thirty-one percent were older by the same number of years in the Noar Oved Velomed, the youth movement of the labor party that leads the government. This movement sends paid leaders into slums and development towns where not enough volunteers can be recruited. In the youth movements, the model hero is and remains the volunteer leader. The proportion of personnel receiving pay is increasing, but many of them work for a bare subsistence wage. They see themselves as giving a public service and are not interested in a career in youth work. Their chief reward is recognition by their peers that the "movement" is being served and that the country as a whole is benefiting.

Youth work as an opportunity structure

There are under-achievers in every society. Their potentialities are not realized, often because of discrepancies between academic preparation and formal requirements for entry into a position. Many kibbutz high schools, although of excellent quality, deliberately avoid preparing students for entry into a university. The parental generation wants their children to remain in a kibbutz. Some parents feel that a university education would tempt their children to choose a professional career that could not be practiced effectively in a kibbutz. There are bright immigrant children who arrived in Israel too late to finish high school. In many an Afro-Asian family, parents do little to reinforce their children's upward mobility strivings through encouragement to complete a proper high school course.

It is for such under-achievers that the youth work structure represents welcome opportunity for entry into a semiprofessional field. In these posts, having kibbutz experience is a functional asset. Youths of Afro-Asian families, even if they lack some of the desired formal education, have a communication advantage, especially with children from their own subculture. Afro-Asian adolescents are under-represented among the youth leaders, but active efforts are being made to recruit them. They represent about one third of the older youth leaders who are nearly always paid (see Table 30).

The under-representation of Afro-Asian youths is most pronounced among the Army Gadna leaders. They can be selected from a large manpower pool of draftees, including many highly qualified youth movement leaders. In contrast, the Beyond School programs and the Gadna Department of the Ministry of Education must hire youth workers in the open labor market, but can offer prospective employees not more than moderate

TABLE 30

Youth Leaders in Israel of
Afro-Asian Origin[a]
(percentages)

Youth program	Number	Young leaders under 20 (N = 586)	Older leaders 20+ (N = 1453)	Percent of all leaders (N = 2039)
Noar Oved Velomed	(536)	10	33	24
All other youth movements	(524)	17	28	26
Beyond School Programs	(569)	37	37	37
Army Gadna Instructors		15	22	19
Ministry of Education Gadna Instructors	(410)	—	36	36

a. Father born in North Africa, Iraq, Iran, Yemen, Aden or other Asian countries.

pay and little chance for advancement. They draw largely on young people who may be socially quite skilled but are not academically qualified and are therefore likely to be attracted to these jobs for lack of alternative career routes.

Idealistic issues

Youth leaders, more than teachers, are free to speak out on controversial issues. On those ideological questions for which attitudinal responses were solicited, there were great variations within each category of leaders. This was true in the area of militarism versus developmental piorities, the virtue of economic efficiency, kibbutz residence and what demands a state may legitimately make in order to get nationally important tasks performed.

Military versus Developmental Priorities: Youth leaders are less militaristic in their outlook than they perceive the public to be. Two-thirds think that the public ranks the role of army commander as more important than other youth work occupations. In their own choices, youth leaders had more developmental oriented priorities. Forty-five percent ranked teaching in the Negev frontier area above all other youth work alternatives. Social workers and army commanders were ranked about equal, but both were considered to be more important than youth movement leaders or youth center directors. Gadna leadership was universally viewed to be the least important. Less than 1 percent of all leaders, including those employed by Gadna were willing to designate this role as the most important (see Figure 28).

Efficiency versus Labor Norms: Few youth leaders would oppose efficiency as an abstract goal. Economic development is an objective of the Zionist movement. The welfare of the citizenry and of immigrants yet to

COMPARISON BY YOUTH LEADERS OF OWN
AND PUBLIC PREFERENCE FOR "MOST IMPORTANT"
OF SIX YOUTH WORK OCCUPATIONS

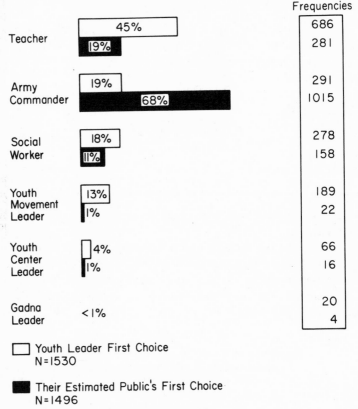

FIGURE 28.

come is dependent on how much is done to make optimum use of the country's resources. Yet a significant minority (18 to 45 percent) would recommend reducing productivity to conform to group standards or to prevailing labor practices, as is evident from their responses to the following question (see Table 31):

> "One of your friends is a very good worker; he is capable of producing more than the average. Some fellow workers resent this, especially since the management is demanding similar performance from them. What would you advise your friend to do?"

The most radical of the socialist youth organizations, the Hashomer Hatzair and Dror were least compliant with group norms. More than any other category of youth leaders, they advocated the moral virtue of work to the best of one's ability. The less socialistically inclined were less imbued

TABLE 31

Readiness to Slow Down Productivity in Response to Work
Norms of Israeli Youth Organization Leaders

(percentages)

Youth organizations	Number	Advice to slow down productivity[a]
Hashomer Hatzair and Dror Socialists	100	18
Scouts	114	22
Gadna Education	a	26
Noar Oved Velomed	577	29
Nationalist Betar Youths	46	37
Gadna Army	a	39
Religious B'nai Akiva	196	45

a. N is large in both categories; total for both is 410.

with values of efficiency and were ready to accept work group policies to
limit productivity.

Pioneering: In the socialist youth movements, more than a majority
of the younger leaders say they plan to join a kibbutz. The Gadna and
Beyond School programs do not stress pioneering. But preferences for
living in a kibbutz were expressed even by a significant minority among
their leaders (see Table 32).

TABLE 32

Proportion of Youth Leaders Planning to Join a
Kibbutz by Age and Youth Program

(percentages)

Youth programs	Number	Youth leaders under 20 (N = 586)	Older Leaders over 20 (N = 1422)
Hashomer Hatzair and Dror	(150)	75	67
Noar Oved Velomed	(574)	70	46
Rural Beyond School program	(222)	38	42
Scouts	(144)	36	28
B'nai Akiva	(223)	17	17
Gadna Army	} (410)	16	13
Gadna Education		None under 20	6
Urban Beyond School program	(285)	6	1

In reviewing the table, the following findings need to be noted: The
interest in joining a kibbutz declines with age. In general, somewhat fewer
leaders over the age of 20 were thinking of joining a kibbutz than those

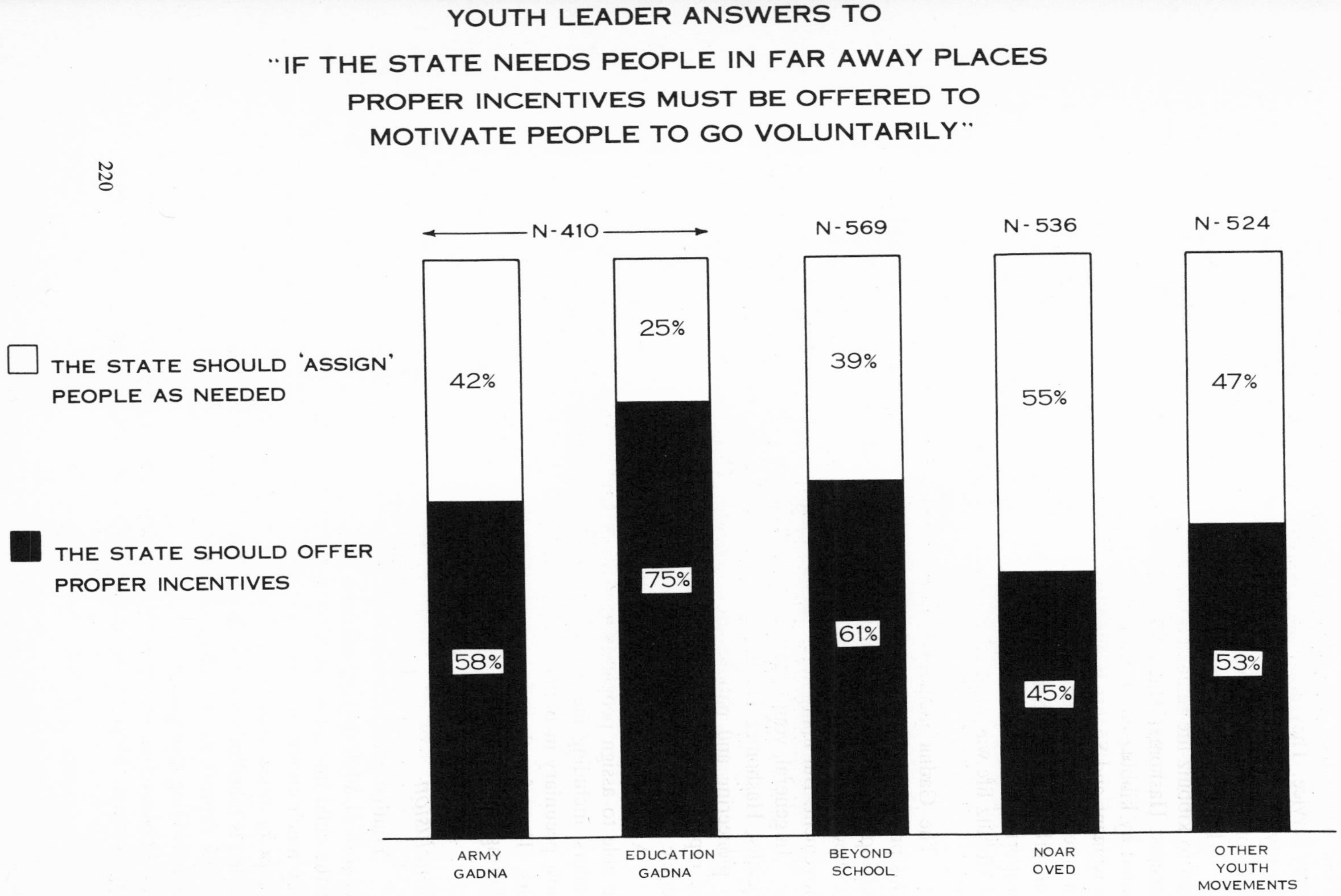

YOUTH LEADER ANSWERS TO

"IF THE STATE NEEDS PEOPLE IN FAR AWAY PLACES
PROPER INCENTIVES MUST BE OFFERED TO
MOTIVATE PEOPLE TO GO VOLUNTARILY"

N - 524   47%   53%   OTHER YOUTH MOVEMENTS

N - 536   55%   45%   NOAR OVED

N - 569   39%   61%   BEYOND SCHOOL

N - 410   25%   75%   EDUCATION GADNA

42%   58%   ARMY GADNA

☐ THE STATE SHOULD 'ASSIGN' PEOPLE AS NEEDED

■ THE STATE SHOULD OFFER PROPER INCENTIVES

FIGURE 29.

under the age of 20. As young adults, they are close to making a decision about where they will actually live. Most of them have completed their army service. They are ready for marriage, if not already married. Some already served in a Nahal unit and decided against kibbutz living on the basis of having tried this way of life.

The ranking of different youth programs on the basis of their orientation to kibbutz life remained the same, irrespective of age. The puritanical socialist Hashomer Hatzair and Dror youth movements are clearly dominated by kibbutz enthusiasts. The Noar Oved Velomed Labor party youth movement and Scouts include many nonkibbutz oriented leaders. There is an interesting difference in kibbutz outlook between employees in rural and urban Beyond School programs. Those in rural areas include a high proportion of persons already living in a kibbutz. In urban areas, the idea of kibbutz life was rejected by practically all of the leaders over the age of 20.

The Gadna includes a minority of kibbutz oriented youth leaders. This probably reflects the army's personnel selection policy. Kibbutz membership is almost irrelevant in the selection of Gadna leaders. They need to show interest in teaching and/or past active involvement in a youth movement. But many other variables are also given weight.[52]

In general, youth movement leaders, especially those in the puritanical socialist Hashomer Hatzair and Dror are most often favorably disposed to pioneering and national development. This inference is reinforced by the replies of youth leaders to the question: "What should the state do if people are needed in far away locations?"

A majority of Noar Oved Velomed leaders thought the state should be able to assign people as needed. A sizable minority of all other youth leaders, including the Army Gadna leaders agreed with this position. The most pecuniary in outlook were the Ministry of Education Gadna instructors. Three-fourths of them thought the state should recruit people by offering material and career incentives (see Figure 29).

Conclusion

Youth organizations in Israel are the most elective part of the country's network of adult-making agencies that are concerned with the socialization of the child into an adult. Children cannot choose their parents. Nor have they much choice in who is to teach them in school. But adolescents can accept or reject their youth leaders. The connection between leader and the led is inherently voluntaristic. Therefore, it becomes a significant means for the expression of preferences about how a youngster wishes to fit into the prevailing youth culture.

Personnel is an important variable that affects how an institution will function. Most of the leaders are amateurs. A few become trained volunteers and still fewer become professionals, since with increasing age, people can function less and less as peer-group leaders.

Amateurs cannot guarantee administrative continuity of an institution, especially in temporary social systems where members change frequently. But volunteers cannot be eliminated without risking the loss of the program's spontaneity. Amateurs also provide a source of recruitment of candidates for professional training. For some, it is a transitional career to support themselves while they are attending a university. Youth work also has much attraction for persons who lack the formal requirements to enter the better established professional fields such as teaching.

The staffing of youth leadership posts is illustrative of the control point planning strategy that predominates in Israel. No effort is made in this multiparty state to enforce nationwide standards for youth leadership. There are no governmental directives governing who can be a youth leader. The youth culture includes many diverse elements. If it is to be influenced organizationally, there must be room for many different youth programs and different youth leaders.

The government takes responsibility for offering training programs and for providing career guidelines to those who will make their livelihood in this field. But there is dissatisfaction with the present training program and career incentives.

There is a shortage of good personnel. Youth leadership commands prestige as a voluntary activity but not as an occupation. The forces now at work to make the field more professional may change this condition.

The coexistence of amateurs and professionals, volunteers and paid workers within the same field gives rise to certain issues of "strategy." What should be the division of labor among volunteers and professionals? Should policy-making power be allocated to volunteers who have no long range responsibility, but who have a normative rather than remunerative interest in their job? Or should it be controlled by the professionals? These and many other unresolved issues confront those who now are responsible for the recruitment, training and hiring of youth leaders.

Youth leadership cannot be viewed only in terms of what leaders do for their members. It provides an opportunity for the leader to get an enrichment education. It yields dividends in the form of peer group recognition at an age when in much of the modernizing world adolescents are viewed by their social system as being too young to be "somebody." Leadership serves to co-opt some of the most enterprising and active adolescents into social roles which give them status in their peer groups and in the adult world.

Chapter 13

Summing Up

Idealists, realists and the detached

Nation building depends on the availability of an idealistic minority backed up by a realistic majority in support of national service objectives.

What happens to the youth of a garrison democracy? What is their reaction to growing up in a land under siege for several generations? A sizable minority, who were designated as *idealists,* express strong attitudes favorable to giving public service. They are self-selected, in part, through youth organizations. When they get older, many will volunteer for difficult and dangerous tasks. A much larger proportion of the adolescents, who were designated as *realists,* balance idealistic values with a high priority for self-centered pursuits. They prefer an easy and well-paid job of limited national significance to one that may be more important but ardous. During a period of crisis, their priorities can shift to considerable identification with nation-building tasks.

Our study did not explore in detail the frustrations which young Israeli often express. They are being voiced but they are not of a magnitude to affect the readiness of most adolescents to work within the system rather than oppose it or drop-out from it. Their overwhelming mood is neither alienation nor fatalistic militarism. Service to their country is part of their life style. But they are concerned with more than physical survival. One can hear much discussion of the question: "Survival for what?" A great deal of emphasis is given to social and economic development and to cultural renaissance. There seems to be a widespread readiness to accept the kind of youth culture traits speculatively identified by Lessinger (1968: 220–221) at an American conference on National Service:

(1) Youth can be trusted.
(2) Youth want to know the world that surrounds them.
(3) Knowing the world and its human agents (adults) is good for youth.

(4) Working with responsible adults in a serving, participating relationship leads to growth and responsible behavior for youth.
(5) Youth enjoys good teamwork, friendship and a place to belong.
(6) Youth is tough and able to "take it."
(7) Youth wants to feel important, to be needed, and to be useful.
(8) Youth does not now feel important, needed, or useful.
(9) Youth would rather work than be idle.
(10) Youth prefers meaningful, socially valued work to meaningless make-work.
(11) Youth likes to be publicly appreciated.
(12) Youth prefers active responsibility to passive dependency most of the time.
(13) Youth would rather be interested than bored.
(14) Youth needs adventure.

Our data suggest that a proportion of the adolescents identify with these values and express their priority for them through youth organization activism. The detached segment of the youth population, who are apathetic or antisocial, is small. They do get headlines in the press and occupy much of the time of police and of welfare officials, but they do not represent a threat to public order or to national morale.

When viewing the Israeli national morale one can easily fall victim to a *uniqueness fallacy:* the belief such a degree of social cohesion in spite of considerable divergency along political and religious lines cannot be compared to any situation. The realities of Israel do indeed differ in many ways from those of any other country. But if common elements of otherwise different complex social systems were without comparability, only artists would have a legitimate role in description and analysis of social phenomena.

No single case can prove a theory, but it can provide insight useful in the analysis of other complex situations that are in some respects similar. It is on such a basis that historians and social scientists have studied social movements, nationalism, social planning and nation building. Within this methodological context, our case study of youth organizations in Israel was conceived. The impossibility of replicating a youth culture makes it necessary to study such phenomena where they occur—in real life, not in laboratories. But this fact does not preclude the formulation of meaningful theorems. A number of generalizations are illustrated by our findings. Some of them with possible applicability for conditions in countries other than Israel will be sketched briefly in this concluding chapter.

Ideology is a nation-building resource

Ideology provides a basis for social cohesion and joint action.

Israel was revived after a hiatus of 1,900 years by a human group whom Arnold Toynbee (1957: 171–172) unflatteringly designates a "fossilized relic of a (Syriac) civilization that was extinct in any other shape." This "fossil" sustains a powerful utopian social movement, Zionism. Its advocated a territorial solution to end the victimization of Jews by anti-Semitism, social exclusion, economic harassment and the occasional mass killings.

For over half a century, this ideology inspired a sizable manpower supply of socialist pioneers. They came from all over the world, often at great sacrifice in their standard of living. With the help of ideologically less committed Jewish immigrants, who needed a refuge from persecution, the Halutz youths succeeded in transforming the land of their father's prayers into a Zionist state. People from very diverse backgrounds and many countries learned to work together to achieve common ideological objectives. Their state has come close to achieving some of its planned-for cultural, spiritual and material goals.

As in so many epic change situations, some of the ideological challenges of the parents have become "old" history to their children. All new nations confront similar issues of continuity. The search for a new ideological goal might well be more active than it is if there were not much unfinished business to tax the new generation.

No revolution is permanent

A revolutionary ideology and action program inspiring one generation cannot be transmitted without much change to another, once many of the objectives of a social movement have been achieved.

Zionism is losing meaning for the children and grandchildren of the pioneers who settled Israel. The Hebrew equivalent, Ziyonuth, has come to connote the idea of misplaced sentimentality. The native born *Sabras* have no personal experience with Jewish homelessness. More and more must learn second-hand about the alienation of Jews in the diaspora, which helped give rise to the Zionist utopian dream. Gas chambers, World War II and the uncertainties of life under the British Mandate are topics studied in a history course.

Israel is no longer an experiment. It now faces new problems—peace, cultural integration and materialism. The average Israeli is today much concerned about having a nice apartment. He complains about heavy taxes, levied in part to finance apartments for immigrants. Doctors have been known to go on strike for higher wages. Jewish Agency officials, charged with encouraging the absorption of new immigrants, have been accused of careerism, of being more worried about working conditions than doing their job well.

There are still chronic "emergencies." The borders need be defended. There are many economic problems, or a new town fails to develop according to plan. But public services to deal with these problems are more and more often met by allocation and assignment and less by voluntarism. Adolescents can now concentrate more than many of their parents could on the more routine and personal problems of human existence. Policy makers of the adult-making institutions confront the question: Will youth movements, once the matrix from which culture heroes emerged, lose out in their influence to the hedonism of James Bond? He seems to believe in nothing other than the loyalty to his organization, personal comfort and sex, devoid of love. Movies about James Bond and similar characters are played to capacity audiences throughout the country. Many of the salacious "best sellers" from Europe and America have been translated into Hebrew.

Numerically youth movements are still flourishing. But there is considerable uncertainty about their long-range influence. How many of the country's youth will continue to be identified with its core ideology? And if there is verbal identification, what will be its practical consequence when young people grow up?

There can be no permanent revolution. A social movement which has succeeded in attaining its objective, like the proverbial sinner, can be saved only once. The fervor that was generated when the parents built a new way of life cannot affect their children in the same way. Revolutionary goals become traditional for the generation that follows. They are expected to be conservative to fall in line with what has been accomplished.

As long as Israel's security remains in doubt and strategic areas remain to be protected, Zionism can have a strong appeal to a minority of youngsters. Frontier areas are being settled by volunteers through Nahal service in the army followed by joining a kibbutz. But most of the volunteers stay only for the duration of their required national service period.

The youth movements do not offer a comprehensive framework for peer group organizations for the country as a whole. They have been slow to adjust their program to the multitude of career alternatives in a modern society. Youth movements cannot recruit doctors in new towns, sailors to man Israel's new merchant marine and administrators with the courage to violate agency traditions to get their work done.

Containment of the achievement crisis

Successful organizations become vestigial unless new programs are adopted to achieve as yet unreached objectives.

When organizations attain a goal, the exhilaration with having reached it often is dampened by awareness that there are new problems. By designating this process as *achievement crisis,* attention is called to the fact that resolution of one or several problems makes it possible for a social group to give priority to others that had been played down previously or had not then existed.

Our generation has witnessed the attainment of independence of nearly all areas of the world. Some new states, formerly ruled by colonial power, barely have emerged from the iron age. Sovereignty leads to a shift in power to make decisions. It does not guarantee closure of the gap of so many new countries between their capacity to aspire to modernization and their technical resources to reach this goal. Some of the new nations have actually experienced a drop in national income after independence though precise data is hard to come by. Certainly when political freedom is given to the many different tribes, races and religious groups in a new country, some were stimulated by their freedom from outside constraint to pursue previously repressed goals, even at the price of civil war. This is what occurred in Pakistan, India, Indonesia, the Congo and Nigeria. The severity of the crisis is, in part, a function of how much prior planning could be done to anticipate such potential confrontations of previously ignored but always latent difficulties or to deal with new problems that can be expected to develop.

Achievement crisis symptoms have emerged in Israel, but their disturbing consequences for the public have been circumscribed. For instance, independence reduced the military importance of youth work. To keep youth organizations relevant, new objectives were adopted such as emergency efforts to help in the absorption of young immigrants and extra-curricular hobby programming. These welfare and educational goals, along with the fact that paramilitary training can still be justified by Israel's embattled condition have served to preserve the Gadna. Only a small proportion of the country's older adolescents now choose kibbutz living. Their number plus the influx of volunteers from overseas has been sufficient to maintain a growing number of communal settlements. They still retain some of their socialist utopian appeal as a framework for idealistic group living. Changes are being agreed upon to make kibbutzim more attuned to new generations. Policies of child care, university studies and private property are under dynamic review (Bashon, 1969: 16).

Many of the urgent developmental challenges that now confront Israel require the services of professional, technical and administrative civil servants who approach life planning more individualistically. They want to live in cities. They plan their lives in terms of personal career, family and primarily self-centered objectives. The army, industry and the Government have recognized these realities by supplementing public service appeals with material and career incentives.

Youth culture acceptance

Acceptance of the theory that the future is determined by the younger rather than the older generation facilitates the maintenance of a vital youth culture.

Zionism began as a youth-oriented revolutionary social movement. One generation, rejecting the way they were brought up, went to a new country and evolved a social system quite different from any other previously known. Tradition, while not rejected in toto, ceased to be the infallible guide. Often it was only a point of departure for planned change or for giving ancient symbols to twentieth century practices.

Youth continues to be important in Israel. The parents achieved independence. Their children have to defend it. At age 18 young men *and* women are transformed into citizens with the prestigious status of being soldiers defending the total society and pioneers who settle strategic areas. Adolescence comes to a sudden end.

There are still many problems. Aspirations for a high standard of living are being frustrated by the absence of peace and a sparsity of natural resources. Multiple ethnic groups including Israel's Arabs need to be integrated around common national objectives along with autonomy for development of their own cultural heritage. Some of these challenges may remain for decades. Young people will have to address themselves to them, just as their parents helped solve other problems that were critical when they were young.

When Israeli policy makers discuss their interest in viable youth organizations, it is often in terms of what these programs can contribute to role learning by adolescents to perform tasks valued in the past. But they also recognize—at least in theory—that young people need to share power in setting goals for the future. Youth organizations function within the "establishment," but are less adult controlled than are the schools.

Socialization through co-optation

Co-optation of peer groups enables adult-making agencies to influence the youth culture with only occasional resistance to the generational transmission of esteemed social values.

After reviewing the Israeli strategies of adult intervention in the youth culture, the following generalizations are suggested:

(1) Adolescents are attracted to an organization as a peer group milieu, where they can learn adult roles without having to compete with adults or meet adult standards. The youth programs allow for a good deal of choice about the nature and intensity of participation. Trial and error are tolerated with fewer sanctions than would be imposed on adult deviant behavior. Being an adolescent provides a partial moratorium on being held to adult responsibilities.

(2) The school and the family have many shortcomings for providing these maturation experiences. Power in these adult-making institutions is centralized. It is primarily exercised by adults to insure that their institutional objectives are achieved. The way adolescents participate in schools and in the family are in large measure imposed. Opportunities for voluntaristic involvement and social change are limited.

(3) When adult-making agencies try to direct informal peer groups, their control can be easily resisted. Adolescents can always resign. More than in the schools, therefore, the officials concerned with the planning of youth organizations reserve for young people the posts of secondary leadership. They accord such leaders considerable middle range power in policy formation, in return for accepting basic guidelines that conform to the expectations of the adult sponsors.

(4) Adolescent status in a modernizing society is increasingly influenced by merit, which Michael Young (1959) has defined as a function of "I.Q., plus effort." The school plays a major part in merit differentiation by providing much of the required technical knowledge and skill. For instance, Israeli children worry much about examinations, especially the Sekker screening test, administered on a nationwide basis in the eighth grade. It helps to stratify students educationally and occupationally. Admission to an academic high school is very difficult for those who score poorly on the Sekker.

In contrast, Israeli youth organizations have no examinations. Those who cannot reach the top of the educational merit scale are welcome. In youth organizations status can be attained on the basis of more diversified standards than at school. Participation is nevertheless correlated positively with social status, including academic merit. But no programs exclude youngsters who are academic underachievers.

Functional change with structural stability

A well established organizational structure can be highly resistant to change, even when there are major shifts in the functions that are being served.

The Gadna Youth Corps was set up in response to the need to train adolescents for para-military service. It survives in spite of the existence of a universal military service at age 18.

Youth movements came to Israel as extensions of the political parties that sponsored them. Their structural arrangements persist to this day, in spite of the fact that conditions in the country and the political parties have changed much since the achievement of statehood. There is a continued preference for volunteer leaders, despite the fact that their number is insufficient to meet the demands. Also the time of volunteer leaders is very limited. There are competing demands to do well in high school.

Can the innovative thrust of change oriented organizations be maintained over a long period of time? Membership organizations that want to retain their hold on the young people benefit from an image of being progressive and revolutionary. Our findings suggest that innovation is a self-limiting process. The more an organization achieves its objectives, the less reason for it to retain an innovation thrust. The struggle for relevancy can never be considered ended.

The capacity to introduce change is therefore an important variable for guaranteeing organizational continuity. There have been shifts in functions to meet new youth culture realities. Youth organizations are more consumer (members) oriented than a generation ago. They place less stress on ideological conformity and more on having fun while participating. But each program also has structural and ideological requirements which impose limits on the capacity of the organization to incorporate youth culture trends. Efforts are made to infuse the traditional structures with new and more relevant functions. But in time even the structure may have to change, as new generations are growing up in Israel's third decade of statehood.

The multiplicity of sanctions

Organizations can hold members by means of a variety of sanctions— normative, remunerative, and coercive (Etzioni, 1961: 4–6). Their potential for arousing enthusiasm for public service is greatest when normative incentives are supplemented by remunerative and coercive ones.

The Gadna Youth Corps has patriotic—a primarily normative—appeal. Its program is seen as being not only good for the member, but also for the country. To insure minimal participation by all those enrolled in a school, including those not sufficiently influenced by this appeal, a part of the Gadna program is made compulsory for all those enrolled in a high school. This coercive approach is supplemented by remunerative and normative benefits. Youth Corps members can be rewarded for involvement beyond the required level by opportunities to make vacation trips to interesting parts of the country, by training in leadership techniques and by free access to hobby clubs and other fun activities. Normative or idealistic meaning is attached to these activities.

Remunerative elements are even more explicit in the appeal for active participation in Beyond School programs. Activists in Beyond School programs are offered chances to learn a skill and/or have fun. In contrast, the youth movements rely to a much greater degree on normative sanctions. They place much emphasis on what the member can do for his movement, less on what the movement will do for him. This "elitist" character helps to explain why there is a high youth movement resignation rate, especially among realistically inclined segments of the youth culture. For them, these volunteer programs fail to offer enough remunerative incentives.

Diversified programming

If organizations are to have an impact on the youth culture, they must provide a wide range of programs and modes of adolescent participation.

A youth culture is a composite of many patterned ways, each enjoying some adult sanction. In the Israeli network of youth programs, young people can gain recognition as peer-group leaders from both young and old. They can do this in many alternate frameworks, in the puritanical socialist Hashomer Hatzair or in an orthodox religious group like Ezra. In the first organization, the goal of joining a kibbutz will be held as being highly desirable. In Ezra, boys are expected to keep all religious rituals, but they can wear short trousers and shave their sideburns to make some of their mothers wonder: "Where is this generation going?"

Youths also are free to shift their identification and resign from such organizations to explore new youth culture fads, the world of movie stars, soccer stars and the latest social dances.

No person or organization could issue an order affecting all adolescents, not even in the para-military Gadna Youth Corps. There is no Komsomol Pravda which could assert that it is writing "authoritatively" about what young people think without open contradiction from many quarters. Youth organizations reach over ninety percent of the country's adolescents by not trying to cast them into one mold. Influence is exercised more through co-optation than through direction.

There is a core ideology which is widely shared and believed. All the youth programs are influenced by youth movement traditions, in part, because so many of their leaders share this experience. But only a minority remain actively associated with a youth movement in later adolescence. The vitality of a youth culture is indicated not only by the extensiveness of the existing organizational apparatus, but also its diversity, including the frequency with which young people resign from a program.

The predominantly voluntaristic participation pattern in Israeli youth programs is consistent with the fact that no young person can discover his interests, capabilities and limits without a degree of freedom. He must have opportunity to experience what it is to defy parental wishes, follow a course different from that recommended by his school, kiss his first girl, and seek friendships outside the circle of prior acquaintance. He needs to think about the goals of living on his own, no matter how adequately the parental generation think that the goals of "the good life" have been defined for him.

Some observers of the Israeli scene claim that the significance of youth movements has declined since the establishment of the state. We

have no way of testing this hypothesis. There are no data about the significance of these movements before 1947.

Many a totalitarian country operates a more unified organizational
structure for the guidance of the youth culture. In the Soviet Union or in
East Germany, the state exercises tight control over the school and the army.
Its organs also try to regulate the family and youth organizations. We lack
data to compare such a negativistic and directive youth culture orientation
to Israel's more co-optative pattern. It seems plausible that when there are
multiple programs, youth organizations can elicit voluntarist participation
from a high proportion of their target populations. Activists remain by
choice because they derive personal satisfaction from their involvement.
They can differ greatly in what they want out of life, their intellectual potential, their social opportunity structure and their family subculture.

Peer group role learning

*The existence of leadership roles in the youth culture facilitates the
learning by adolescents of adult rights and duties.*

Adolescents anywhere, as they grow and mature, are confronted by
adult roles that they cannot assume immediately. They cannot become
teachers or parents. Rarely can they find responsible jobs. But in Israel
they can become youth leaders as early as latency period, after the age
of thirteen and above. This road to social status is open without formal
prerequisites and tests that govern progress in school. Irrespective of his
school record, a young boy or girl can volunteer as a Madrih in a youth
movement or may become eligible for selection to a Gadna summer course
for squad leaders.

The experience is one of a number of maturation experiences for
most of the young youth leaders. For a few it provides the underpinning
of their career. Most professional youth leaders in the Gadna Youth Corps
and in the other youth programs had been volunteer leaders. Others apply
their experience in teaching and social work, especially groupwork.

Paid youth workers are not yet professionalized. There is no labor
union to advocate better working conditions and higher levels of compensation. The process of professionalization, especially in recruitment for
lower echelon administrative posts, is being contained by the high value
placed in Israel on voluntaristic participation. Youth leaders are expected
to be a young *Haver* (friend), close in age and status to those whom they
try to influence. Full fledged professionalization would soon destroy the
co-optative element of this informal educational network.

On being somebody or nobody

*Major problems can serve to strengthen rather than weaken the iden-
tification of adolescents with the parental generation, provided that*

the source of the problem is believed to be outside of the social system and there is a basis for optimism that the problems can be ameliorated.

"Antiestablishment" sentiments in Israel are limited, in spite of the existence of many reasons why young Israelis can be dissatisfied with present conditions. The following are some of the reasons for discontent.

(1) High school education is not free. Except in border regions and development towns, tuition must be paid by the parents on a sliding scale. Admission to academic programs is not open to all who wish to study. It is subject to stringent competitive standards.

(2) War exacts a heavy price from the on-coming generation. Casualty rates in the army and from guerilla attacks are in excess of those experienced by Americans during the Korean and the Vietnam wars. Youths cannot begin their technical education until army service, at the age of 21, when many also wish to get married. Work and study often must be combined.

(3) Housing, cars and other comforts are expensive. Rapid advancement in the world of work and career is rare.

Grumbling and criticism are common. No Israeli institution, policy or leader is immune from being questioned, in private and in public forums. Nor are those who criticize of one mind. But very few react to their frustrations by detachment or "dropping out." They seem to have accepted the dictum: "It may not be the best of worlds, but it is ours."

From our findings a good case can be made for the theory that the infrequency of alienation may be related to the existence of organized programs to relate adolescents to challenges confronting their society. Esteemed social roles are within reach of a large segment of the country's youth. The bright as well as the less bright, the oldtimers and the newcomers, the rich and those who grew up in poverty can be *somebody* rather than *nobody* even during their late adolescent years.

Youth movements and organizations encourage adolescents to identify with the future of their society by a combination of fun activities, the learning of skills and the nurturance of national service attitudes. One does not have to be an exceptionally endowed person to be a Halutz or a youth leader. Ordinary young people can perform roles which have status in the larger social system. Adolescents, not quite ready to enter the adult world, can visit locations and help in tasks which make newspaper headlines. For a few days or weeks they can participate in land reclamation, tree planting, harvesting cotton or establishing a new village that will add to their country's sense of security. Peers and public figures will recognize these tasks as concrete contributions to the national welfare. These opportunities for adolescent participation in the performance of prestigious social tasks supplement the conventional avenues for gaining recognition in the home or in school. Youngsters can choose in which of these institutions they want to strive for recognition. The opportunity structure is thereby made more open than would otherwise be the case.

Control point planning

Through planned intervention at selected points of a social system, it is possible to have predictable influence on peer group programs without imposing central direction and total operational responsibility.

All Israeli youth organizations depend to some degree on adult influence. Government units offer subsidies, organize leadership courses and publish program materials. But decision making for using these resources is decentralized. The multiparty coalition in power for decades restricts its efforts to influence youth programs to selected control points, such as leadership training. Many operational details are left to local and peer group initiative. Each youth program allows some choice among available resources, as its leaders see fit. Initiative can be taken at many administrative levels and by volunteers. Each local branch can be innovative or respond differently to local demands.

Youth organizations, like all social structures, are resistant to formal change, but their multiplicity facilitates competition between programs. Youth movements, which once had a near monopoly on peer group organizations, now have to compete increasingly with less structured "salon" cliques. They attract youngsters because they include popular youth culture objectives in their program. The Gadna Youth Corps at one time operated an extensive group work program in immigrant settlements. It has now been disbanded. Within a paramilitary framework, it could only be ancillary. Beyond School programs under educational control have replaced them.

The existence in Israel of a variety of organizational frameworks provides most individuals with alternate structured peer group programs. Young people are free to indicate approval or disapproval of one or the other program by voting with their "feet," by entering or leaving the program.

Central planning is limited to selected organizational variables or control points. This allows for many local and personal options on how to use the available organizational resources. Such control points—in contrast to total planning—keeps small the hiatus that could develop if the youth organizations were subject to a high degree of bureaucratic and centralized control.

Social change is system related

Planning for change can proceed more quickly than implementation. Few specific problems can be "solved" rapidly because they affect the total social system.

One of the frustrations that complicates planned social change is the inherent differential between the capacity for aspiration and the possibility of achievement. Israeli officials planned the "in-gathering of exiles" to provide the benefits of territorial therapy to as many Jews as possible. After 1948, when mass immigration reached massive proportions, doubling the population of Israel within thirty months, its resources were strained to the utmost. Among the immigrants were many disadvanaged families, including more than 100,000 illiterates. Some of them later learned how to read and write. But comprehensive education to adjust to life in a modern country could be given only to the children. Even among this new generation, many grew up with a limited capacity for "achievement" in terms of the expectation of a technological society.

There is no deliberate barrier to the participation of the poor. In contrast, youth organizations are an avenue of social mobility for some of the children of recent arrivals. Here they can learn to achieve in an expanding society where there always is need for new talent. But the youth programs have difficulty in reaching the children who do poorly in school, those of Afro-Asian families, recent immigrants and the poor. Such youngsters are less likely to acquire the communication skills necessary for them to fit comfortably into adult sponsored peer group programs in which there is an expectation of conformity to group discipline and the acceptance of a core ideology. Equally hard to reach are the children of tradition-oriented families, especially girls and youngsters of Afro-Asian origin. The Israel experience would indicate that youth organizations that require a relatively high public service component will not flourish in tradition-oriented subcultures. The patriarchal family structure, for instance, is built on an expectation that women stay close to home and that men will devote themselves primarily to the needs of their own family. The idea of peer-group loyalty cannot have the same attraction for youths in such subcutures as among families whose traditions encourage formal associations of age mates.

The capacity to take advantage of existing opportunities is not randomly distributed in any multicultural population. Indeed, if such an objective were to be pushed hard, the price in alienation might outweigh the potential gain. If children were to be taught that their parents have a competely outdated way of life, the authority of the family as an adult-making agency would be undermined.

The planning process in a democracy can never be unidimensional so that—in the interest of a technical objective—all cultural deterrents can be ignored. Planning involves more than the determination and public enforcement of relevant priorities. Allowance must be made for the fact that there are traditions—many of them widely cherished—even though they introduce considerations in the planning process that are contrary to the achievement of its technical goals.

Those who view Israel from without may see little of these conditions that limit planned social change. They can be over-impressed by the country's pace of development to ignore the evidence of its limits. It would seem that man's technical capacity for planned modernization is much greater than his capacity to absorb its consequences in the social system and its institutional components.

Military and development priorities

Military and developmental public service objectives, when combined, can attract nonmilitaristic and innovative elites to the defense establishment.

Most armies are led by professionals who think largely in terms of nonproductive tasks. They are rarely concerned with adding resources to the national product. It is uncommon to find persons in the military establishment who are strongly development oriented.

Not so in Israel. The army is composed of "temporary" soldiers, who are drafted for a limited period. It is coordinated by small cadres of career officers most of whom are expected to retire in their forties and pursue a second nonmilitary career.

Except during periods of dire military threat, certain resources of the military establishment are devoted to land settlement, the improvement of communication, vocational training, teaching, foreign aid, manpower and industrial development which have a feedback to the civilian economy. Military leaders have opportunities to achieve public esteem on the basis of nonmilitary accomplishments. Many of the higher staff officers were trained in agricultural schools, in kibbutzim, and in academic pursuits. They identify with production oriented pioneer values.

The symbiotic combination of military and developmental objectives begins in youth organizations. The youth movements stress the development of resources. Even when its members enter the military service, many serve in the development-oriented Nahal pioneer corps. One of the bitter ironies of our era is the fact that these children of socialist utopians who went to their holy land to build a better world now start adulthood as soldiers.

Challenge and national morale

Intergroup conflict increases group cohesion. Can innovative core values perform the same function?

Zionism has flourished in spite or perhaps also because of dedicated opposition from a competing pan-Arab movement. Would there be less cohesion and more intergenerational alienation if the country were less threatened or when peace comes? Such a change could be anticipated if one accepts the plausible generalization that outside conflict increases group cohesion. This theory reasons that when the perception of outside threat declines, a society will lose much of its morale.

Prospects for peace in the Middle East seem remote at this time. But what if peace were to come? Could the country's youth culture maintain its present level of identification with the ideals of the previous generation? Can adolescents grow up with a strong sense of commitment to defense as well as development when the only threats are those inherent in the human condition, such as sickness, poverty and anomie? Is war or the belief in its imminence a necessary prerequisite for national morale?

There have been Arab nationalists who urge that the conflict with Israel be ended, on the assumption that without external threat the national morale of Israelies would decline. The population, so they reason, would then emigrate to other countries in larger numbers, while the Arabs in Israel with their high birthrate, would increase in number and power. In time the demographic balance would shift in their favor. They would come to dominate, without war, in contrast to the present strategy of belligerency, which reinforces the social cohesion of the otherwise polyglot Jewish population.

The theory that peace can undermine social cohesion can be supported by much illustrative evidence. For instance, in the United States, during the Joseph McCarthy era, efforts were made to silence dissident thinkers by appeals to the fear that they would lead the country toward communism, consciously or through "guilt by association." Russia and China seem to reinforce their appeal for citizen loyalty with the warning that differences that may exist must be suppressed to combat dark and hostile forces, like "imperialists," "cosmopolitans" and "revisionists." Priority in social planning is given to the negative goal of defeating the "enemy."

The question: "Can there be a moral equivalent to war?" is of importance for those who yearn for peace. Until there is peace, the opportunity to test this alternative will not occur in Israel. There was a recession and lapses in national morale in Israel during a period of relative calm before the military crisis in May–June, 1967. But even then, there was cohesive social action to fight against internal "enemies"—ignorance and poverty. The integration of diverse ethnic groups and the pursuit of enriched cultural opportunities retained high priority. Utopian socialist ideas remained meaningful for an activist minority.

Universalist and renaissance values that once inspired the parental and grandparental generation of Israel continue to enjoy some support in the youth culture.

This evidence provides a basis of entertaining the theory that social cohesion and national morale need not dissipate in times of peace. While it is almost certain peace will bring an achievement crisis, as occurred in all of the affluent nations of Europe and North America, Israeli officials say they would welcome such a "problem" in place of their current concern with defense.

Questions of a moral equivalent to war cannot have high priority until peace comes. But they are being thought about even now. Many Israelis feel deeply the sentiments of their grandmotherly Prime Minister, Golda Meir: "I can almost forgive the Arabs for killing our sons, but I can never forgive them for having forced us to teach *our* children to kill." A significant segment of the youth stand *for* a core ideology, rather than just *against* an enemy. The high priority assigned to developmental ideals, even in the midst of a chronic military confrontation makes Israel's experience with youth culture management and national service relevant for those in search of patterns for substituting the unifying side-effects of bloody conflict with cohesiveness based on peaceful challenges.

NOTES

Chapter 1. Education for Commitment

1. The distinction between co-optation and other modes of social control was first presented by Philip Selznik (1949: 13–15).

2. Since the completion of our research, a depth survey of the beliefs of American college-educated youths 18–24 sponsored by and reported in *Fortune Magazine* (1969: 68) observed a somewhat similar differentiation. There seems to be a division between a majority who are *practical minded* and a minority of about two-fifths who are defined not by any particular belief system but mainly by their low emphasis on making money. *Fortune* designates them as *forerunners*, who are greatly concerned with idealistic issues. For the *practical* youths, the college route is primarily a route to a high-ranking job. In general, their feelings about what they want from life and their beliefs about many public issues are remarkably similar to those young men and women who have never attended college. The so called *forerunners* are more inclined to be against the establishment. Unlike the Israeli *idealists*, who view themselves as guardians of the values of their present society, the *forerunners* of the American campuses are more often critical of the existing system and predominantly opposed to it.

3. William James, "The Moral Equivalent to War," first published in 1910 (1940: 193–194). James' proposal for a national service for peace and development is similar to the "Community Service" that Theodor Herzl proposed eight years earlier (1902) in his utopian novel, *Old-New Land* (1959: 79).

4. See McDiarmid, "Japan and Israel" (1966: 136–143). Both countries increased the Gross National Product in excess of ten percent during the preceding decade.

5. Expectation of idealism is particularly explicit in the official program of Russia's Komsomol. Adolescents cannot join; they must be chosen. See, for instance, Davis (1944: 156); Bowen (1962); Bereday et al. (1960).

Chapter 2. Youth Organizations

6. The social expectation that children do well tends to have a self-fulfillment effect. See, for instance, Rosenthal and Jacobson (1968).

7. For more up-to-date data on Germany, see Federal Ministry for Family and Youth Affairs (1968).

8. Harry Sorotkin (1960: 607–617) reports selected membership statistics provided by several national federations. For example, the Boy Scouts of America had 4,950,885 members in 123,549 clubs as of December 31, 1958. The Boys Clubs of America had over 500,000 members in 522 clubs in 1959. The Camp Fire Girls reported over 500,000 in over 400 local units. The 4-H Clubs had 2,254,000 in 1958 with 28,000 adult volunteer leaders and 101,000 older boys and girls as junior leaders.

The Girl Scouts of America had 3,295,000 persons including 765 adults and the Young Men's Christian Association had 3,342,931 individuals in 1,823 local associations.

About one boy in every four, aged 11–13, is a Boy Scout; one in ten belongs to a farm organization like the 4-H Club. Forty-one percent of a national sample reported that they did not belong to any club and 5 percent were not members of any athletic team. One-fourth of the preadolescent sample were not members of any organized group, but only 3 percent indicated that they had neither gang, clique or best-friend associations. See Survey Research Center (1960: 6–10).

Among girls 11 to 13, only about one-third reported not belonging to a club or organized group (University of Michigan, Research Center, n.d.: 157–161). The unaffiliated girls, as in the comparative study of boys, came from primarily low status and rural families and from very high status families.

Because of the great variations in the way records are kept, it is doubtful that these reports document much more than that these organizations reach large numbers of youngsters, including preadolescents.

9. For details, note the youth culture analyses by Friedenberg (1965); Gordon, (1957); Goslin (1965); Havighurst and Neugarten (1967); Keniston (1960); Coleman (1961); and Goodman (1956).

Chapter 3. Co-optative Planning

10. From a report of the Department of International Cooperation, Ministry of Foreign Affairs, *Israel's Cooperation with Developing Countries in the Field of Volunteer Pioneer Movements and National Service Organizations,* 1959–1964, Jerusalem, State of Israel, 1965, mimeographed, 19 pages. Data to update this report to 1969 were supplied in a personal communication to the author from the Department of International Cooperation.

11. The planning process in Israel, although extensive, has never been studied comprehensively. Much of it is contained in unpublished documents. Some of the published reports are: Ruppin (1926); Lowdermilk (1944); Nathan et al. (1946); Esco Foundation for Palestine, Inc. (1947); and Orni and Efrat (1964: see especially Bibliography 305–319).

12. For an illustration of one area of divergency, see Goldman (1964).

13. Precise statistics about Halutzim are not available. The attributes of being a Halutz are not clearly defined. Also during much of the pre-statehood period, the encouragement of immigration was decentralized. Eisenstadt (1967: 11) cites an estimate of 152,000 to 157,000 immigrants between 1904 and 1931 and 265,000 from 1932 through the end of 1944. Pioneering-oriented workers were in a minority, but their social cohesion had a disproportionate influence on the organization of the country's emerging institutions.

14. Communist leaders do not allow dissemination and free discussion of information about the socialist experiments of Israel. The findings would raise too many questions about what happened to socialist dreams for a utopia. In Russia, Labor Zionists have been imprisoned and executed for "counter-revolutionary" ideas.

15. There are many accounts of this era. See, for instance, Yaari (1958a); Dayan (1961); St. John (1959: 1–39); also Fishman (1957).

16. For an apt characterization of Israel, see Hurewitz (1969: 357).

Chapter 4. Generational Transmission

17. Marcus Garvey, the first proponent of a territorial solution, electrified Blacks by proclaiming the possibility of a territorial solution to their outcaste status. He was a Jamaican who appealed to fellow blacks after World War I with a call to

strike out against their bondage by moving to Africa, where they could be part of the majority rather than a disadvantaged minority.

The emotional upsurge made Garvey the leader of the largest black mass movement in American history. He was the first to stress racial pride, black history and "blackness" as sources of ego-identification rather than ego-rejection. His emphasis on the territorial roots of power continues to be reflected in the contemporary civil rights struggle.

Chapter 5. The Research Setting

18. In Jerusalem, for instance, the municipality provided a subsidy of 15,000 Israeli pounds for the 1967–68 fiscal year. Hapoel, the Mapai Labor Party sports club, received 45 percent of this sum; 25 percent went to Betar, the nationalist party club. The Religious Party Club, Elitsur received 12 percent; and 13 percent went to ASA, a nonpartisan student sports class club, supported by the Liberal Party. These allocations were made in accordance with the number of registered members.

19. For details about the nature of this Holon sample, see page 95.

20. Camp Marcus School was named after Colonel "Mickey" Marcus, a West Point graduate who served as Israel's first field commander-in-chief during the War of Independence.

21. A similar social rehabilitation effort was instituted by the United States Army in 1966, *Project 100,000*. About one third of the approximately 300,000 men, who each year are screened out as mentally or physically unfit, were, nevertheless, accepted for military service. Preliminary findings in 1969 indicate that these men do as well as other servicemen. While some of them received literacy training, they were not part of any special unit or socialization program (*New York Times,* February 17, 1969: 1, 19).

This finding may reveal more about the inadequacy of present screening techniques than any other variable.

22. Seven percent accelerated—under 13; 5 percent were 15 and 1 percent was 16 years old or older.

23. For a detailed description of the study population, field procedures and the representativeness of our sample, see Chen (1967).

24. The differential underenumeration of poor youngsters and marginal students was even more pronounced with respect to certain questionnaire items. Only 65 percent of our 1965 respondents of low socioeconomic status responded to the question "In which unit would you prefer to do your army service?", as compared to 82 percent of the highest socioeconomic scale group.

Chapter 6. Pioneering

25. The absence of synchronization in social changes was first noted by William F. Ogburn in *Social Change* (1922). It has been refined and broadened since, by Ogburn and other writers. The first formulation concentrated on differences in rates of technological and normative patterns. The differences in rate of change noted here are between the youth movement ideology and administrative or governmental policies.

Chapter 7. Youth Movements

26. The same proportion was estimated to be enrolled in 1959 by Hillel Barzel *The Youth Movement. Its History Among the Nations and in Israel* (1963: 81).

27. Somewhat more than half (38 percent of the 70 percent) had already re-

signed when the eighth grade survey was made. Membership turnover of high school students was also large, but at a slightly lower rate. As many as 84 percent reported to have been in a youth movement in the 1963 leisure time study reported in Chapter 5. Nearly half of them indicated that they had re-resigned by the time the survey was made when they were in the first or third year of high school. In the Holon area sample of tenth grade level students, 75 percent of the respondents reported having joined a youth movement at one time. But four out of five had dropped out at the tenth grade level when our survey was made.

28. Young leaders were underrepresented in our sample. They can serve as volunteers for a year or two before their name will appear on the central roster of their movement, which was used in the study to identify who should be interviewed.

29. See Chapter 1, pp. 24–26.

30. In the public schools with a religious orientation the Scouts never did enjoy this favorite position. In theory, no youth movement was supposed to recruit in the schools, but in actuality many principals gave encouragement to youth leaders of the traditional B'nai Akiva movement because it has a program in harmony with their own orientation.

31. Figure 9 is based on answer to the question: "What should be a leader's attitude towards a youth with an outlook different from certain basic principles of his organizations?"

(1) Expel him from the program
(2) Put the issue up to the group
(3) Explain to him he would have to be expelled if he continued to hold his point of view
(4) Try to persuade him to change his mind, but do nothing else

32. According to the survey proportion of tenth-grade level Holon youths by youth program affiliation reporting parents "who do not understand the problems of young people," in percentages was as follows (N = 805):

Youth Movement Activists (ex-members excluded)	17
Gadna Youth Corps Voluntary Program Activists	30
Nonschool Related Extracurricular Program Activists	29
All other youths	28

33. Our findings are similar to those of August B. Hollingshead and David P. Ausubel who found that in the United States participation in formal and informal youth programs is often related to socioeconomic status and school achievement. See Hollingshead, *Elmstown's Youth: The Impact of Social Classes on Adolescents* (1949); Ausubel, *The Theory and Problems of Adolescent Development* (1954).

Chapter 8. Institution Building: The Gadna

34. For youths who were working and who were not enrolled in a high school, a different administrative arrangement was needed. It was called Gadna, the Hebrew initials of the term, "youth corps." Its name ultimately was to be applied to the school related units as well.

35. This estimate, quoted by Heiman without revealing its source, appears plausible, although it represents between 13 and 14 percent of the entire Jewish population. Even the major powers, which scraped the bottom of their manpower barrel in World War II, seldom approached a 10 percent mobilization rate (Heiman, 1967: 21).

36. Israel's ideological particularism was even more pronounced before statehood than today. Many schools were under the auspices of a political party. Each

youth movement strongly advocated its own general, socialist or religious prescription for a better world. But a high measure of unity could be obtained around one issue: survival.

Chapter 9. Gadna Today

37. Tel Katzir is a village that had been exposed to frequent Syrian shelling for nineteen years until Israeli occupation of their Maginot line type gun positions during the June War.

38. The Welfare Department sample included a large number of non-respondents: 47 percent could not be located. The percentages reported are based on the number who answered each question, about half of the total sample.

39. Four out of ten of the 54 percent of the Welfare Department sample, who "never were in youth movements" reported themselves in *Gadna*. Only about 10 percent in the general sample of adolescents in Holon reported "never having been in *Gadna* or a youth movement," but the proportion of non-involvement was more than twice as great (24 percent) for the Welfare Department youths who were in a secondary school. The non-involvement ratio of school drop-outs was even greater. Fifty-five percent of those, who at age 16 had not gone beyond elementary schooling or failed to complete it, were never enrolled in either Gadna or the youth movements. Both of these programs require youths to accept a great deal of organizational discipline. One can also read these findings in reverse. Forty-five percent of these very-hard-to-reach youths reported to have been enrolled in Gadna, a youth movement or both.

40. The high morale and effectiveness of the Israeli military forces may well be related to its reliance on civilian initiatives.

41. Table 14, as well as Figure 16 that follows it, is based on responses to the following question, which was repeated for each of the youth programs:
"What is your evaluation of Gadna (youth movements, Beyond School) activities and experiences and their impact on you when you were a member?"

(1) Never participated   (4) So so
(2) Very important   (5) Unimportant
(3) Important   (6) Negative influence

"Unimportant" and "Negative influence" were coded as "Critical View" in preparing Figure 16: "Gadna Leaders Expressing Critical Views About a Youth Program in Which They Had Been a Member."

42. A loose network of programs to help young people to discover their own abilities. There are five schools in the United States. The students undergo the physical toughening training similar to that required of soldiers in basic training. Outward Bound combines the idea of teaching survival skills and rescue techniques with exposure to the idea that man must be able to work hard and confront the forces of nature. Students live primitively in the mountains, near the ocean or in the desert.

Chapter 10. The Beyond School Programs

43. Personal communication of the Director of the Youth Department of the Israel Ministry of Education and Culture. During a survey of unspecified date, the age distribution of the participants in percentages was as follows:

Under 11	23
12–13	45
14–17	10
Over 18	22

44. Technical club participants were more often younger than those in Youth Centers. An age breakdown reported by the Ministry of Education and Culture in 1968 in percentages was as follows:

Under 11	30
12–13	41
14–17	27
Over 18	2

45. Fewer programs are open to youths just completing grade school than to those of high school age. Also, between 1963 and 1965, when the Holon area survey was made and 62 percent were found to be enrolled, Beyond School programs were expanded.

46. The following were the choices for answering the question: "Who can advance and succeed in the State of Israel?"

___ people with luck	___ hard workers
___ professionals	___ people who have "pull"
___ children of the Vatikim	___ members of the Ashkenazi
___ educated people	community
___ members of wealthy families	___ strong willed people

Chapter 11. The Hard-to-Reach

47. Ministry of Education and Culture (1965:10). At the start of the adult campaign there were 226,000 illiterates, Arabs and Jews. All are entitled to vote. These statistics do not include the Arab population of the areas administered by Israel since the Six Day War in 1967.

48. The intermarriage rate rose from 11.8 percent in 1955 to 15.3 percent in 1965. See Central Bureau of Statistics, *Statistical Abstract of Israel*, Table C/12 "Persons Marrying, By Bride's and Groom's Continent of Birth," Jerusalem, No. 19, 1968: 63. Brides and grooms born in Israel were classified on the basis of the ethnic derivation of their parents.

49. Not all of the Welfare Department clients are living in poverty. On a nationwide basis 39.4 percent of the families known to their local social welfare bureau receive nonmaterial services. They suffer primarily from noneconomic handicaps. See Central Bureau of Statistics (1968: 561).

50. *The Jerusalem Post,* September 29, 1968: 6, reports that the armed forces adopted a special program for soldiers from Afro-Asian families to facilitate their attending "special preparatory courses" to enter a university after completing their period of national service. In 1968, this scheme was extended to cover also young persons from slum areas, immigrant settlements and development towns. However, the scheme is restricted to students who come close to meeting the stringent requirements for university admission.

Chapter 12. Leadership

51. From a personal communication from an American teenager, who belonged to a youth movement at age 14 and revisited his Israeli friends two years later.

52. For instance, boys who have perfect health scores and the leadership qualities required for Gadna are usually given a combat assignment.

BIBLIOGRAPHY

AKZIN, B. and Y. DROR (1966) *Israel, High Pressure Planning*. Syracuse: Syracuse University Press.

ALCALAY, R. and M. NUROCK (1968) *Israel Government Yearbook 1967/68*. Jerusalem: Israel Government Printing Press.

ALLILUYEVA, S. (1969) *Only One Year*. New York: Harper & Row.

ALMOND, G. (1950) *The American People and Foreign Policy*. New York: Harcourt, Brace.

ARIES, P. (1962) *Centuries of Childhood, A Social History of the Family*. New York: Alfred A. Knopf.

AUSUBEL, D. P. (1954) *The Theory and Problems of Adolescent Development*. New York: Grune & Stratton.

Babylonian Talmud (1935) "Pirkei Avoth." *Babylonian Talmud*, Vol. 4, p. 8. London: Soncino Press.

BADEN-POWELL, R. (1931) *Scouting and Youth Movements*. London: Jonathan Cape.

BARCLAY, W. (1950) *Educational Ideals in the Ancient World*. London: Collins.

BARNARD, C. (1950) *Functions of the Executive*. Cambridge: Harvard University Press.

BAR-ON, M. (1966a) *Education Process in the Israel Defense Forces*. Tel Aviv: Israel Defense Forces.

———— (1966b) "A nation-building army." *Israel* No. 6: 37–38.

BARZEL, H. (1963) *The Youth Movement: Its History Among the Nations and in Israel*. (In Hebrew) Jerusalem: Youth Department of the Jewish Agency.

BASHON, R. (1969) "Interview of the week with Mrs. Senta Yosephthal, Secretary of the Ihud Kibbutz Federation." *Maariv* (August 9): 16. (In Hebrew)

BEN SHAUL, M. [ed.] (1968) *Generals of Israel*. "Mordechai Hod," pp. 133–141. Tel Aviv: Hadar Publishing House.

BEREDAY, G.Z.F., W. W. BRICKMAN and G. H. READ [eds.] (1960) *The Changing Soviet School*. Cambridge: Riverside Press.

BOWEN, J. (1962) *Soviet Education: Anton Makarenko and the Years of Experiment*. Madison: University of Wisconsin Press.

BRAHAM, R. L. (1966) *Israel: A Modern Education System*. Washington, D.C.: U.S. Government Printing Office.

BRENAN, H. [ed.] (1968) *The Military Intervenes: Case Studies in Political Development*. New York: Russell Sage Foundation.

BURG, Y. (1968) Statement in the Knesseth (parliament) by Welfare Minister Yosef Burg, February 7.

CENTRAL BUREAU OF STATISTICS (1968) *Statistical Abstract of Israel*. Vol. 19. Jerusalem: Central Bureau of Statistics.

———— (1967) *Statistical Abstract of Israel*. Vol. 18. Jerusalem: Central Bureau of Statistics.

CHEN, M. (1967) *Educational Concomitants of Adolescent Participation in Israeli Youth Organizations.* Ph.D. dissertation. Pittsburgh: University of Pittsburgh.

CHEN, M. and D. ORMIAN (1965) *Some Findings of the Youth Movements Survey.* (In Hebrew) Jerusalem: Youth Department, Ministry of Education and Culture (mimeo.).

CHURCHILL, W. S. (1930) *My Early Life: A Roving Commission.* London: Fontana Books.

COHEN, A. K. (1965) "Foreword." In F. Musgrove, *Youth and the Social Order.* Bloomington: Indiana University Press.

COLEMAN, J. D. (1965) "Voluntarism: a constructive outlet for youthful energy." *Journal of Marriage and the Family* 27: 171–175.

COLEMAN, J. S. (1961) *The Adolescent Society.* New York: The Free Press.

Commandant Levy Aperçu Sur Les Activites Du Service (1967) Bouake, Ivory Coast (mimeo.).

COSER, L. (1956) *The Functions of Group Conflict.* New York: The Free Press.

CRANKSHAW, E. (1968) "Children of the revolution." *London Observer* (January 14): 9.

DAVIS, K. (1944) "Adolescence and the social structure." *Annals of the American Academy of Political and Social Sciences* (November).

DAYAN, S. (1961) *Pioneers in Israel.* Cleveland: World Publishing.

DEAN, M. (1965) "Hatikvah, police and delinquency." *Jerusalem Post Weekly Magazine* (December 10): 7.

DEKEL, E. (1959) *Shai: The Exploits of Hagana Intelligence.* New York: Thomas Yoseloff.

DILAS, M. (1963) *The New Class—An Analysis of the Communist System.* New York: Frederick A. Praeger.

EATON, J. W. (1969) "Socialism and higher education." In *University and Social Welfare, Proceedings on the occasion of the formal opening of the Paul Baerwald School of Social Work, Hebrew University,* pp. 74–82. Jerusalem: The Magnus Press.

——— (1970) "Reaching the Hard-to-Reach in Israel." *Social Work* 15, No. 1 (January): 85–96.

——— (1968) "National service and forced labor." *Journal of Conflict Resolution* 12, No. 1 (March): 129–134.

——— (1967) "Education for public service." *School and Society* 95, No. 2294 (October 14): 358–360.

——— (1962) *Prisons in Israel.* Pittsburgh: University of Pittsburgh Press.

——— (1952) "Controlled acculturation." *American Sociological Review* 17, No. 3 (June): 331–340.

——— (1950) "Is scientific leadership selection possible?" In A. Gouldner [ed.] *Studies in Leadership.* New York: Harper.

——— (1943) "Utopian group farms of the past." In J. W. Eaton, *Exploring Tomorrow's Agriculture,* Chapter 27. New York: Harper.

EATON, J. W. and N. GILBERT (1969) "Racial discrimination and diagnostic differentiation." In R. R. Miller [ed.] *Race, Research and Reason: Social Work Perspectives,* pp. 79–88. New York: National Association of Social Workers.

EATON, J. W. and S. M. KATZ (1942) *Research Guide on Cooperative Group Farming.* New York: H. W. Wilson.

EATON, J. W. in collaboration with R. J. WEIL (1955) *Culture and Mental Disorders: A Comparative Study of the Hutterites and Other Populations.* New York: The Free Press.

EBERLY, D. J. (1966) *A Profile of National Service.* New York: Overseas Educational Service.

EISENSTADT, S. N. (1967) *Israeli Society.* New York: Basic Books.

———— (1956) *From Generation to Generation: Age Groups and Social Structure.* New York: The Free Press.

ELKINS, D. P. (1968) "Imposed anonymity." *The American Zionist* 58, No. 6.

ESCO FOUNDATION FOR PALESTINE, INC. (1947) *Palestine, A Study of Jewish, Arab and British Policies,* 2 volumes. New Haven: Yale University Press.

ESMAN, M. J. (1967) *The Institution Building Concepts—An Interim Appraisal.* Pittsburgh: Research Headquarters, Inter-University Research Program in Institution Building, University of Pittsburgh (lithographed).

ETZIONI, A. (1961) *A Comparative Analysis of Complex Organizations.* New York: The Free Press.

European Seminar on New Methods of Working with Youth Groups (1956) Geneva: United Nations.

European Seminar on New Methods of Working with Youth Groups (1955) Helsinki, Finland: United Nations, Marjaniemi (August).

FAINSOD, M. (1951) "The Komsomols—a study of youth under dictatorship." *American Political Science Review* 45, No. 1 (March): 18–40.

FEDERAL MINISTRY FOR FAMILY AND YOUTH AFFAIRS (1968) *International Youth Meetings, Germany.* Köln: Europa Union Verlag.

FIGHTERS' CONVERSATION (1968) A compilation of comments of Kibbutz youths about their personal feelings in the Six Day War. Privately printed by a committee of Kibbutz members. (In Hebrew)

FISHMAN, A. [ed.] (1957) *The Religious Kibbutz Movement.* Jerusalem: The Religious Section of the Youth and Hechalutz Department of the World Zionist Organization.

Fortune Magazine (1969) January: 68.

FRIEDENBERG, E. Z. (1965) *Coming of Age in America.* New York: Random House.

FRIEDMAN, G. (1968) "The Sabras: the crisis of values." In G. Friedman, *The End of the Jewish People?* pp. 117–131. New York: Anchor Books, Doubleday.

GLICK, E. B. (1967) *Peaceful Conflict: The Non-Military Use of the Military.* Harrisburg, Pa.: Stackpole Books.

GOLDMAN, E. (1964) *Religious Issues in Israel's Political Life.* Jerusalem: Jerusalem Post Press.

GOLOMB, E. (ca. 1940) *The History of Jewish Self-Defense in Palestine 1878–1921.* Tel Aviv: Lion the Printer, The Zionist Library, Vol. 4.

GOODMAN, P. (1956) *Growing Up Absurd.* New York: Random House.

GORDON, C. W. (1957) *The Social System of the High School.* New York: The Free Press.

GOSLIN, D. A. (1965) *The School in Contemporary Society.* Glenview, Ill.: Scott, Foresman.

GROSS, B. (1966) "Preface." In B. Akzin and Y. Dror, Israel, *High Pressure Planning.* Syracuse: Syracuse University Press.

GROSS, M. (1967) *Learning Readiness in Two Jewish Groups: A Study in Cultural Deprivation.* New York: Center for Urban Education.

HAILIE SELASSIE I UNIVERSITY (1966) *Handbook of Ethiopian University Service* (mimeo.).

HANNING, H. (1967) *The Peaceful Uses of Military Forces.* New York: Frederick A. Praeger in cooperation with World Veterans Federation.

HAVIGHURST, R. J. and B. NEUGARTEN (1967) *Society and Education.* Boston: Allyn & Bacon.

HEIMAN, L. (1967) "Can Israel build defense industries?" *The American Zionist* 58, No. 4: 21.

———— (1964) "Israeli infantry." *Infantry Magazine* (May–June): 44–45

HERZL, T. (1960) *Alt-Neuland* (P. Arnold, translator). [First published 1902.] Haifa: Haifa Publishing.

—— (1959) *Old-New Land* (L. Levensohn, translator). [First published 1902.] New York: Herzl Press and Block Publishing.

—— (1943) *The Jewish State* (S. D'Avigdor, translator). [First published 1902.] New York: Scopus Publishing.

HEYMONT, I. (1968) "The Israeli career officer corps." *Military Review* 48, No. 10 (October): 13–19.

—— (1967) "The Israeli Nahal program." *The Middle East Journal* 21, No. 3 (Summer): 314–324.

HOLLINGSHEAD, A. B. (1949) *Elmstown's Youth: The Impact of Social Classes on Adolescents.* New York: John Wiley.

HOROWITZ, D. (1965) "Israel and the developing nations." *Jerusalem Post* (December 3): 10.

HUDSON, M. (1969) "The Palestinian-Arab resistance movement: its significance in the Middle East crisis." *The Middle East Journal* 23: 291–307.

HURWITZ, J. C. (1969) *Middle East Politics: The Military Dimension.* New York: Frederick A. Praeger, published for the Council on Foreign Relations.

INTERNATIONAL PEACE CORPS SECRETARIAT (1964) *International Volunteer* 2, No. 1 (March).

ISAACS, H. R. (1967) *American Jews in Israel.* New York: John Day.

ISRAELI, N. (1965) *The Madrih: The Israeli Youth Leader: Roles, Training and Social Functions.* Pittsburgh: University of Pittsburgh Graduate School of Social Work (mimeo.).

JAMES, W. (1940) "The moral equivalent to war." [First published in 1910.] In W. Thatcher and F. P. Davison [eds.] *American Youth.* Cambridge: Harvard University Press.

Jerusalem Post (1969) *State Controller's Annual Report summary* (April 28).

JEWISH AGENCY (1968) *Report of the Jewish Agency to the 70th Zionist Congress.* Jerusalem: Jewish Agency.

JEWISH AGENCY, YOUTH ALIYAH DEPARTMENT (1964) *The World Conference Youth Aliyah.* Jerusalem: Jewish Agency.

JONES, E. (1963) *The Life and Works of Sigmund Freud.* New York: Anchor Books, Doubleday.

KANOWITZ, S. (1927) "Zionistische Jugendbewegung." In R. Thurnwald [ed.] *Forschungen Zur Völkerpsychologie und Soziologie.* Leipzig: C. L. Hirschfeld Verlag.

KAUFFMAN, J. K. (1963) "Youth and the Peace Corps." In E. H. Erikson [ed.] *Youth: Change and Challenge.* New York: Basic Books.

KENISTON, K. (1960) *The Uncommitted.* New York: Dell Publishing.

KENNEDY, J. F. (1964) *Profiles in Courage.* New York: Harper & Row.

KOHN, H. (1934) *Encyclopedia of the Social Sciences.* New York: Macmillan.

LACQUEUR, W. Z. (1962) *Young Germany, A History of the German Youth Movement.* New York: Basic Books.

LAUFER, L. (1967) *Israel and the Developing Countries.* New York: Twentieth Century Fund.

LAWRENCE, V. H. (1962) *History and Role of the Jamaica Youth Corps in the Social and Economic Development of Jamaica.* Master's thesis. Pittsburgh: University of Pittsburgh.

LEARSI, R. (1951) *Fulfillment: The Epic Story of Zionism.* Cleveland: World Publishing.

LEISSNER, A. (1969) *Street Club Work in Tel Aviv and in New York.* New York:

Humanities Press with the British National Bureau for Cooperation in Child Care.

—————— (1967) *Research Project on Forces Acting on Street Corner Groups,* Vols. I & II. Jerusalem: Ministry of Social Welfare. (Prepared under a grant from the Welfare Administration, U.S. Department of Health, Education and Welfare.)

—————— (1965) *Street Club Work in New York and Tel Aviv.* Tel Aviv: Ministry of Social Welfare.

LERNER, M. (1940) *Ideas are Weapons.* New York: Viking Press.

LESSINGER, L. M. (1968) "A role for socially valued service in the education process." In D. J. Eberly [ed.] *National Service, A Report of a Conference.* New York: Russell Sage Foundation.

LEVIN, L. C. (1967) *Report from Iron Mountain on the Possibility and Desirability of War.* New York: Dial Press.

LEVITAS, G. (1967) *Nahal: Israel's Pioneer Fighting Youth.* Jerusalem: Youth and Hechalutz Department, World Zionist Organization.

—————— (1966) "On the fringe." *Work* 17, No. 45 (July) [published by the Histradruth General Federation of Labor in Israel].

LORCH, N. (1961) *The Edge of the Sword.* New York: G. P. Putnam.

LOWDERMILK, W. C. (1944) *Palestine, Land of Promise.* New York: Harper.

McDIARMID, O. J. (1966) "Japan and Israel." *Finance and Development, International Monetary Fund Quarterly* 3, No. 2 (June): 136–143.

MARDOR, M. M. (1957) *Strictly Illegal.* London: Robert Hale.

MATRAS, J. (1965) *Social Change in Israel.* Chicago: Aldine Publishing.

MERTON, R. K. (1964) *Social Theory and Social Structure.* New York: The Free Press.

MILES, M. B. (1964) "On temporary social systems." In M. B. Miles, *Innovation in Education,* pp. 437–490. New York: Columbia University, Teacher's College, Bureau of Publications.

MINISTRY OF EDUCATION AND CULTURE (1965) *School Comes to the Adults.* Jerusalem: Government Printer.

MORRIS, Y. (1953) *Pioneers from the West.* Jerusalem: Youth and Hechalutz Department, World Zionist Organization.

NATHAN, R. A., O. GASS and D. CREAMER (1946) *Palestine: Problem and Promise: An Economic Study.* Washington, D.C.: American Council on Economic Affairs.

NATIONAL ADVISORY COMMISSION ON SELECTIVE SERVICE (1967) *In Pursuit of Equity: Who Shall Serve, When Not All Serve?* Washington, D.C.: U.S. Government Printing Office.

OGBURN, W. F. (1922) *Social Change.* New York: Viking Press.

ORNI, E. and E. EFRAT (1964) *Geography of Israel.* Jerusalem: Israel Program of Scientific Translations.

PERES, Y. (1967) "Type of youth cultures in Israel." In *Utilization of Youth in Preventing Juvenile Delinquency: Proceedings of the Fifth Conference, Council for the Prevention of Delinquency and the Treatment of Offenders.* Jerusalem: Ministry of Social Welfare (in Hebrew).

PERLMUTTER, A. (1968) "The Israeli army in politics: the persistence of the civilian over the military." *World Politics* 20 (July): 606–643.

THE PRESIDENT'S TASK FORCE ON MANPOWER CONSERVATION (1964) *One-Third of a Nation: A Report on Young Men Found Unqualified for Military Service.* Washington, D.C.: U.S. Government Printing Office.

RABIN, Y. (1968) "Israel does not claim right of victor but right of equality."

Address of the Ambassador of Israel to the United States before the Ninth Annual Policy Conference of the American Israel Public Affairs Committee, Washington, D.C., March 11.

RAPHAEL, A. (1964) "Why we failed in Tokyo." *Jerusalem Post* (October 29): 3.

ROSENTHAL, R. and L. JACOBSON (1968) *Pygmalion in the Classroom.* New York: Holt, Rinehart & Winston.

RUPPIN, A. (1926) *The Agricultural Colonization of the Zionist Organization in Palestine.* London: Hopkinson.

ST. JOHN, R. (1959) *Ben Gurion.* London: Jarrolds Publishers.

SCHUL, Z. (1968) "All quiet on Syrian front as Nahal unit moves unto land." *Jerusalem Post Weekly Magazine* (January 5): 8.

SEBALD, H. (1968) *Adolescence: A Sociological Analysis.* New York: Appleton-Century-Crofts.

SEELEY, J. R. (1967) "Introduction." In M. Gross, *Learning Readiness in Two Jewish Groups.* New York: Center for Urban Education.

SELIGMAN, L. G. (1964) *Leadership in a New Nation.* New York: Atherton Press.

SELZNIK, P. (1949) *TVA and the Grass Roots: A Study in the Sociology of Formal Organizations.* Berkeley: University of California Press.

SHAPIRO, S. (1968) "Search for bright young men." (report of Aharon Becker's remarks to the Histadruth Central Committee on September 13, 1967). *Jerusalem Post* (January 18): 5.

SHILOH, A. (1968) "Population Problems and Programs in Israel." A paper read at the Middle East Studies Association, Austin, Texas, November.

SHOHAM, S., Y. KAUFMAN and M. MENAKER (n.d.) *The Tel Mond Follow-Up Research Project,* Part I. Haifa: Damon Prison Press. (This study was conducted in the late 1960s.)

SHRIVER, S. (1966) *Account of the testimony of Sargent Shriver to the U.S. National Advisory Commission on Selective Service.* Washington, D.C., October 7 (mimeo.).

SHULDINER, H. (1965) "Wanted: skilled hands for the Peace Corps." *Popular Science Monthly* (June): 73–75.

SIMMEL, G. (1955) *Conflict* (K. H. Wolf, translator). New York: The Free Press.

SIMON, E. (1961) Über militarisch erziehung." In E. Fromm, H. Herzfeld and K. P. Grossman [eds.], *The Search for Peace: Festgabe für Professor Dr. Adolf Leschnitzer.* Heidelberg: Verlag Lambert Schneider.

SMITH, N. B. "Combat motivations among ground troops." In S. A. Stouffer [ed.] *The American Soldier* 1949, Vol. II. Princeton: Princeton University Press.

SOROTKIN, H. (1960) "Youth services." In *Social Work Yearbook 1960,* pp. 607–617. New York: National Association of Social Workers.

SPIRO, M. E. (1965) *Children of the Kibbutz.* New York: Schocken Paperbacks, Schocken Press.

——— (1963) *Venture in Utopia.* New York: Schocken Press.

SULZBERGER, C. L. (1968) "Foreign affairs; the shape of dreams." *New York Times.* Sect. E (April 28): 18.

SURVEY RESEARCH CENTER, UNIVERSITY OF MICHIGAN (1960) *A Study of Boys Becoming Adolescents.* Ann Arbor: University of Michigan and Boy Scouts of America.

SYKES, C. (1965) *Crossroads to Israel.* Cleveland: World Publishing.

TAMIR, S. (1968) *Everyday Life in the Kibbutz.* Jerusalem: Ahva Press.

TAX, S. [ed.] (1967) *The Draft: A Handbook of Facts and Alternatives.* Chicago: University of Chicago Press.

TAYLOR, D. A. (1968) *Institution Building in Business Administration.* East Lansing: Michigan State University Press.

THURNWALD, R. (1927) "Die Neue Jugend." In R. Thurnwald [ed.] *Forschungen Zur Völkerpsychologie und Soziologie.* Leipzig: C. L. Hirschfeld Verlag.

TOYNBEE, A. J. (1957) *A Study of History.* London: Royal Institute of International Affairs. (Abridgment of Volumes L–X by D. C. Sommervell.)

UNIVERSITY OF MICHIGAN, RESEARCH CENTER (n.d.) *Adolescent Girls: A Nation-Wide Study of Girls Between Eleven and Eighteen Years of Age.* Ann Arbor: University of Michigan.

WEIGERT, G. (1968) "Young Druse to Gadna: want to join Nahal as well." *Jerusalem Post Weekly Magazine* (July 19): 19.

WEINGROD, A. (1966) *Reluctant Pioneers: Village Development in Israel.* Ithaca: Cornell University Press.

YAARI, A. (1958a) *The Goodly Heritage.* Jerusalem: Youth and Hechalutz Department, World Zionist Organization.

——— (1958b) "Hashomer." In A. Yaari (ed.) *The Goodly Heritage: Memoirs Describing the Life of the Jewish Community in Eretz Yisrael from the Seventeenth to the Twentieth Century* (I. Schen, translator and abridger), pp. 264–282. Jerusalem: Youth and Hechalutz Department, World Zionist Organization.

YADIN, Y. (1966) *Masada: Herod's Fortress and the Zealot's Last Stand.* London: Weidenfeld & Nicholson.

YOUNG, M. D. (1959) *The Rise of Meritocracy, 1870–2033.* New York: Random House.

INDEX

256   *Index*